Three Eras of Political Change
in Eastern Europe

Three Eras of
Political Change
in Eastern Europe

GALE STOKES

New York   Oxford
OXFORD UNIVERSITY PRESS
1997

Oxford University Press

Oxford   New York
Athens   Auckland   Bangkok
Bogota   Bombay   Buenos Aires   Calcutta
Cape Town   Dar es Salaam   Delhi
Florence   Hong Kong   Istanbul   Karachi
Kuala Lumpur   Madras   Madrid   Melbourne
Mexico City   Nairobi   Paris   Singapore
Taipei   Tokyo   Toronto

and associated companies in
Berlin   Ibadan

Copyright © 1997 by Oxford University Press, Inc.

Published by Oxford University Press, Inc.
198 Madison Avenue, New York, New York 10016

Library of Congress Cataloging-in-Publication Data
Stokes, Gale, 1933–
Three eras of political change in Eastern Europe /
Gale Stokes.
p.   cm.   Includes bibliographical references and index.
ISBN 0–19–510481–1. — ISBN 0–19–510482–X (alk. paper)
1. Europe, Eastern—History.
2. Yugoslavia—History.
I. Title.
DJK36.S85   1997   947—dc20   96–33655

1 3 5 7 9 8 6 4 2

Printed in the United States of America
on acid-free paper

This book is dedicated to Uncle Sam, without whose support it, and most other post–World War II scholarship on the former Soviet Union and Eastern Europe, could not have been written

Fulbright and Fulbright-Hays Programs
National Endowment for the Humanities
The Soviet and East European Research and Training Act (Title VIII)
National Defense Education Act (Title VI)

The American Council of Learned Societies
Joint Committee on Eastern Europe of the ACLS and Social Science
     Research Council
Council for the International Exchange of Scholars
International Research and Exchanges Board
Woodrow Wilson International Center for Scholars
National Council for Soviet and East European Studies

Contents

Introduction

When I meet new people and tell them that I am a Balkan historian, they almost always ask me, with some surprise, how I got into the study of Balkan history. The question could be interpreted as merely polite conversation. I have come to believe, however, that it reveals the depth of ethnic consciousness that permeates modern thinking. Questioners usually are quite specific: my non-Slavic name has confused them. They assume that only those with an appropriate ethnic background could be interested in the arcane history of Southeast Europe. If my name were, say Miloš Marković, it apparently would be obvious to them why I chose Balkan history as my subject—ethnics are interested in their own history. But of course everyone is an ethnic. We are all part of a community in which we have been nurtured and feel comfortable. And not all of us chose to be historians. Nevertheless, I cannot recall a single instance of someone asking me why I chose to be a professional historian rather than to pursue some other career.

I have my dinner party answer to why I chose the Balkans. It goes like this: The Christmas before I graduated from college, my mother gave me one thousand dollars to visit Europe the summer of my graduation, after which I was to enter the Air Force as an ROTC second lieutenant. Her condition was that I travel with the Experiment in International Living, which placed young people with families in host countries. I chose Yugoslavia and spent several weeks in Ljubljana (the student I stayed with remains a good friend), following which our group traveled around Yugoslavia.

After a number of years' service as a regular officer, I realized I wanted to leave the Air Force. One of the things I did to think more clearly about this decision was to list all the books I had read over the previous two years. To my astonishment, most of them were history books. Even though I had been convinced since my undergraduate days that history was boring, I had read Florinsky's two-volume history of Russia and even B. H. Sumner's history of the Eastern Crisis almost without realizing it.

In due course I applied for a Woodrow Wilson fellowship, given at the time to encourage young people to go into college teaching. When I arrived at the interview, the committee asked me what area I intended to specialize in. Well, I said, modern European history. Fine, but what history? French? Russian? Eighteenth-century? Nineteenth-century? Having failed that interview I went home and undertook another survey. I realized this time that I had been keeping scrapbooks on Tito, that I was still in touch with my friend in Ljubljana, and that there was something quite fascinating about the murky history of Yugoslavia. I decided to try Balkan history, and at the next year's Woodrow Wilson competition I was prepared. When Indiana University offered me an assistantship, I resigned my commission, and my wife and I, along with our two children, packed up for Bloomington.

There is nothing inaccurate about this story—it happened more or less like that. But like most dinner party stories, it leaves out more than it puts in. It does not mention the profound sense of inexperience and ignorance that I felt during that first visit to Yugoslavia, nor does it express the sense of unease I felt at my privileged position. Even as an ordinary American student I was blessed with material goods beyond most Yugoslav families in 1954. I even left my razor to my friend when I left. My choice of the Balkans, then, was not primarily a rational selection of an intriguing region but rather a way to overcome the naiveté of youth, to force myself to learn languages, and to expiate my guilt at having been born to a prosperity that others could only dream of.

Whatever my youthful emotions, history as a discipline proved far more important to me than region. Human experience is intrinsically interesting, by whatever route we approach it. The choice of how we do so is a matter of personality, of quirk, of the inexplicable confluence of sensibilities that constitutes an individual. In my case, I find it enormously grounding to have a grasp of how those who have come before have shaped my world. Knowing something about the emergence of the state system, the flowering of the ideal of equity, the elaboration of the worldwide economic system, and the creation of pluralist political systems makes me feel solidly embedded in a vast human experience that extends far into the past and, one hopes, will extend far into the future. The study of history has also enlarged my sense of responsibility. I see that acts have consequences, that time does not stop, and that what one does today has an impact on those who follow. For me, then, history has proven to be not only an academic subject, but also a way to make myself comfortable at my particular site in the ongoing sweep of the space-time continuum.

The most important experience in achieving this end has been teaching an introductory European history course, which I have done continuously since my arrival at Rice University in 1968. Honing my personal interpretation of Europe's five-hundred-year explosion into the world from 1500 to the present has afforded me the luxury of reconfronting issues of historical placement every year. The main theme of that course, quite obviously, has been the reordering of human values, personal relations, social structure, political organization, ideology, work habits, living styles, and all the rest that has constituted the great transformation from agricultural to industrial society. Only recently have I realized that this theme of transformation permeates my work on Eastern Europe as well. Alerted to the difference between development and underdevelopment by my 1954 visit, I have centered almost all of my work on the question of how East Europeans, Yugoslavs, and specifically Serbs have coped with the great transformation. In other works, I have dealt primarily with the political implications of backwardness.

This collection of essays presents three aspects of that general theme. The first group found in Part I, are experiments in large-scale explanation. One of the challenges of East European studies since its professionalization after World War II has been the variety of languages and the richness of cultures that make up the region. Especially for nonnatives, the difficulty of learning enough languages to do original research in more than one or two countries has limited cross-national research. In part for this reason, the historiography of Eastern Europe has been rich in single-nation studies and poor in areawide efforts. None of the three articles in Part I were intended as full-scale syntheses. The second and third of them, however, use two different paradigms to argue that confronting backwardness has been the fundamental theme of modern East European history. Challenged by the creeping advance of the Dual Revolution (Industrial and French) that reformulated the definition of what constituted a fully human existence, East Europeans had no choice but to react in ways consistent with their varied pasts and within their specific social structures.

The articles in Part I concern all of Eastern Europe except Poland. The specialized body of my work, however, which is represented in Part II, has concerned Yugoslavia, especially Serbia. Until recently, Serbian history has constituted one of the more obscure byways of the European past. Nevertheless, it has always seemed to me a particularly telling case of development (or nondevelopment) toward modernity. The Serbian conundrum is this: if we believe that political outcomes are closely related to social and economic conditions, how could Serbia develop modern political institutions when its social structure changed very little? The first article in this section attacks that problem directly, while the remaining essays analyze several key moments in the creation—and eventual destruction—of Yugoslavia. The discussion of Yugoslavism in the 1860s shows how differences between Serb and Croat ideas of Yugoslavism surfaced at least two generations before the formation of the first Yugoslavia, and the essay describing Yugoslavism during World War I shows how this difference continued to underlie interactions between Serbs and Croats into the twentieth century. The next to last essay in Part II brings the narrative up to 1991, setting the stage for the wars of Yugoslav succession, while the final article assesses the chances for stability in the former Yugoslavia by looking at the character of nationalism

Both Part I and Part II deal with historical issues of development and continuity, normal subjects for a historian. But the revolutions of 1989 brought every East Europeanist up short. Specialists dealing with the region knew the weaknesses of those societies, but few realized how brittle the regimes really were. Falling into the trap of believing that the times we knew were natural and appropriate, we failed to read the signs clearly. I do not feel the need to lament this failure, because I do not take predictive models very seriously. If there is a given in this world, it is that we cannot predict the future. (This does not mean that it is not fun to try—witness the final article in this collection entitled "Is It Possible to Be Optimistic about Eastern Europe?") And yet the events themselves were so dramatic, so sudden, so shattering of the political and economic structures of a generation that they compelled the interest of scholars from every field.

Despite the new data involved, and their contemporary focus, the articles in Part III follow the same two themes that have always interested me: (1) the struggle with backwardness, which after 1989 has been called the transition to democracy and market economies; and (2) historical placement, or the siting of current events in a sweep of time that extends far into the past and will extend equally far into the future. The article on modes of opposition leading to revolution in Eastern Europe suggests, like my work on Serbian history, that ideas and structures are at least as important as social determinants in generating modernizing change. In the same vein, the discussion of the lessons of the revolutions of 1989 argues that one of the reasons so many people failed to see the collapse coming was that they emphasized hard-nosed rather than soft-nosed analysis. That is, they concentrated on quantifiable phenomena, foreign policy issues, and technological balances, rather than on the seemingly ineffectual ideas of novelists, playwrights, essayists, and other intellectuals. The last essay presents a generally optimistic scenario for the future of Eastern Europe.

Historians understand the falsity of the cliché that those who do not know history are bound to repeat it. The practice of history is not a decision-making technique or a discipline that we master and are done with. It is instead a process of deepening our understanding of our own lives by vicariously experiencing the past as it has been lived by people who, despite their apparent distance, were, in the biological sense, our exact equals. The study of history is the study of ourselves in different settings. As we back into the silent future like Walter Benjamin's angel of history and look at the chaos opening at our feet, we can see an infinitude of possible pathways leading toward us. Picking a point on one of those pathways and following it for a while is the experience and the pleasure of history. If the journey adds nuance and richness to our world, or helps us with that most important of all questions, "How do I live my life?" so much the better.

Note

All the articles in this collection have been edited slightly. Diacritical marks have been added where necessary. I would like to thank Nancy Lane of Oxford University Press for her help and good counsel. Over the years her encouragement has meant a great deal to me.

Three Eras of Political Change
in Eastern Europe

I

THE ORIGINS OF EAST EUROPEAN POLITICS

In this section I argue that the history of Eastern Europe differs in significant ways from that of Western Europe. In itself this view is unexceptional, because even within Western Europe the history of each country, indeed of each region, differs significantly from that of every other country or region. Every people in the world has had to confront the challenges of the French and Industrial revolutions in terms of its own historical background, geographical position, natural resources, and social norms. This was just as true of France and Germany as it was of Romania and Bulgaria. Nevertheless, a few of the views expressed in this section are problematic for some people. For starters, many believe that the term "East European" implies an inappropriate linkage of the region to an allegedly inferior Russian cultural sphere, rather than being primarily a geographic designation. This form of orientalism lies behind the preference for terms like Central Europe, East Central Europe, Southeastern Europe (instead of the Balkans, where the orientalism is linked to Ottoman culture), or simply, Europe.

I hold, however, that Eastern Europe is a distinct historical entity, perhaps divided into northern and southern parts, with its own identifiable characteristics. It has persistently been economically more backward than Western Europe, and its southern part has always been a region of political and cultural dependency. Another characteristic discussed in this section is that Balkan elites in the nineteenth century used the ideology of nationalism and the instrument of the state to serve their own interests rather than to forward economic development. The terms "backward," "dependency," and "nationalism" could be interpreted as normative statements, but I do not intend them as such. I consider them simply analytical theorems that have proven useful in discussing developments in other parts of the world and that seem functional in illuminating East European realities.

As a specialist in Yugoslav history, I am well aware of the dangers of the orientalist fallacy. In the 1990s, many claimed that ancient ethnic hatreds lay behind the wars of Yugoslav succession. If the Yugoslav wars were the result of a quasi-genetic fault ("these people have been fighting each other for centuries"), one would be justified in not intervening in the "irrational" behavior of people below the civilized level. This lazy argument was not only false, for despite recurring tensions, Serbs, Croats, and Bosnians rarely actually fought each other, but it also made understanding the actual interests involved in the Yugoslav wars difficult. The claim had a particularly hollow ring to it when it came from Europeans who had spent the years 1914 through 1945 killing tens of millions of their brethren in imaginatively brutal ways.

One of the controversial concepts used in this section is "dependency." John Lampe, among others, has successfully argued that dependency theory, as developed by scholars such as Emmanuel Wallerstein and André Gunnar Frank, does not work well in the Balkans.[1] Indeed, Southeastern Europe does not fulfill the criteria of dependency theory, which in its classic form concerns the political and social consequences of economic domination of a periphery by a core. Nevertheless, the political structures created in the nineteenth century in Eastern Europe were derivative, not organic outgrowths of indigenous socioeconomic change. As the countries of Southeastern Europe emerged from under Ottoman rule, they created new states on the model of those they found in Western Europe. However one interprets the role and impact of these states, this fact seems to me indisputable.

Because the new states in Southeast Europe emerged in socially undifferentiated countries, the state apparatus had few internal competitors for power. Rather than representing accurately the social composition of their countries, state structures became the domain of the educated elites. This state class dominated the social and economic structures of the new countries, using its power to maintain and increase its control. Diana Mishkova has argued with considerable force that the new states performed an active modernizing function, rather than being simply the agents of the educated elites.[2] Balkan parliaments were not "mere facades," she writes, but opened up real possibilities of political contestation. The policies Balkan states pursued in education and military service in particular helped integrate each nation. My only disclaimer in agreeing with Mishkova would be that these processes were themselves adopted from Western Europe, as she herself suggests when she compares them to those going on at the same time in France. But it would be incorrect to assume that these successes had something to do with economic development or with changing social structures. Mishkova comments that it is impossible to overestimate the impact of increased exports, monetization of some sectors, and the construction of railroads. But Peter Sugar and Michael Palairet have shown that the impact of these phenomena has routinely been overestimated.[3]

Indeed, one of the tragedies of Southeastern Europe in the nineteenth century was that nationalism acted as a substitute for economic development. Forced to use newly introduced electoral processes to get or maintain control of the powerful state apparatus, the contending members of the state class in each country found nationalism to be their most useful tool. For this very reason, however, they had difficulty in using the state directly to effect socio-economic change, because the ideology of nationalism has very little social or economic content.[4] Lack of these elements partially explains why nationalism has been such a successful ideology. It is useful for those who employ it whether a state is organized as a dictatorship, a democracy, a centrally planned socialist economy, or a market system, but it does not alert its practitioners to social or economic issues.

Development in Southeastern Europe prior to World War I remained primarily in the political sphere, not in the social or the economic realms. Thus the articles in Part III implicitly argue that terms like backwardness, dependency, and nationalism are descriptive rather than normative, useful in analyzing the history of Eastern, especially Southeastern, Europe.

1

Eastern Europe's Defining Fault Lines

The term "Eastern Europe" as it is used in this book refers to a strip of thirteen countries (at the time of writing) that runs north and south in an uneven band several hundred miles wide from the Baltic Sea in the north to the Aegean Sea in the south.[1] The region's approximately 140,000,000 people speak even more languages than the number of countries involved; comprise five major religious groups, three of which are Christian; and have experienced a variety of national histories that in some cases go back more than a thousand years. All the peoples of the region can be considered in a fundamental sense to be Europeans, and yet in another way they have historically been separate from the great transformations that characterized Western Europe. The Renaissance, the Reformation, the scientific revolution, the Enlightenment, the creation of limited government, and the French Revolution all had their reflections in and impacts on the region, but they were not generated there. On the other hand, despite a strong linguistic connection to Russia and a cultural linkage to Orthodox Christianity, the region did not participate directly in the unique Russian historical trajectory either. Even though the Soviet Union dominated Eastern Europe over most of the post–World War II era, historically the region was not subject to direct Russian control.

Eastern Europe consists of the lands between, as Alan Palmer styled them.[2] Linked by many important connections to cultures to the east, to

From Sabrina P. Ramet, ed., *Politics and Society in Eastern Europe* (Bloomington: Indiana University Press, forthcoming). Reprinted by permission.

the south, and to the west, the East European peoples were not fully part of any of them. Three fundamental historical fault lines that divided the European continent define the region.[3] These are (1) the line that separates Orthodox Christians from Catholics; (2) the line that separates the Ottoman cultural area from that influenced by the great Christian empires, primarily Habsburg Austria, but also Prussia and Russia; (3) the line that divides the socioeconomic conditions of Western Europe from those of Eastern Europe. In addition, Eastern Europe has been one of the most important laboratories of the quintessentially modern political ideology, nationalism, a fact made especially salient by the region's extremely confused ethnic situation. Eastern Eupope is a shatterzone whose ethnic map in 1900, if indeed one could be drawn, would resemble the cracked bottom of a dried mud puddle. A discussion of these three fault lines and of the consequences of ethnicity and nationalism in Eastern Europe constitutes the introduction to this volume.

Neolithic settlements have been uncovered in the area we now call Eastern Europe, anthropological finds confirm the presence there of prehistoric peoples, and Greek and Roman ruins dot Southeastern Europe in particular. But the history of the region as a specifically European entity began with the migration of the Slavs in the sixth century and the conversions to Christianity at the end of the first millennium. Originally, the Christian church was one unit, Jesus and his disciples, and for the first three hundred years of its existence internal theological and political struggles had merely local interest. But in the fourth century of our era the Roman Empire, which dominated the Mediterranean world, adopted Christianity as its official religion. The newly authoritative position of Christianity made it imperative to define the faith accurately. Over the next two hundred years, by means of several ecumenical councils, the Christian emperor and his bishops defined the character of the Trinity and settled a number of theological issues. In doing so they lost the easternmost portion of the church, such as the Copts, but in return they provided the church a coherence and a mission that it had lacked previously.

At about the same time these Christological controversies were being worked out, the Roman Empire collapsed under the weight of its own size and under the pressure of the Germanic peoples on its periphery. The traditional date given for the fall of Rome is 476, but in fact the process took place over several centuries. Furthermore, it was not the entire empire that collapsed, but only the western part, centered in Rome. The eastern half of the empire, the center of which was Constantinople (today Istanbul), survived as the Byzantine Empire until its final conquest by the Ottoman Turks in 1453. The consequences of this bifurcation were enormous. In the West a single Christian patriarch in Rome faced a disintegrating political situation, whereas in the East several patriarchs (in Jerusalem, Antioch, Alexandria, and, eventually, Constantinople) attended a rich and powerful state. Over time the Roman church filled the political vacuum in which it found itself and became the organizational and spiritual heir to the

Roman Empire. The Pope ruled over a hierarchical church organization modeled on that empire; canon law took its lead from Roman law; and the church adopted the language of the empire, Latin. Eventually, when strong secular kings arose in northern Europe, the struggle between pope and king became a fruitful source of Western political theory and practice, while monastic movements and church councils periodically produced both moral cleansings and crises of authority within the church.

In the East, however, where there was no political vacuum, the Christian church worked in "harmonious concert" with the Byzantine emperors, retaining at the same time a strong sense of community. Patriarchs maintained their local authority. When new peoples converted to the Byzantine rite they were permitted to have their own national churches, to use their own languages in the liturgy, and even to write their holy works in their own alphabets. Monasticism in the East remained a personal matter, a going into the desert for purification, and never developed the organizational dimension that characterized the Western church. Neither did the Eastern church recognize any church councils after the seventh ecumenical in the year 787. The different spirits of the diverging churches are captured in their names and in the style of their affirmations of faith. The Western church called itself the Catholic, or universal, church and began its creed "I believe," that is, I, the believing citizen of this hierarchically organized religious successor to the Roman Empire, believe. The Eastern church called itself the Orthodox Church, since it perceived its goal as preserving the faith of the early church fathers intact. It began its affirmation of faith "We believe," that is, we, the members of this community banded together as believers in the ancient faith, believe.

Between approximately A.D. 800 and A.D. 1200 the two centers of Christianity, Rome and Byzantium, competed to convert the pagans of northern and eastern Europe to their brands of Christianity. The ragged line separating those who chose Orthodoxy from the those who chose Catholicism is roughly equidistant between Rome and Constantinople. Thus the Greeks, Bulgarians, Serbs, Romanians, Ukrainians, and Russians became Orthodox, while the Croats, Slovenes, Hungarians, Czechs, Slovaks, and Poles became Catholic. Among the latter peoples, educated persons learned and used Latin well into the nineteenth century, as did educated persons throughout the Catholic West. Among the former peoples, however, almost no one knew Latin, since the Eastern churches did not use that language in their liturgies. Because the Renaissance was fueled in good measure by the rediscovery of Latin texts from the Roman past, Orthodox lands did not participate in that awakening. Naturally the Reformation, which was fundamental not only in a religious sense but also in fomenting the conflicts that led to be the beginnings of the European state system in the seventeenth century, could not occur in the Orthodox East either, although abortive reform movements did occasionally arise. Neither did the scientific revolution, the Enlightenment, the Industrial Revolution, nor the French Revolution arise in the East. Russian history in particular, which consisted in good measure of the imposition of Russian imperial rule on the region that eventually became the Soviet Union, followed a radically different trajectory from the West. One of the most important reasons was its cultural isolation from the creative discontinuities of Western development brought about by its adherence to Orthodoxy.

The Orthodox peoples of Southeastern Europe did not experience the same kind of historical development as did the Orthodox Christians of Russia because, between the fourteenth and the sixteenth centuries, Southeastern Europe came under the rule of the Ottoman Empire. This created the second major fault line running through Eastern Europe, a division between the cultural and political area of the Ottoman Empire to the south and that of the three European empires to the north: the Russian, the Prussian, and, especially, the Austrian. The Ottomans originated as one of many warrior societies of Turkic origin populating the Anatolian peninsula. In the thirteenth century a particularly able leader, Osman, gathered a successful group of fighters around himself and took control of much of western Anatolia. Early in the fourteenth century his successors began to achieve military success in Southeastern Europe. Well organized under able leadership, the Ottoman troops were more than a match for the medieval states of the Bulgarians, the Serbs, and the Bosnians. In 1453 the Ottomans captured Constantinople, thus accomplishing the fall of the second Rome, and by the sixteenth century, under the leadership of their greatest Sultan, Süleyman the Law Giver, they had conquered all of Southeastern Europe and even besieged Vienna. Beaten back from Vienna, the Ottomans settled into Hungary and Southeastern Europe. In time, conquests in North Africa and the Near East extended their empire from the border of Morocco to the edges of Persia. The Ottomans ruled over Hungary for only 150 years, but they dominated Serbia and Bulgaria for approximately five hundred years and ruled in some parts of the Balkans, such as Bosnia and Macedonia, into the twentieth century.

The Ottoman Empire was a Muslim empire of conquest, "the divinely protected, well-flourishing, absolute domain of the House of Osman," as they styled it.[4] It succeeded as a patrimonial state, that is, one in which the state and all within it were in theory the property of the prince, or in this case the Sultan, in part because it experienced ten successive generations of able rulers from Osman through Süleyman. These rulers commanded a new-style standing army, the janissaries, that was well trained and well armed, and a cavalry of feudal knights, called sipahis, whom the Sultan rewarded with estates in conquered territory. The administrators of the empire were the Sultan's slaves, literally. Often these persons had been recruited as young boys from Balkan peoples, converted to Islam, rigorously trained, and then permitted to rise as far in the Sultan's service as their talents allowed. One of the strengths of the Ottoman Empire at its peak was this administration, in which ability, not family background or wealth, was the secret to personal success.

The Ottoman Sultans ran their empire according to the precepts of the Qur'an as interpreted by holy law, the Sheri'a, and by the chief justice of the realm, the Seyh-ül Islam, who could and did advise the Sultan as to the ethical and legal consequences of his actions. Because of Islamic law, the Sultan considered himself the direct ruler of all the people in his realm and took steps to permit even ordinary subjects to remonstrate with him and his court about injustices. Paradixically, the Islamic character of the Ottoman Empire was the reason that Southeastern Europe did not become Muslim. According to the Qur'an, before God vouchsafed his final revelation to Mohammed he made earlier revelations to Adam, Abraham, Moses, and Jesus, as told in the Old and New Testaments. Muslims therefore consider Jews and Christians to be "peoples of the book" whose religions, while incomplete, are revelations of God nevertheless.

The Ottomans never made a concerted effort to convert the Christians or Jews of Southeastern Europe to Islam. Of all the peoples on the Balkan peninsula only the Albanians, who are today 70 percent Muslim, and some Bosnians converted over time. Instead the Ottomans established the millet system, whereby the Orthodox Christians, and eventually the Jews as well, maintained their religious organizations and were permitted to adjudicate civil differences among their own believers. The Greek, Bulgarian, Serbian, and Romanian Orthodox churches survived the Ottoman period and remain today living parts of national sensibilities in each of those countries. Jews expelled from Spain in 1492 established strong communities in the Ottoman Empire, especially in Thessaloníki and Sarajevo, where Ladino speakers survived until World War II.

The Habsburg lands absorbed the main thrust of the Ottoman push into Central Europe. The Habsburg family established itself around Vienna in the thirteenth century. In the fifteenth and sixteenth centuries, by a series of fortunate marriages, it created by far the most extensive medieval holdings of any European dynasty. Charles V (1500–1558) was not only the senior member of a family with claims to Austria, Hungary, and Bohemia in Central Europe and holder of the crown of the Holy Roman Empire of the German Nation, but he also ruled over Burgundy, Milan, Naples and Sicily, the Netherlands, Spain, the Spanish New World, and the Philippines, among other places. Despite this extensive realm, Charles and his brother Ferdinand, who administered the Central European, or Austrian, part of this family realm, were not able to push the Ottomans out of Hungary. The Habsburgs accomplished this only at the end of the seventeenth century, by which time the Ottoman Empire had begun to decline. The Treaty of Karlowitz in 1699 drew a new line between the Ottomans and the Habsburgs that left Croatia, Vojvodina, Hungary, and Transylvania in Habsburg hands, whereas Bosnia, Serbia, Romania, Bulgaria, and Greece remained in Ottoman hands. This east–west line divided the peoples of the East Central Europe from those of Southeastern Europe. The decline of the Ottomans opened what became known as "The Eastern Question," which was, basically, which great power would step into the vacuum developing in the Balkans: Russia or Austria.

The new Habsburg realm confirmed at Karlowitz included two of the three major kingdoms of medieval East Central Europe, Bohemia and Hungary. Both had become Christian about the year 1000, and both had a complex medieval history. The Czechs, who live primarily in Bohemia and Moravia, particularly celebrate the Protestant movement of Jan Hus. Early in the fifteenth century, one hundred years before Martin Luther, Hus inspired a successful insurgency of reforming Czech Christians against the Roman church and its German defenders. The Hungarians, who do not speak an Indo-European language, entered Central Europe at the beginning of the tenth century and established themselves in the plains surrounding the middle course of the Danube River.[5] Becoming Christian in the year 1000 under King Stephen, the Hungarians created a state and society based on a strong feudal aristocracy. The Habsburgs established a claim to the Hungarian crown in 1526, when the Ottomans defeated the Hungarian nobility at the battle of Mohács and killed Louis, their reigning monarch. Ferdinand of Austria had married Louis's sister, while Louis had married Ferdinand's sister, under an arrangement that permitted the surviving monarch to succeed to the other's throne. Since Louis was also king of Bohemia, Ferdinand now claimed that crown as well.

The Habsburgs were not able to dominate the Czech lands completely until 1620. In that year they defeated rebellious Czech forces at the battle of White Mountain and assumed hereditary control of Bohemia and Moravia. Control of the lands of the Holy Crown of St. Stephen, as the Hungarian holdings were known, came with the Treaty of Karlowitz. The Habsburgs were able to Germanize Bohemia and Moravia by dispossessing the Czech nobility in favor of deserving members of the Habsburg aristocracy, but in Hungary their Germanization policy failed. The Hungarian nobility retained its privileges and sustained aristocratic and gentry-class cultures that dominated Hungary up to World War II.

The third of the great medieval states of Central Europe was Poland. After its dynastic union with Lithuania in the fourteenth century, Poland became the largest kingdom in Europe. The main characteristic of this kingdom, or commonwealth as it became known in the seventeenth and eighteenth centuries, was the success of its landowning class in establishing its rights and privileges over against those of the king. While Poland's neighbors, particularly Prussia and Russia, were becoming more powerful by rationalizing their military and administrative structures, the Polish nobility kept their king weak and their administration minimal. The Polish nobility considered themselves the freest men in Europe, and they were, but they also ruled what increasingly became the weakest state in Europe. At the end of the eighteenth century their powerful neighbors—Russia, Prussia, and Austria—simply divided up Poland among themselves in three "partitions," leaving no Polish state at all by the time of Napolean.

While Austria was establishing its hegemony in East Central Europe,

Southeastern Europe remained a peripheral area of the great Ottoman state that dominated the Near East. For the Balkan peoples, the model of culture and politics, and the center of economic intercourse, lay to the south in Istanbul. They were able to maintain their Orthodox Christian traditions, but even in this case the orientation was southward, since the ecumenical patriarch was located in Istanbul. The orientation of the peoples of East Central Europe, on the other hand, was toward Vienna, Berlin, and points west. This cultural divide between those peoples oriented toward the Ottomans and those oriented toward the Habsburgs, which cuts across the north–south line dividing Othodox Christians from Catholics, constitutes the second historical fault line dividing Eastern Europe.

A third fault line of economic differentiation runs approximately along the Elbe River south and west to Trieste. After the year 1000, the time by which most of Europe had been converted to Christianity, economic divisions between the territories east and west of that line begin to emerge. Western Europe experienced a demographic and economic boom in the twelfth and thirteenth centuries. Population grew; new methods of cultivation using the three-field system and the deep plow increased agricultural production and inspired the retreat of serfdom; towns emerged as trading centers; and commerce boomed. East of the Elbe River, however, all of these tendencies were attenuated. Population densities were much lower, making commerce more difficult; towns grew up primarily as military and administrative centers rather than as autonomous trading units; and agricultural technology spread much more slowly. In the fourteenth century population declined throughout Europe, in part because of the Black Death. But when the demographic climb started again in the fifteenth and sixteenth centuries an entirely new element entered the picture. Starting about 1450 the Portuguese and Spanish took to the seas, exploring the west coast of Africa, discovering a sea route to India and Asia, and landing in North America. The Atlantic-facing communities of Europe entered a completely new era of commercial possibilities. By stripping the New World of gold and silver and by bringing home luxury products from Asia, they began the process that created the world trading system of capitalism.

Central Europeans, not advantageously situated geographically, did not participate directly in this economic boom nor in the elaboration of property rights that accompanied it, although the economic changes produced by the successes of the Atlantic-facing communities had a great effect on them. In Poland the main impact came through the grain trade. Since medieval times Polish landowners had exported grain through the Hanseatic system of ports, particularly from Danzig to the Netherlands. In the fifteenth and, especially, sixteenth centuries this trade became the dominant fact of the Polish economy. The Vistula River became the great highway by which the Polish nobility took its grain to the German and Dutch merchants who made Danzig (today Gdańsk) a great trading city. Since the Polish nobility was already strong, the opportunity for profits in the grain trade encouraged its members to insure the labor supply they needed to produce the grain by imposing serfdom on the Polish peasants. Whereas in Western Europe serfdom had been eliminated as a legal category by the sixteenth century, in Poland it became imposed at that time. This outcome was not solely the result of the grain trade, as is demonstrated by the fact that Russia, which did not participate heavily in that trade, also imposed serfdom at the same time, but the sociological outcome was to rigidify the Polish social structure and to condemn its agriculture to a backward style of extensive grain production. While the French port cities, the Netherlands, England, and North America were developing new and productive commercial devices, Poland was saddling itself with a backward social and agricultural system that greatly widened the already large economic gap between it and Western Europe.

Hungary felt the impact of the Atlantic opening too. One of Hungary's main exports in late medieval times was live cattle, which were driven to markets in southern Germany. As those German towns became increasingly linked to the new world economy, their need for Hungarian cattle greatly lessened, and the Hungarians had to look to Vienna or even to the Ottomans for markets. In both cases this cut them off from integration into the changing Western economies. When Hungary became part of the Habsburg lands in the eighteenth century, it assumed the role of an agricultural producer. Hungary finally began its industrailization only late in the nineteenth century.

Bohemia, much of which actually lies to the west of the Elbe-Trieste line, was the only place in East Central Europe that became more or less integrated into the West European trade system. In the middle ages, Bohemia already exported textile products, primarily linens, and in the early modern period it exported wool products successfully as well. Whereas the Habsburgs assigned Hungary an agricultural role, they considered Bohemia one of their main industrial and commercial centers. In the eighteenth century, Bohemia was among the first parts of Europe to turn to the mechanization of textile production, as even noblemen introduced proto-industrial production facilities into the countryside. Early in the nineteenth century, mechanized cotton production took off, so that by World War I, Bohemia and Moravia were the most industrialized parts of Eastern Europe, on a par with many parts of the West.

The economic picture in Southeastern Europe, of course, was quite different. The Romanian lands supplied Istanbul with grain produced on large estates by tenant peasants, while Bulgaria developed a small-scale commerce and a modest textile industry supplying Ottoman needs. Greece had the most varied economy. It had its wretched peasants and primitive mountain people, as did the rest of the Balkans, but Greek shipowners were able to take advantage of the opening of the Black Sea in 1774 to prosper during the Napoleonic wars. Upper-class Greeks living in Istanbul, the so-called Phanariots, ruled the Romanian lands as adminstrators in the eighteenth century and dominated the Orthodox millet, often including even the national churches of the Bulgars, the Romanians, and the

Serbs. With these exceptions, by the time of the French Revolution the Balkans were economically in an even more undeveloped state than most of East Central Europe.

The transformation of Eastern Europe into the region we are familiar with today began with the French Revolution and the entire nexus of ideas and institutions that grew out of it. Of these the most important has been nationalism. England was the first country in which a community spirit encompassing the people as a whole became the justifying idea behind the state, and France was the second. The French Revolution provided the world with a wealth of texts identifying the nation as the sovereign. Under Napoleon, the doctrines of the Enlightenment spread throughout Europe. In both England and France, the sense of nation matured within the boundaries of an already existing state. But the notions of liberty, equality, and fraternity, coupled with the idea of popular sovereignty, entered an Eastern Europe in which no states existed that could be considered "national." Instead, four multinational empires based on variations of the medieval principles of kingship, nobility, and deference ruled over a vast variety of religious, ethnic, and traditional groups. Until the ideas of the Enlightenment and the French Revolution began to spread in Eastern Europe most of the peoples there did not grant saliency to their ethnic or linguistic background. Educated Christians spoke Latin, French, German, or Greek, and the important differentiating characteristic was religion.

The conclusion of the Napoleonic period brought political reaction to Central Europe under the leadership of Clemens von Metternich in Vienna, Prussian conservatives in Berlin, and Nicholas I in Russia. But underneath the apparently calm surface maintained by these leaders small groups of intellectuals of varying social backgrounds began to investigate the implications of Enlightenment ideas. Often basing their efforts on the work of Germans such as Herder rather than on French or English authorities, they undertook to codify their languages, to discover and transcribe folk poetry, and to study history. Slavic speakers in both Russia and Eastern Europe started to become aware that their languages were related. In some places this created a Panslavic enthusiasm, while in others nascent nationalists developed a fear of domination by the Russians or the Poles. In Croatia, for example, the Illyrian movement of the 1840s suggested that all speakers of Serbian, Croatian, and Bulgarian were South Slavs who had a fundamental cultural unity, while among the Czechs Karel Havlíček became convinced that the Slavs were not one nation. He argued that the Czechs were better off supporting the multinational but Western-oriented Habsburg empire than they would be pursuing a long-range goal of Slavic unity that risked subjugation to Russia.

The revolutions of 1848 created an opportunity for liberal and nationalistically minded Germans and Hungarians, as well as for the Slavs. Since educated Slavs in Eastern Europe were few in number, poorly organized, and without a state apparatus, the best they could do in the revolutionary situation was to hold a conference in Prague and reject affiliation with the

Germans and the Hungarians. Some Slavs, particularly the Serbs and Croats, even joined forces with the Habsburgs. The Hungarians, however, with an ancient tradition of an independent aristocratic state behind them, went much further. Under the leadership of the revolutionary Lajos Kossuth, the Hungarians declared their independence from the Habsburgs and set out on their own path of national development. Within little more than a year, however, the Habsburgs rallied and, with the military help of the reactionary Russian tsar Nicholas I, reincorporated Hungary into their lands.

The failure of the revolutions of 1848 ushered in a ten-year period of reaction in Central Europe, but it did not end the growth of a sense of nation among the educated strata of the non-Germanic peoples of Central Europe. In the 1860s, their aspirations received an enormous boost, both psychologically and practically. Italian and German unification more than offset the failure of the Polish revolt of 1863. In 1867 the Hungarians were able to achieve autonomy. By the *Ausgleich* of that year, Austria and Hungary became separate realms linked together only by the person of the ruler and by common policies in foreign affairs, military governance, and finances. From that moment on the two halves of the Dual Monarchy followed separate paths in their domestic politics, although they continued to act as one state in international affairs.

The terms "Hungary" and "Austria" hide the important fact that both elements were themselves multinational medieval agglomerations of great variety. Therefore, during the rest of the century both Austria and Hungary faced not only their mutal conflict, but also growing political movements inside their own realms that were based on nationality. In the Austrian lands perhaps the most important of these was the regeneration of the Czechs, who assumed by the end of the nineteenth century a key role in the Austrian parliament. Polish nobility from Galicia also found a way to achieve political importance, but they were less nationalists than they were traditionalists who socially dominated their backward region and found a way to make their local dominance pay off in Vienna. In Hungary the most difficult ethnic problems concerned the Croats, who had had a special relationship with the Hungarian crown since A.D. 1102, and the Romanians, who constituted a majority in the traditionally Hungarian region of Transylvania. Themselves increasingly nationalistic, the Hungarians pursued a policy of Magyarization (forcing Hungarian language and culture on populations whose mother tongue was not Hungarian) that alienated these and other ethnic groups under their rule.

Jews played a significant role in both the Austrian and the Hungarian halves of the Dual Monarchy. By the end of the nineteenth century they even began to develop their own brand of nationalism, which they called Zionism. Despite the emergence of anti-Semitic politicians and parties in Austria (the mayor of Vienna from 1897 to 1910 was explicitly anti-Semitic), Jews played a key cultural and economic role in Vienna. In Budapest, the aristocratic Hungarian leadership pursued an assimilationist policy that permitted rich and successful Jews to enter the nobility, so that the most successful Jewish community in Eastern Europe became the Hungarian one, especially that of Budapest. In other parts of Eastern Europe, especially in Romania, however, anti-Semitism grew more widespread at the end of the nineteenth century.

While national movements were coalescing in Habsburg lands, new national entities were emerging in the Ottoman region as well. The Eastern Question had originally been which of the Great Powers, Russia or Austria, would take the place of The Sick Man of Europe (the Ottoman Empire) in the Balkans. But during the nineteenth century a third possibility arose: that the Ottoman Empire would be replaced by national states. The first people to revolt successfully against the Ottomans were the Serbs, who achieved autonomy within the Ottoman Empire by 1830. The Serbian uprisings were probably based more on Ottoman models of political behavior than they were on French revolutionary traditions or nationalism, but they provided an administrative basis for the growth of a Serbian state. By 1878 Serbia achieved full statehood and began adopting European standards rather than Ottoman ones, turning, that is, from a southward orientation of cultural and political dependency to a northward-facing orientation. Serbs adopted a constitution, formed political parties, created a court system, built a bureaucracy, and, of course, adopted the legitimating notion of nationalism.

Greeks too achieved their independence through revolution, although in the Greek case that independence (also achieved in 1830) came only with substantial international involvement, so that throughout the nineteenth century, Greece, while adopting forms of Western public life, came under the strong influence of foreign states, particularly of England.

The Romanians achieved their independence in 1859 by clever tactical politics. The two main Romanian regions, Wallachia and Moldavia, were borderlands of the Ottoman Empire. Ruled in the eighteenth century by Greek surrogates from Istanbul, in the early nineteenth century they came under the domination of Russia, which paradoxically introduced the first elements of Western-style rule there. After Russia's defeat in the Crimean War the Great Powers decided that rather than reimposing either the eighteenth-century Greek representatives of the Ottomans or the nineteenth-century Russian administrators, they would permit the Moldavians and Wallachians to elect their own local princes, while remaining under Ottoman rule. But the Romanians outfoxed the Powers by electing the same man as prince in both regions, thereby de facto uniting Moldavia and Wallachia into one country. In 1878 the Treaty of Berlin recognized Romania as an independent state.

In Bulgaria a movement of renascence that began in the 1830s was in full flower by the 1870s. When war broke out between the Russians and the Ottomans in 1877, it was the Bulgarians who benefited most. In 1878 the Russians forced the defeated Ottomans to recognize Bulgarian independence in the Treaty of San Stefano. This treaty created a large Bulgaria that included the entire territory known as Macedonia. But the Great Powers found the creation of a strong Russian client astride the Balkan peninsula unacceptable and forced the Russians to back down. The Treaty of Berlin granted Bulgaria independence but deprived it of Marcedonia. Therefore, the very origin of the Bulgarian state was flawed by disappointment and a sense of loss. Three times since then the Bulgarians regained Macedonia—in the Balkan Wars, in World War I, and in World War II—but each time only temporarily. Since Greece and Serbia also entertained aspirations to Macedonia, it remained a volatile part of Europe.

The first stirrings of Albanian nationalism came near the end of the nineteenth century, and an independent Albania came into existence only in 1912. This new country included about 60 percent of the Albanians living on the Balkan peninsula. The rest remained in Serbia, Bosnia, Montenegro, and Macedonia, all of which at the end of World War I became parts of Yugoslavia. During the interwar years Albania became a client of Italy and after World War II it retreated into almost complete isolation from both Eastern and Western Europe.

World War I and the collapse of the Habsburg Empire brought independent national states to life in Central Europe. The origins of World War I are complex and long debated. Certainly the ambitions of Germany to exercise power on a world scale and its fears of being encircled by enemies were important to the specific way in which the war expanded. Both Russia and Austria also entertained fears about their Great Power status. But the one problem that no amount of negotiation could have solved was the underlying contradiction between nationalism and the medieval principle of *Kaisertreue*, or loyalty to the emperor. The Habsburg realm relied on *Kaisertreue* to draw the disparate Austro-Hungarian Empire together. The nationality principle held that for popular sovereignty to have full meaning the state should be organized for the protection of the nation. Putting this principle into effect would mean the end of the Habsburg Empire. The specific arena in which this confrontation between the old and the new turned into actual politics was the conflict between Serbia and Austria.

After becoming independent in 1878 Serbia became an Austrian client, but in 1903 it began to pursue an independent policy. Austria-Hungary reacted in 1905 by restricting Serbian imports, and in 1908 it annexed Bosnia and Herzegovina, parts of which the Serbs coveted. An emotional wave of anti-Austrian nationalism bubbled to the surface of Serbian public life. The success Serbia enjoyed in the Balkan Wars of 1912–1913, in which Greece and it seized the lion's share of Macedonia, greatly enhanced its prestige among all the non-Germanic peoples of Austria-Hungary, especially among the Serbs and Croats, and correspondingly intensified Austro-Hungarian fears that the Serbian example was intensifying the centrifugal forces in the empire. When some very young Serbs from Bosnia assassinated the heir to the Habsburg throne in Sarajevo, Austria-Hungary decided to act. The Germans, seeing in the Serbian-

Austrian conflict a way to overcome their frustrations through war, encouraged the Austrians to act decisively, giving the Austrians what historians have called "a blank check" to take whatever action they felt appropriate. When the Serbs did not accept the resultant Austrian ultimatum unconditionally, the war started.

No one expected the Great War to destroy all four of the ancient states that had dominated Eastern Europe for so long, but that is what happened. A secular Turkey under the leadership of Kemal Atatürk replaced the Ottoman Empire, while a Bolshevik revolution brushed the Russian Empire aside and established the Soviet Union. The defeated German Empire was replaced by a frail democratic republic, which suffered various insults before giving way to Hitler's Third Reich. And a string of independent states stretching from the Baltic to the Adriatic took the place of the Austro-Hungarian Empire.

Even though the victory of the allies in World War I in a sense vindicated the nationality principle over *Kaisertreue,* all the new and changed states of Eastern Europe that came into existence in 1918, with the exception of Hungary, were very diverse ethnically. Poland reemerged from more than a century of nonexistence and, after a successful war with the new Bolshevik regime, pushed its eastern border far into Belarus and Ukraine. Poland, especially urban areas such as Warsaw, also contained a significant number of Jews and Germans. Czechoslovakia, a completely new state that had never existed before, comprised two ruling groups, Czechs and Slovaks, but it also contained large and compact German, Hungarian, Ukrainian, and Jewish minorities. The Romanians doubled their territory by seizing Transylvania, where the underprivileged Romanian peasantry constituted a majority, but Transylvania was traditionally Hungarian and had a compact and prosperous German community. The Romanians also took Bukovina and Bessarabia, both of which were dominated culturally by significant Jewish and Ukrainian populations. The most diverse state was Yugoslavia, where no national group constituted a majority. There the successful efforts of the Serbs to dominate the new country set the other peoples on edge, particularly the Croats, and established a pattern of ethnic conflict that has endured.

The interwar years in Eastern Europe were dominated by several conflicts the East Europeans could have controlled if they had found the wisdom, and several major developments over which they had no control. The issues over which the East Europeans had some control were territorial questions, economic relations, and internal political organization. The issues over which they had no control were the international economic situation, the rise of the Nazis, and the power of the Soviet Union. If ever these lands were "in between," it was during the 1930s and 1940s. It is difficult to blame the East Europeans for not being able to focus on policies that might have brought stability to the region during the 1920s and 1930s. The problems they faced in organizing new countries out of the heterogeneous remnants of ancient states were enormous; very few had any experience in the politics of accommodation; many of them were excited and rash in the first flush of national self-determination; and, with the exception of Bohemia and Moravia, all of them were economically undeveloped. At first, it seemed that political parties designed to appeal to the peasantry, such as the Bulgarian Agrarian National Union under the original leadership of Alexandûr Stamboliski, or the Croatian Peasant party under Stjepan Radić, might find original solutions to the problems faced by the main social class of the region. But the success of the intelligentsia and state class in seizing and maintaining power, the corrosive power of nationalism, the erratic personalities of the peasant leaders, and the antimodern thrust of their programs doomed these efforts to failure.

At least two of the new East European countries were extremely dissatisfied with their fate. The Bulgarians had entered the war on the side of the Germans in order to seize Macedonia. Having lost, many of them, including terrorist emigrés from Macedonia, nursed violent grievances through the 1920s. The victorious allies forced the Hungarians to accept the Treaty of Trianon by which they lost many of the traditional lands of the Crown of St. Stephen, such as Croatia, Slovakia, and Transylvania, to their newly independent or expanded neighbors. Bitter rejection of Trianon tainted Hungary's entire interwar psychology.

Challenged by the difficult task of integrating varied administrative procedures inherited from the departed empires into a single state system, disrupted by ethnic controversy, debilitated by weak economies, misguided by attempts to protect infant industries through tariff measures, wracked by bitter border disputes, and lacking a useful democratic past, it is no surprise that the first approximations of modern democracies in Eastern Europe failed. But even had the East Europeans been more successful in the interwar years in their efforts to cope with new and difficult problems, they probably would have failed anyway in the fifteen years between 1933 and 1948 under the extraordinary pressures placed on them first by the depression, and then by the expansionist policies of Germany and the Soviet Union.

During the 1920s the revisionist powers, Hungary and Bulgaria, along with Austria, looked to Mussolini's Italy for help and guidance, but in the 1930s Hitler's Germany took over that role for all of Eastern Europe. East European countries could not emerge from the Great Depression by themselves, but during the 1930s they found that the Western democracies were not inclined to help them through credits or acceptance of their agricultural products. Hitler's Germany, however, attracted East European custom with credits and outright purchases. By the end of the 1930s Germany had become Eastern Europe's largest trading partner.

In the political arena, East European politicians, who by the time of Hitler tended toward authoritarian solutions in any event, realized by the mid-1930s that they could expect little support from the Western democracies. If France would not react to such an obvious threat to its vital self-interest as Hitler's occupation of the Rhineland in 1936, the chances that the West would protect its East European allies from Hitler's initiatives were negligible. The final proof of this came with the crisis of September 1938, when Prime Ministers Neville Chamberlain and Eduard Daladier met with Adolf Hitler and Benito Mussolini in Munich and agreed, without the participation of Czechoslovak Prime Minister Edward Beneš, to permit Nazi Germany to occupy the ethnically German parts of Czechoslovakia. This British and French act of appeasement only encouraged Hitler and demonstrated that, for the West, Eastern Europe was, as Chamberlain put it regarding Czechoslovakia, "a far away country . . . [of which] we know little."[6] It is little wonder that Slovakia, Hungary, Romania, and Bulgaria reached their accommodations with Hitler and entered World War II as Germany's allies.

Eventually, of course, the West did react against Hitler. When the Nazis occupied Bohemia and Moravia in 1939, the British unilaterally guaranteed the integrity of Poland, so that when Hitler invaded that country on September 1, 1939, the British and the French declared war. Just as in World War I, Germany and its central European allies could not sustain the massive costs of their aggression. By 1943 the tide of war had changed, and in 1944 the Red Army entered Eastern Europe from one direction while the Americans, British, and Free French invaded France from the other. In May 1945 the victorious allied armies converged over the prostrate body of a crushed and defeated Germany, and within a short time the cold war began. This is not the place to enter into the details of the imposition of Stalinist rule in Eastern Europe, which was one of the main causes and consequences of that cold war, but in general it can be said that, unlike Western Europe, the countries of Eastern Europe lost the opportunity for restructuring in a democratic way that the great ceasura of 1945 afforded Germany, France, and Italy. Whereas the defeated Germans took the creative and constructive steps of ending their long-standing enmity with France and of joining with the other Western states in a voluntary and pluralistic European Community, East Europeans were forced to submit to coercive dictatorships that closed the door to debate and reconciliation. Forty years later the negative consequences of closing off Eastern Europe to a generation of reconciliation and remembrance have become apparent.

Eastern Europe constitutes a specific arena of European historical development defined by three long-standing and fundamental fault lines and strongly influenced by nationalism and ethnic diversity. A religious fault line separates Orthodox Christianity from Catholicism and its Protestant heirs. Russia and the Orthodox East pursued a very different historical trajectory than did the Catholic countries. Crosscutting this more or less north–south line is the roughly east–west line separating the Ottoman Empire and the European empires, particularly the Habsburgs. Whereas Greeks, Serbs, Bulgarians, and Romanians looked south and east for cultural and political models for hundreds of years, central Europeans looked toward Rome, Vienna, and Berlin. The third fault line, the economic one, ran southeast along the Elbe River and then south to Trieste, but lay several hundred miles to the west of the Orthodox-Catholic line. It separated the commercial and developing West from the agricultural East. In the generation following World War II, it sometimes seemed that these ancient fault lines had been erased by the homogenizing internationalism of Stalinism and Communism, not to mention by industrialization and modernization, but after 1989 it became clear that they had not.

2

Dependency and the Rise of Nationalism in Southeast Europe

A successful theory of nationalism in Southeast Europe must incorporate all three lines of approach that hitherto have been taken to the problem: parallel interpretation, diffusion theory, and structual explanation. The first of these approaches seeks to identify in Ottoman Europe processes similar to those that produced nationalism in Western Europe, emphasizing indigenous developments and often concentrating on a single country.[1] Diffusion theory is associated with the name of Hans Kohn, who suggested that East European nationalism was the intellectual stepchild of the German romantic enlightenment, which was itself a reaction against French rationalism; categorization is the speciality of this school and typologies are its strength.[2] Finally, structural explanations see nationalism as only one aspect of large social and economic changes that occurred over long periods of time and in several places.[3]

The salient aspects of all these approaches can become part of a theory of nationalism in Southeast Europe that is based on the idea of dependency. The Balkans have always been a dependent area in the sense that a cultural or political system sufficiently strong to become a model for others has never arisen there. The Balkans were borderlands of the Roman Empire and cultural appendages of the Byzantine Commonwealth. With the coming of the Ottomans, they remaned oriented toward the metropole to the South, Constantinople, now in its Muslim and Turkish form, Istanbul. But during the nineteenth century, by which time the Ottoman Empire

From *International Journal of Turkish Studies*, 1 (1980), pp. 54–67. Reprinted by permission.

had become only peripheral to the world market economy, the Balkans became a dependency area of northern Europe. This turn to the north did not alter Balkan social and economic relations significantly, but it did bring about the introduction of a new political system in emulation of European models. This system was the nation-state, and its ideology was nationalism. The contradiction between the unchanged traditional norms and the new national political system shaped Balkan politics in the nineteenth and twentieth centuries.

This view is essentially structural, as it sees nationalism in Southeast Europe as being one aspect of the spread of capitalism throughout the world, but it is also diffusionist, as it postulates that modern Balkan political ideas came directly from northern Europe. The elaboration of the theory beyond what is presented in this article would introduce autonomist or parallel elements as well.

The origins of nationalism in Western Europe trace back to the creation of the state, a development that had three basic elements. The first of these was the lengthy process of internal consolidation that transformed the diffuse relations of medieval Europe into structured systems of routine adminstration. The second was the creation of an international system within which these well-defined polities could interact. The third was the emergence of an ideology that authenticated the state as a legitimate replacement for the traditional Christian model, empire.

The continental European state emerged by means of the consolidation of power over a well-defined and contiguous territory by a king supported by an administrative organization created gradually but specifically for that purpose. The king's claim to be ultimately responsible for justice led to the creation of a legal system that tended to overpower local law. The centralizing authority usurped the position of guarantor of rights and liberties from the local or class agencies that protected them in medieval Europe. Equally important were the king's efforts to raise money. The necessity of keeping up with technological and organizational changes in the military sphere, coupled with the unwillingness of the population to respond voluntarily, fostered the creation of coercive devices for raising revenue, which in turn led to the centralization of military power, the assumption by the central authority of many of the order-keeping mechanisms of society, and the penetration of that authority into the economic affairs of the realm. By these means, a coherent system of administration with the qualities that Charles Tilly has called "stateness" ("formal autonomy, differentiation from nongovernmental organizations, centralization, and internal coordination") emerged by the sixteenth century and was well established by the eighteenth century.[4] This went on in several places simultaneously; at no time did there emerge a center of sufficient strength to subdue Europe and create an empire, or to recreate the Roman Empire.

In actuality, Rome had of course been long dead by 1500, even in its Byzantine form.[5] But the idea of empire retained its power into the sixteenth century because of its close connection with medieval aspirations toward unity, and because the notion that contemporary circumstances might be fundamentally different from Roman times was only just beginning to emerge in 1500. But the formal unity of the Christian Commonwealth was shattered by the Reformation, and a new consciousness of historical process was produced by sixteenth-century humanism:[6] these two developments, as well as many other factors, paved the way for the realization of a nonimperial way of organizing Europe that corresponded to the emergence of individually powerful states. The Treaty of Westphalia was the first great international agreement that envisioned the interaction of states with incompatible ideological bases as a normal course of events. After Westphalia, one could speak of a state system in Europe, for Westphalia "was not simply an ad hoc agreement between two or three enemies, settling a few disputed issues. Rather it was conceived of as . . . a once-and-forever settlement, agreed to by *all* the major powers. . . . Wars and maneuvering continued of course, but they were now understood within the context of an ordered diplomatic system, whose connections and assumptions were universally accepted."[7]

The state system achieved its mature formulation in the eighteenth century as the idea of the "balance of power." This concept arose in Italy in the fifteenth century and entered Europe by the sixteenth century, but it did not become an operating principle until about the time of the treaties of Utrecht.[8] The concept has no meaning in an imperial setting, but it had important implications for sovereignty. Each of the participants in the balance-of-power system had to recognize the autonomy and equal sovereignty of the other participants. Soon the most powerful states arrogated to themselves the authority to define sovereignty, that is, to rule on who could participate in the system. By the nineteenth century, the independence of a new state required formal international sanction, as today it requires admission to the United Nations or formal diplomatic recognition.

Thus the emergence of the centralized state by the eighteenth century was a twosided phenomenon. Internal political consolidation within individual states was matched by the creation of an international system within which the states could operate.

Inevitably, the accretion of power in several European centers spawned supporting ideologies. The authority of rulers in most human systems, and certainly after the time of Christ, has been thought to derive from supernatural sources.[9] The emperor ruled over his realm much in the way God did over the universe at large. But with the disintegration of the ideal of empire, especially during the sixteenth century, new justifications began to arise. At first these maintained, and even stressed, the king's similarity to God, as did Jean Bodin, for example. But in seventeenth-century England, the Civil War, especially the overthrow, trial, and execution of Charles I, suggested that reason or natural law would provide a better justification of rule.[10] John Locke eventually wrote that natural law, if rightly understood, gave some members of the realm the right to replace the king if it were necessary as a matter of justice, that is, to protect property. Locke's theoretical step, which grew out of English practice, raised up the nation, defined as the property owners, over the king as the final authority in the realm.

The ability to think of the king separately from the nation began to spread in continental Europe in the eighteenth century, especially but not exclusively among French-speaking thinkers, and proved to be one of the solvents that began to dissolve the hierarchical social basis of the *ancien régime*.[11] Hierarchy was the social analogue to the political model of Empire. In the hierarchical state, the place of each group was considered sanctioned by God and was venerated by custom and established by law. Only certain persons were considered eligible for participation in public affairs, and in the end only one had the authority to rule. Inequality was not simply the result of this system, it was its purpose. There was no embarrassment in the autocratic state that some received more rewards than others simply because of birth; the system was designed to work that way.[12]

The philosophes of the eighteenth century were not democrats or necessarily egalitarians. But they did believe that man was an autonomous figure who could find his way to truth through reason. They envisioned "the possibility and proclaimed the desirability of a society open to talent."[13] In other words, the philosophes concluded that all were equal before natural law. Accordingly, no group in society should have special political privileges, including that unique group, the king. By the 1780s the political idea that incorporated this insight, Rousseau's "general will," had become a widely discussed alternative to the royal will as the source of legitimate rule. The delegates of the Third Estate in 1789 wasted little time in rejecting the principle on which the consolidation of the state had rested for many centuries. In place of Louis XV's statement that "sovereign power resides in my person alone," the Declaration of the Rights of Man and Citizen declared that "the principle of sovereignty resides essentially in the nation."[14] The dramatization of popular sovereignty by the French Revolution ushered in the era of "nation-building," defined as the process of creating a political situation in which "the people" can assume a political role.[15]

The fact that nation-building occurred during the nineteenth century in the Balkans as well as in Western and Central Europe could mislead one into thinking that the Balkan nations were created by a process similar to the one I have described for Western Europe. This, however, was not the case. None of the European developments, at least until the nineteenth century, were part of the Balkan experience. If we first consider state-formation, for example, an entirely different process shaped Southeast Europe. At the time of the differentiation of states in Western Europe, the small medieval Balkan kingdoms were being conquered by a single center, the Ottoman Empire. By the middle of the seventeenth century, Europe had completely sloughed off the ideal of empire as a practical form, and the idea of natural law was beginning to erode the principle of hierarchy. In Southeast Europe, however, not only the ideas of empire and hierarchy lived on: the actuality did too.[16]

The Ottoman Sultan occupied a much more exalted position than any European king. He was the head of the family to whom Turkish tradition had given the right to rule and the duty to defend Islam. His task was to preserve the social order, provide justice, and expand the world of Islam. To do that he needed power, and, as the Turkish belief went, "a ruler can have no power without soldiers, no soldiers without money, no money without the well-being of his subjects, and no popular well-being without justice."[17] The circle was completed by the absolute ruler, without whom justice would be impossible. Therefore, everything and everyone in the Sultan's realm belonged to him, and his power over all things and persons was absolute. This included his rule over the social order. Ottoman society was rigidly hierarchical, the object of statecraft being to preserve the orders into which law and the Sultan had placed men. Upward mobility was possible early in the Empire through service to the Sultan and, later, through becoming a successful local notable; but rigid adherence to rank was the rule.[18]

This design, providing an absolute military and religious leader atop a hierarchical society, was not unusual in an empire. The Ottoman Empire did not differ fundamentally from other imperial political systems created at various times in human history. However it did differ greatly from Western Europe; and when, after the sixteenth century, the Ottoman Empire began to experience a degeneration of the center that weakened the ability of the Sultan and his viziers to control events far away from Istanbul, the result was not the emergence of consolidated sovereignties, as it had been in northern Europe. It was, rather, the creation of local power centers nominally under the Sultan but actually under the control of local notables called *âyans*. Some *âyans* came in the eighteenth century to hold considerable power and autonomy, referring to their families sometimes as "dynasties"; but their regimes were not organized on any new principles. They did not think in terms of "stateness," but depended on the traditional principles of family links, clientage, wealth, and force, covering themselves perhaps with a figleaf of legality extracted from a weak Sultan. They operated, that is, within the Ottoman paradigm.

Only once did the *âyans* actually threaten the empire's organizing principles rather than just its stability. In 1808 the *âyan* class extracted an agreement from the Sultan recognizing its right to local rule and placing limits on the Sultan's authority to remove local leaders. Some have suggested this *sened-i ittifak* (Covenant of Union) was analogous to the Magna Charta in its limitation of the Sultan in favor of the *âyans*.[19] However, Mahmud I began to suppress the *âyans* only a few years thereafter, restoring his own dominance by the 1820s. So it is true that some local figures did begin to achieve rudimentary training in rough and ready politics by the end of the eighteenth century, a fact that was of some importance for nation-formation later.[20] This internal development was not comparable to that which separated Western Europe into individual states, however.

Naturally, therefore, as no states appeared and no admission was made that such a thing could happen, a state system did not emerge either. Indeed, quite the opposite occurred. The Ottoman Empire as a whole began to be considered by Europeans to be a state in itself. In the Ottomans' own view their empire was not simply another state: it was the divinely sanctioned realm of Islam. In theory there could be no peace between it and other claimants to this title, or with the non-Muslim world into which it was Islam's mission to expand. But with the emergence of the state system in Europe by the nineteenth century, the Ottoman Empire lost its unique status.

This fundamental change was the result of many factors, but two external pressures were central: military reverses suffered at the hands of the Romanovs and the Habsburgs, and the emergence in Europe of an entirely new sort of economic system, capitalism. The first of these is well known to all students of the "Eastern Question," and therefore needs little discussion, but the second factor has only recently emerged as a subject of research.

For millenia preceding 1500, the centers of political and economic strength in the European part of the world were in the Mediterranean. In the few centuries before 1500, the Baltic trade achieved strong local significance; but the Mediterranean remained the focus of the most extensive European trade, as well as the locale of the acknowledged, if no longer extant, classical political models. But as the Ottoman Empire expanded to take control of a large portion of this economic system by the middle of the sixteenth century, the center of European economic and political importance began, for the first time, to move westward and northward.

This shift had a number of causes. First, of course, was the discovery of the new world, which, from its effect on European development, might be called the Atlantic breakout. The initial result of the new discoveries was the enormous but temporary enrichment of Spain, which became the dominant European power of the sixteenth century.[21] In the seventeenth century, the ability of England and the Netherlands to turn the windfalls of new world trade to permanent advantage made them the strongest economic powers of the century, while France under Louis XIV became the dominant political force.

England achieved its strong economic position in good measure because it was there that a powerful new mode of economic activity, the market, took hold most effectively.[22] Based on principles probably first elaborated in a Mediterranean setting in the Italian city states, the idea that resources could be allocated by supply and demand within a legal system of property protection was established in practice in northwest Europe by the late sixteenth century. At first Antwerp had been the center of this activity, but by the seventeenth century the combined forces of England and Northern Netherlands made Amsterdam and London the bourgeois cities *par excellence* of this new system. The English Civil War, rather than deflecting this process, as perhaps the religious wars had in France, created a favorable political arrangement for British entrepreneurs. On the one hand they received free rein to seek commercial gain inside Britain without interference from the government and, indeed, with strong protection for private property. On the other hand the government provided aggressive protection for British commercial interests abroad.[23] This happy combination, when coupled with simultaneous improvements in agriculture, set the stage for the most fundamental transformation of the European experience, the Industrial Revolution. Although British circumstances may have been favorable for this breakthrough, the Industrial Revolution was not a parochial British event. It occurred within a market system that had been in the process of formation for centuries and that encompassed not only the core states of northwest Europe, but also other European states and non-European areas in peripheral and subordinate roles.[24]

While this dynamic development was taking place in northwest Europe, the Ottoman economy remained static. The Ottomans were not indifferent to commerce and trade. On the contrary, they were well aware of its necessity to the success of the realm, and they sought with considerable success to encourage it.[25] But the Ottoman elite, like the upper classes of agricultural societies elsewhere, understood very little about how wealth was generated. Ottomans accepted the traditional view that three activities produced wealth: commerce, handicrafts, and agriculture. Since the purpose of the economy was to produce the revenues that would support the power of the Sultan, the government strictly regulated all three, squeezing them as necessary for income. Thus, for example, guilds were encouraged and protected despite their long-term inhibitory effect. A desire to maximize current income often led the Sultan to take steps that created structural barriers to economic development. Imports were stressed, for example while exports were strictly regulated, even prohibited, thus producing a balance-of-trade deficit.[26] Tax farming emphasized current income at the expense of long-term efficiency. Capitulations to foreign traders were another concession that had a long-range deleterious impact. The hierarchical social ideal encouraged stasis in the economy. Finally, underlying all as a basic cause for the Ottoman failure to develop economically, was the insecurity of property rights: in the final analysis all property belonged to the Sultan, and he did not hesitate on occasion to exercise his right, to the sudden and complete ruin of even the most powerful commercial or political figures.[27]

Traditional though this system may have been, at least for much of the fifteenth and sixteenth centuries it was not subordinate to any other system. The Empire traded with European states, and it suffered from the impact of the price revolution,[28] but it also participated in a highly developed trade in the Black Sea region, the Eastern Mediterranean, and Arab lands.[29] Psychologically too the Ottomans were independent. The privileges

granted to Europeans through capitulations were not humilating concessions of sovereignty, but bestowals of the all-powerful Sultan designed to
provide for the prosperity of the realm or to achieve some political or
diplomatic end.[30]

However, when the unprecedented expansion of Europe started in the
sixteenth century, the economic balance began to tilt. The first European
country to achieve concessions from the Ottomans was France, in the
sixteenth century. At the end of the century the British founded the Levant
Company, which lasted into the nineteenth century, and the Dutch began
also to compete for the Mediterranean trade.[31] From the beginning the
Ottomans exported primary goods, such as wool, cotton, and silk, and
received in return finished goods, usually cloth.[32] By the seventeenth century this trade had become important to both sides. At this time about half
of France's maritime trade was with the Levant, and at its peak in the
seventeenth century 10 percent of Great Britain's total trade was with the
Ottoman Empire.[33]

But as the Western economies grew stronger they began to exert an
overwhelming influence on Ottoman trade, while, at the same time, the
volume of Ottoman trade declined as a proportion of total trade for the
Western countries. By the middle of the eighteenth century, 50 to 60
percent of Ottoman trade was with France, but less than half the trade of
Marseilles, the greatest French link with the Levant, and only 20 percent of
all French trade, was with the Ottomans.[34] European influence was not
limited to the economic sphere. Capitulations in the seventeenth century
began taking on the character of extracted one-way privileges, and European culture made its first serious inroads on the Sultan's court early in the
eighteenth century.[35]

In short, the great expansion of European trade was turning the Ottoman Empire into a link in a worldwide market system dominated by the
countries of northwest Europe. The precise moment when the Ottoman
Empire became a dependency area of this system is not certain. Some say
the Empire already was in an inferior position to northern Europe in the
sixteenth century; a more conservative estimate would be that by the time
of the French Revolution, at the very latest, the Ottoman Empire had
changed from a freestanding economic system into a peripheral adjunct to
the world market system.[36]

While this was going on, the Sultan's armies were suffering defeats at
the hands of the as yet economically undeveloped states of central and
eastern Europe. The treaties of Karlowitz and Kuchuk Kainardji were the
milestones in this Ottoman military decline.

The culmination of these developments came in the nineteenth century. Early in 1856 the Sultan was forced to issue a constitution that gave
the empire a European form.[37] Later that year the empire was formally
"admitted to participate in the advantages of the Public Law and System
(*Concert*) of Europe."[38] Having developed neither a state nor a state system, the Ottoman Empire was forced to accept both in 1856. Its ancient

historical task redefined by stronger adversaries, the empire lost its originality and, as a so-called Great Power, became fair game for those who had
forced this status on it.

In Europe, the development of the state and its corresponding state
system produced ideologies to match, including eventually the idea of
popular sovereignty. Nothing comparable occurred in the Ottoman Empire. At the beginning of the nineteenth century no idea of popular sovereignty had emerged in Southeastern Europe through any indigenous process, nor had it penetrated the Balkans from Europe, with perhaps the
exception of the communities of the Greek diaspora.[39] Almost entirely cut
off from the Enlightenment, Balkan leaders depended on Ottoman
models. Pasvanoglu, Ali Pasha, even Miloš Obrenović, were local strongmen with no more notion of the constitutional state than Stefan Dušan,
and perhaps less.[40]

But as the Ottoman Empire itself was by 1800 becoming more and
more dependent economically on northern Europe, it was inevitable that
the Balkan peoples, the dependents of the dependent, so to speak, should
begin to realize that the new strength in Europe lay to the northwest.
Pasvanoglu could look to Istanbul and to his warlord colleagues for
models. The sons of a Romanian boyar who went to school in Paris in
1830 could not. The ideas found by the young boyar in Paris, the young
Serb in Berlin, ot the young Bulgar in Kiev all made a frontal assult on the
basic authenticating theory of the Ottoman Empire. Naturally, the Ottomans themselves had a great deal of difficulty accepting these new ideas;
they adopted state-creating reforms only under heavy European pressure
and were slow in coming to the idea of a national consciousness. The
Balkan peoples, however, were under no ideological restrictions; in fact,
quite the opposite. They had always known that the Ottomans were their
conquerors. While they resented this, they could accept it until the ideas of
popular sovereignty, constitutionalism, civil liberty, and social equality
taught them that Ottoman rule was not justified by natural law, that it was
not inevitable. Once they discovered this idea, they were well armed to
pursue political ends at the expense of what suddenly seemed to be an
outmoded empire.

The history of nation-formation in Southeastern Europe, therefore, is
the history of a turning toward the north. In each region the reorientation
occurred in its own way, but there were basic similarities. First came the
discovery by a handful of individuals that Istanbul was not the center of
European power and strength. This created a desire to adhere in some way
to the new core region. On the basis of that desire, and of a basic understanding of European politics and economics, the committed few would
succeed in imposing a European-style political organization, which they
defined in terms of nationality, on their region. This arrangement was then
sanctioned by the Great Powers, as for example in the Treaty of Berlin
(1878). Having successfully imposed a foreign model on top of an as yet
unmobilized population, the committed few would then begin an effort to

create the national consciousness they believed would complete the transition to modernity. In other words, nation-formation in the Balkans was a process of emulation, or of restructuring a peripheral area according to the political and intellectual norms of a dominant area.

But a basic contradiction in these norms haunted the national states of the Balkans. The essence of the political message that emerged from the French Revolution was that "the people" could and should participate in political affairs. However one defined the term "people," whether it meant a layered system of propertied voters or a mass of peasants, the implication of the ideal of popular sovereignty in a state system was that the people of one state were just as able to legitimize political authority as the people of any other state. In actuality, however, the people of the Balkan states provided only a neccessary, not a sufficient, sanction for political authority. Final recognition of the right to have a state was granted by the Great Powers, who could do so not because of any intrinsically greater worth, but because they were the most powerful states of Europe and therefore the arbiters of the state system.

This lack of power in the newly recognized Balkan states was not only political. The direction of economic activity of Southeast Europe was shifting to the north as well. Trade in the near hinterland of Istanbul remained oriented toward that enormous city, but the Balkan states established typical colonial relations with the capitalist states of Europe.

It is difficult to establish just when each Balkan area turned northward economically. For Romania, it was perhaps after the Treaty of Adrianople (1829); for Serbia, in the 1840s; for Bosnia, after the Austrian occupation (1878); for Bulgaria, perhaps not until after World War I, at which time tobacco became the critical export. Salonica did not become a major port until the eighteenth century, when wool became an important export to Europe from Macedonia and Greece, but it is not clear that the Greek economic turn northward was delayed until that time; Albania never turned to the north. In any event, the Balkan countries became suppliers of basic commodities, often relying heavily on a single crop (currants in Greece, swine in Serbia, grain in Romania).

Because of their utter lack of indigenously accumulated capital, by the end of the century the main sections of Balkan nonagricultural economy, including some of the revenue-producing resources of the states themselves, had been captured by aggressive European investors. Thus, at the very moment when the committed few were imposing a political ideology based on the liberating ideas of the French Revolution, economic reorientation was simply substituting subordination to northern Europe for subordination to Istanbul. Southeastern Europe remained in the position it has always occupied, importing luxury goods and exporting primary goods in the classic colonial fashion.

Political and economic dependency produced psychic and cultural strains as well. The certainty of the core countries that they were involved in "progress" made Europeans contemptuous of the periphery. The condescension of those engaged in the "civilizing mission" and bearing the "white man's burden" was not exhibited only in faraway colonies. The Balkans too were considered utterly backward, their politics fitting them for farce, perhaps, but not for full-scale membership in the modern world. In the Balkans the committed few themselves half accepted this view. Their sense of inferiority, bred by political and economic subservience and fostered by the complacent pride of the northern Europeans, was a third aspect of the dependency relationship.

The dark sense of powerlessness that hovered over nineteenth-century Balkan political life accounts in good measure for the quality of nineteenth-century Balkan nationalism. There was no shame in being peripheral in the Ottoman Empire, because the system was organized on the basis of an inequality that all accepted and worked with. Neither was there a need for a well-defined ideology, a language, a history, or a state. Religion provided the basic differentiating factor. But the underlying premise of the new ideas from the West was equality, and it became no longer acceptable psychologically to be peripheral. Because they accepted the European view of themselves as backward, the Balkan elite sought to prove their own worth in what they could think of as a more important area, the area of national spirit. Perhaps there were no other possibilities. "Mobilization had to be in terms of what was there; and the whole point of the dilemma was that there was nothing there—none of the economic and political institutions of modernity now so needed. All there *was* was the people and peculiarities of the region. . . ."[41] Accordingly, they produced the spiritual attributes that national greatness demanded: a glorious past, a beautiful language, a powerful literature. And if these were found mainly in potential rather than achievement, all the better, since it meant that the new states were in the adolescent stage of youthful vigor, ready in the not too distant future to achieve the power and prestige of the model states.

But this effort to modernize through the creation of a myth of the nation was doomed to failure or, if not to failure, to successes that did not enhance the economic or political future of the Balkan states or change their social conditions. Perhaps some, or even many, of the Balkan politicians who espoused nationalist justifications and ideas hoped that by adopting these Western notions before the social and economic changes that had produced them in the West had occured in their own countries they could pull their lands into the modern world. But this did not happen. The ideas that justified the creation of the nation-state were not appropriate for understanding Balkan social realities. These ideas had emerged when, in Western Europe, the hierarchical society had collapsed under hammer blows from all sides and, in place of the collapsed hierarchical system, there developed what Max Weber called a "class" society, that is, one in which impersonal rules, principally those of the market, came to determine social position.[42]

The class system so defined is the antithesis of the hierarchical system. Under it, all men were in theory equal before the law, and birth declined dramatically as a determinant of status. However, while the political norms of class society were being imposed in the Balkans through the creation of the nation-state, hierarchical society had barely begun to be questioned there. Simply changing the direction of dependency from south to north did little to dislodge traditional ideas, which remained characteristic of what Weber called "status" societies. Authority in such societies is a matter of birth. One's family is the source of strength; clientage systems are the basic social network; and largess is a characteristic trait of the leader. Since this *mentalité* remained strong, the creation of centralized nation-states in the Balkans permitted the committed few simply to substitute themselves for the departed upper classes of Ottoman times.[43] Justifying itself in new terms as the representative of the people, the new class acted much like the old regime. Bureaucratic offices were not considered "civil service" jobs, but as something akin to benefices which could be used to profit one's family and friends. Loans from abroad did not go in full measure to economically rational ends, but flowed through successful clientage systems. The impact of introducing sovereign nationhood and its institutional accoutrements in a region that remained economically dependent was to substitute for the Ottoman rulers a native bureaucracy that had almost as little interest in changing the social system as the hierarchs they replaced.

In this way a gap developed between the theoretical equality that was basic to the new political norms and the real social situation. That is, while in the old system inequalities were considered proper, in the new system inequalities were, in theory at least, not in accord with natural law. However, this basic difference escaped nineteenth-century politicians for several reasons. First, the new class did not want to encourage social change that would threaten its dominance. Second, nationalist ideology traditionally lacks social content; nationalism has been a fruitful device for politicians of almost all persuasions because it performs the functions of legitimizing and mobilizing without neccessarily implying a social program. Both socialists and fascists can be nationalists. Nationalism as such, therefore, is not a good tool for understanding social problems. Finally, the spiritual quality of the nationalist efforts, mentioned above, turned nationalists away from social and economic problems. Therefore, even though social equality was one of the latent promises of the French Revolution, nationalism was not an appropriate ideology for realizing it in the Balkans.

The undetected gap between theory and reality resulted in a lack of equilibrium that dictated the political options available in the Balkans in the twentieth century.[44] Both the corporative and the peasant parties accepted the contradictions of the social situation generated by dependency. The corporativists tried to achieve equilibrium by rejecting the ideal of equality before the law, claiming for example that the peasants were not and should not be equal, while the peasant parties simply tried to make peasants the bureaucratic class. Only the socialists and communists sought to bring about a new equilibrium by changing the social reality. All three movements, reflecting to a greater or lesser degree that emulation of the core area that characterizes dependency, found the technical ideology of nationalism useful in pursuing their goals, which themselves had been set for them by the process of nation-formation in Southeast Europe.

It seems then, that the notion of dependency provides a fruitful framework for the study of nationalism in Southeast Europe. Use of this concept places Balkan developments in the widest possible context of modern history. Basically a structural explanation, the notion nonetheless allows for national differences and accepts the diffusion of ideologies as one of the most important features of the process. The argument can be summarized in nine propositions:

1. A nation-state system was created in Western Europe at the same time as capitalism.
2. Indigenous political and economic forces in the Ottoman Empire of the eighteenth century were not leading toward a similar result.
3. The people of Southeast Europe have always been in a dependency relationship with a greater power. In the eighteenth century this dependency was oriented toward Istanbul.
4. In the nineteenth century, however, individuals among the Balkan peoples began to realize the enormous power of the northern European states. They succeeded in introducing political arrangements to Southeast Europe based on the nation-state system.
5. At roughly the same time the traditional economics of the Balkan states were being reoriented to dependency on northern Europe. Thus little or no social change accompanied the introduction of new political forms.
6. The interplay between traditional society and the imposed political system resulted in the creation of a dominant bureaucracy that acted as a status organization but appeared formally as a class system.
7. Externally, the dependency position of the Balkan states contrasted with the modern theories of equality of nations and pushed local nationalists to define the nation in spiritual terms as a counterweight to actual powerlessness.
8. Internally, the nationalist ideology thus produced served to legitimize the authority of the bureaucracy, but did not assist it in solving social and economic problems.
9. In the twentieth century corporativist parties sought to close the gap between political ideology and social reality by changing the ideology; socialist parties, by changing the reality; and peasant parties, by seizing the bureaucratic apparatus.

3

The Social Origins of
East European Politics

In considering the problem of how East European societies have been transformed in the past two centuries it is proper to start with the fundamental impact of external influences, particularly the Industrial and French revolutions, as well as to take into account the state system within which Eastern Europe awakened to these two revolutions. There is nothing demeaning in this, even though such analysis sometimes goes by the name dependency theory, because every society in the world, even including to a certain extent the core countries of northwestern Europe, has had to participate in this same confrontation. Despite the well-deserved criticisms that modernization theory has undergone, it remains true that the history of most societies includes a lengthy period that precedes the coming of industrialization, a brief transitional period of initial contact and confrontation, and the present, which contains the first moments in what may be another lengthy period of a new relationship between man and nature.[1] It goes without saying, therefore, that the most fundamental questions of modern history are those surrounding the main developments in northwestern Europe since 1500. But when we turn to the specifics of each society's confrontation with the inevitable, endogenous factors must receive equal attention to exogenous ones. When industrialism forced its way unwanted, uninvited, and unexpected into the kitchens of every society in

From *Eastern European Politics and Societies,* 1 (1987), pp. 30–74, copyright © by The American Council of Learned Societies. Reprinted by permission.
I would like to thank Peter Gunst and the late Stanley Pech for their comments on an earlier version of this article.

the world, the soups that resulted, while all created from the same stock, each had their own individual flavors.

This is certainly the case in Eastern Europe, where the gamut of political cultures in the first half of the twentieth century included functioning democracy in Czechoslovakia, vigorous peasant political parties in Serbia and Bulgaria, aristocratic bureaucratism in Hungary, and authoritarian governments in Poland and elsewhere. Despite the normal drive of contemporary scholars to find coherence in diversity, students of Eastern Europe have not often transcended these differences. It has proven difficult to avoid simply marking off each East European example as a special case, so that individual scholars working separately have produced what amounts to a listing of instances rather than an overall analysis.

The problem is not limited to Eastern Europe, of course, and only the greatest synthesizers or theorists have dealt with real diversity successfully. One of these successes has been Barrington Moore's *Social Origins of Dictatorship and Democracy*. Why, Moore asks, did the Industrial and French revolutions create such dramatically different political solutions as English and French parliamentary government, aristocratic monarchy in Germany, Communism in Russia and China, and militarist dictatorship in Japan? His answer is that the political outcome of development depends on the relationship among three main classes at the moment when a society has to confront industrialization. The existence of a strong and independent urban commercial class that can seize control over national policy will result in democratic capitalism. If a strong bourgeoisie is lacking and the landed class sponsors the commercialization of agriculture while at the same time taking control of the state, a fascist style will emerge. If the landed class fails to commercialize agriculture before market relations intrude into the countryside, however, peasant revolution is likely, but only where the relationship between the landlord and the peasant is weak. This last is likely to produce a communist society, with the leadership in the hands of the intellectual elite that provided the peasants with the organizational skills needed to run their revolution.

In working out this system in detail Moore does not discuss small countries, such as those in Eastern Europe, because, as he puts it, "the decisive causes of their politics lie outside their own boundaries."[2] Moore's assumption, apparently, is that only large countries have a social system of sufficient autonomy to affect decisively the structure of posttransition political organization. Germany provides the example of a landed upper class in position to introduce capitalist agriculture before a bourgeoisie could establish itself strongly, with a conservative political result. The English bourgeoisie was already in place by the time industrialization began, so the tendency was toward democratic results. In China peasant, or communist, revolution resulted when capitalist relations were introduced into the countryside under conditions of weak landed upper-class control.

And yet in a fundamental way large countries and small countries do not differ in the era of transformation: they must face the pressures of

exogenous change, whenever it comes, with a given set of social arrangements. There seems to be no *a priori* reason the critical elements at work in
Moore's model might not have their impact on small entities as well as
large ones. At least it seems plausible that democracy in Czechoslovakia,
aristocratic bureaucratism in Hungary, peasantism in Bulgaria, and perhaps even mixed results elsewhere may be in part the result of the social
configuration in those countries when they entered into the not too warm
embrace of the state system. That is the hypothesis of this article. To test
it I will discuss briefly five examples of East European development:
Czechoslovakia, Hungary, Romania, Bulgaria, and Serbia. Those who do
not wish to follow the argument through the thickets of factual material
may turn to the end of the chapter, where conclusions as to Moore's
applicability to Eastern Europe may be found.

In several regards the political and social history of the Czech lands were
not favorable for the creation of democracy. Urban development of Bohemia and Moravia lagged; servile labor requirements were abolished only
as late as 1848, well after the initial mechanization of the Bohemian textile
industry; and land in Bohemia was maldistributed. As of 1757 only 0.5
percent of Bohemian land was held in freehold, and a report of 1902
showed that the 0.5 percent of the rural population with farms larger than
one hundred hectares owned almost one-third of the land, whereas smallholders with farms under five hectares, who comprised 71.6 percent of the
population, owned a total of only 14.7 percent of the land (medium-sized
farms constituted 28 percent of the farmers and about 50 percent of the
land).[3] The political arrangements of the empire in the nineteenth century
reflected this relationship, with the emperor and aristocracy holding the
major reins of power.

Nonetheless, after World War I Czechoslovakia became, by general
consensus, "the most prosperous, progressive, and democratic state of East
Central Europe."[4] Led by a number of unusually balanced and states-
manlike figures, such as Tomás Masaryk, Eduard Beneš, and Antonín
Švehla, the new republic of Czechoslovakia constructed a political democracy that was able to take difficult steps, such as devaluation of its currency
in 1919, while at the same time providing for the participation of even the
Communist party in public life. Czech democracy may not have been
perfect in its ability to deal with national minorities or in the strictness with
which party discipline and presidential leadership were enforced, and it
was swept away by events beyond its control, but a great many Czechs,
both within the intelligentsia and among the public at large, believed by
the twentieth century in the virtues of parliamentary life.[5] Czech nationalists claim that this was the result of the Czech national character, formed by
history from the time of Jan Hus into a democratic spirit of moderation.
An explanation more in the spirit of Barrington Moore, however, would
be that Czechs achieved national consciousness in the nineteenth century at

a time when industrialization and social differentiation were already relatively advanced.

Textiles were a major industry in which mechanization took place in Bohemia in the nineteenth century, but textiles were not a new industry to the Czech lands. The flax-growing areas of the mountainous parts of Bohemia had produced linens since the Middle Ages. With the creation of a world market in the sixteenth century, Bohemia began to enter that market not only through German traders in Nuremberg and Augsburg, but directly through Milan, Spain, and Portugal. The prosperity this trade brought to Bohemia was destroyed when the Czech nobility revolted against their Habsburg king in 1618. Suffering definitive defeat at the Battle of White Mountain in 1620, the Czech nobility found itself deposed and its estates parceled out over the next century to aristocrats from other parts of the Habsburg realm. This disaster for the Czech nobility was accompanied by the terrible destruction of the Thirty Years War. Whereas it is fashionable now to discount the casualties of that war in the German lands, Czech scholars still estimate that in Bohemia as much as half of the population perished.[6] The change in aristocracy and the demographic disaster, however, did not alter the pattern of social stratification. In fact, as the postwar population grew (it increased by a factor of about 2.5 in the 130 years following the Thirty Years War), the new nobility succeeded in imposing ever stricter work requirements on their serfs. This second enserfment was not related directly to foreign trade in grain, as it may have been in Poland, but it does seem to have had a relationship to the restoration of the linen trade.

Prior to the Thirty Years War German firms made arrangements with urban craft guilds in the Czech lands to purchase their entire linen output, thus preserving the guild system of skilled craftsmen even while involving them in significant international trade. After the devastation of the Thirty Years War, however, much of the linen industry moved into the countryside, where German firms and their agents (factors) established a putting-out system. A firm (or entrepreneur, or factor) procured raw materials for the peasant spinners or weavers, or lent the money needed to purchase such materials, and then bought back all of the production. Feudal landlords were more than happy for the linen industry to shift to the countryside, even if it was organized industrially, since their increasing power included an obligation by their serfs to provide a certain amount of spinning or weaving. An increase in the sales of flax profited the lord also, as did the payments made to him by his serfs for permission to do extra spinning or weaving and the percentage paid the lord on every piece produced. This system did not preserve the concept of individual craftsman but resembled a wage system, and therefore has been called proto-industrialism.[7] Created for purposes of foreign trade, the system worked well internally also. The mountainous, less agriculturally productive areas became heavily involved in linen production, which was sold to the lowlanders for agricultural produce, thus creating a relatively complex division of labor in Austria.

English and Dutch traders in linens penetrated into Saxony and Bohemia by 1660. Raw Bohemian linens were sent up the Elbe to Hamburg and thence to Holland or England, where they were dyed, made into garments, and re-exported. Seventeenth-century Austrian mercantilists realized that this trade was disadvantageous to the crown, since Bohemia was merely supplying the raw linen (or raw wool) to others, who manufactured it into more profitable finished products. Already in 1664 P. W. Hörnigk insisted in his treatise *Österreich über alles wann es nur will* that Austria could greatly prosper if, among other things, it would process its raw materials at home.[8] For Hörnigk and the other mercantilists, this meant not only prohibiting the export of raw materials and the import of finished products, but encouraging manufactories and discouraging guilds, which were seen as a brake on industrial development. It took a long time for mercantilist ideas to be put into practice, however. Not until 1702 were imports of foreign linen forbidden, and only in 1731 and 1739 were the rights of craft guilds curtailed. But by the time of Maria Theresa, mercantilist ideas had become the entrenched orthodoxy.

At the beginning of the eighteenth century, English entrepreneurs saw the potential profitability of conducting all phases of linen production in Bohemia itself and began to establish bleaching and dying factories. Arnošt Klíma describes the enormous success of a certain Robert Allason, who established a very large manufacturing system in Rumburk in 1713.[9] One local nobleman, Count Filip Josef Kinsky, became so enamored of industrial methods that he signed a contract with Allason, becoming in effect an entrepreneur. This was not at all unusual. In the eighteenth century nobility played the major entrepreneurial role in the growing Bohemian proto-industries.[10]

Austrian defeat in the War of the Austrian Succession, coupled with the pressures of population growth, brought important changes to the Habsburg lands. When Frederick II seized Silesia, Maria Theresa began to seek ways of centralizing her state and strengthening her economy, not only because Prussia alarmed her, but because the declining prosperity of the peasantry due to population growth made her realize that the stability of the crown might depend on ameliorating the economic condition of the increasingly restive peasants.[11] Under the influence of Kaunitz, who as administrator of Milan had come into contact with a successful liberal economy and who knew the ideas of the physiocrats, Maria Theresa agreed to the introduction of free trade in the Austrian lands.[12] Until this point linen manufacturers in Bohemia had been able to prohibit the production of cotton goods, but in 1763 the prohibition was lifted.

In 1775, after a particularly large peasant uprising clarified the danger presented by an impoverished peasantry, Maria Theresa went further, limiting the labor services of the serf population. By a decree of that year obligations were divided into eleven categories so that peasants with the largest holdings had to provide substantial labor services, whereas peasants at the other end of the scale, without land, who constituted from 40 to 60 percent of the rural population, depending on region, were required to work for the lord only thirteen days a year, thus freeing them for other labor.[13] The new rules provided that "no one should force a spinner to work against his will for an entrepreneur under conditions disadvantageous to the employee. It was further decreed that the relationship between the domestic worker and his employer should be based on contract. Should one party not fulfill the contract the second party could no longer be held to be bound by it."[14] The decree on labor reflected Maria Theresa's desire, as she expressed it a year later, "to promote as much freedom in trade and industry as possible in all my lands," but its result was to permit the peasantry to increase its income, and thus stave off the Malthusian threat, by participating in proto-industry.[15]

Joseph II was influenced more by the entrenched ideas of mercantilism than by the new ideas of free trade, but he did continue the trend toward creating a more mobile labor force in 1781 with his so-called liberation of the serfs. Servile labor obligations were not finally abolished until 1848, but Joseph's decree permitted serfs to marry, move if they were not indebted to their lord, and learn trades and arts without payment or permission.[16]

The influx of foreign traders, entrepreneurs, and technicians; the interest of the Bohemian nobility in the textile trade; the lifting of the restrictions on cotton manufacturing; and the increase in labor mobility brought about by the reforms of Maria Theresa and Joseph II led to the creation of a substantial proto-industry in textiles in Bohemia in the eighteenth century. By 1789 the number of persons employed in cotton spinning and weaving grew to more than 528,000, with a somewhat smaller number of persons in linens, an indication of the enormous development of textiles in Bohemia even before the introduction of mechanical devices. In Moravia the city of Brno underwent such a rapid transformation in the 1780s that Czech scholars have called it the "Manchester of Central Europe."[17] By the end of the century nonnoble entrepreneurs began to overtake the nobility, hitherto dominant among native entrepreneurs. A growing number of merchants, rich peasants, successful factors, and prosperous artisans began to take the aristocracy's place. Capital was scarce, and no banking system supported their efforts, but the experience and earnings of factors and small-scale traders during the proto-industrial era created a growing group with many of the characteristics of a bourgeoisie.

Mechanization of this already advanced industry began at the turn of the nineteenth century when an Englishman named John Thornton set up a spinning mill in Pottendorf. By 1805 Bohemia had 18,000 mechanical spindles; by 1827, 47,000; by 1850, 550,000; by 1880, 1.6 million; and by 1914, 4.9 million.[18] The introduction of cotton-weaving machinery began in 1815, and mechanized means of spinning and weaving first wool and then flax and linen were introduced as the century wore on. In imitation of Britain's classic example, the mechanization of the textile industry called forth concomitant growth in coal mining and machine production, and innovations began to appear in other industries as well. Among these was the introduction of sugar beets, which after 1848 became one of Bohemia's most advanced and lucrative industrial enterprises. By 1880 more than half a million persons in Austria and Bohemia were employed in modern industrial enterprises, and by 1913 the number was 2.3 million.[19]

This impressive development, which put Bohemia at a level only somewhat below Germany but above France and Italy in some sectors, was not entirely without problems. Urbanization lagged in part because traditionally the textile industries were located in the countryside, in part because the sugar beet industry was rural, and in part because of the lateness of completely relieving the serfs of their obligations. Despite the appearance of many capable native entrepreneurs, there remained a shortage of entrepreneurial talent. The important point, however, is that at the moment when national consciousness arose in Bohemia, industrial development with its concurrent social differentiation was already well under way. When the intelligentsia necessary for political action began to consider the Czech situation, it had at its disposal a growing class of persons economically outside the lord-serf nexus.

In a curious way the aristocracy, and the emperor who relied on it, were instrumental both in creating an economically independent class and in providing that class with its political education. Both the Bohemian nobility and the crown encouraged proto-industrialization in eighteenth-century Bohemia, Maria Theresa to strengthen her realm and the aristocracy to increase its income. Proto-industrialization acted as a substitute for England's mixed system in creating the beginnings of an independent class of entrepreneurs in Bohemia.

In the nineteenth century, when the number of entrepreneurs had become significant and a working class was emerging, the emperor and the landed aristocracy acted again in a way that permitted middle-class elements to gain a political education. By the Manifesto of 1868 Franz Josef created a two-track system of government for Austria. This system placed a provincial governor in charge of "internal security, taxation, military affairs, the census, judicial administration, and surveillance of self-governmental bodies" in every province. Each governor appointed a district captain to supervise these activities in the districts and communes.[20] The broad authority of these officials derived solely from the emperor. At the same time, however, Franz Josef created a second administrative track, consisting of communal and district governing boards, provincial diets, and executive committees, that was in charge of all local affairs not directly given over to the captains. Although in theory any decisions of local agencies could be overruled by the central bureaucracy, in practice their activities quickly became too varied and broad for real supervision. Local agencies concerned themselves with schools, roads, hospitals, poor relief, and similar matters, and many municipalities went further, establishing public transportation systems and even food-processing plants.[21]

The Austrian two-track system can be contrasted with the Russian *zemstvo* movement, which was established at about the same time. In comparison to Austria, Russian authorities gave the *zemstva,* which were to deal with the same type of problems as Austrian local governments, little leeway, so that efforts of the *zemstvo* workers to enter political life could be repudiated by Nicholas II as "senseless dreams." The Bohemian economy was much more developed in the 1870s and 1880s than the Russian economy, the educational level of the Czech population was higher, and the tradition of local self-administration, a holdover from the era of the *Ständestaat,* was much stronger. As a result, in contrast to their Russian contemporaries, liberal Czechs gained real political experience in local government. "Of forty-five Young Czech deputies elected to the *Reichsrat* in 1897," says Garver, "at least thirty had entered politics through communal or district political organizations."[22] The freer situation in Austria even permitted the emergence of a legal socialist party to represent the growing working class, although the party had to endure persecution analogous to that suffered by the German Social Democrats until 1890. The development of a peasant party completed the picture, so that when universal manhood suffrage for the lower house of the *Reichsrat* was introduced in 1907, Bohemian politicians were prepared to make use of the opportunity.

This is not the place to enter into the details of Czech political life in the decade preceeding World War I, nor into the creation of the Czechoslovak state in its aftermath. A great many factors entered into that success, not least the powerful personality of Tomás Masaryk. It seems clear, however, that Masaryk's success was due in significant measure to the existence of middle-class norms of democratic behavior that had been tested by Czech participants in Habsburg politics. Strong parties, all committed to national democracy, provided the creators of the Czechoslovak state with the raw material of democracy. These parties existed because Czech economic development proceeded from a long history of proto-industry and industrialization that created an alert middle class able to take advantage of the relatively narrow niche assigned to it by the dominant landowning class and its emperor. Although the members of this landowning class participated heavily in the initial introduction of both proto-industry and industrialization into the Czech lands, they did not undertake Moore's "revolution from above." By the time Czech industrialization was accelerating rapidly in the last half of the nineteenth century, middle-class competitors were elbowing noble entrepreneurs aside. Furthermore, no modern state existed for the landed nobility to seize. Instead they participated in the Habsburg system, leaving middle-class Czech politicians to educate themselves in the new norms of democratic behavior in local and regional politics. Therefore the demise of the centralized Viennese apparatus in 1918 did not create a vacuum of experience, but opened an opportunity to a prepared stratum. A group of middle-class parties existed that could seize power and introduce a democratic political solution. This result has a strong resonance with Moore's analysis. Central European industrialization was strongest in the Czech lands; it grew out of a developed proto-industrial tradition; it produced a middle class with substantive political experience; and interwar Czechoslovakia became a democracy. Only a good deal of further work could lend substance to this syllogism, but it is a plausible sequence, one suggestively close to what Moore's model might lead us to anticipate.

If Czechoslovakia was the most democratic state in interwar East Central Europe, Hungary was the least democratic. When in October 1918 the Habsburg Empire disintegrated, one of Hungary's few truly democratic politicians, Mihály Károlyi, sought to form a liberal government that the Western democracies would see as moderate, but he received almost no support from the public or from Hungarian political elites. Under severe pressure from foreign invasion and leftist revolutionaries, Károlyi lasted only until March 1919. The Soviet Republic of Béla Kun stayed in power until August, when an invading Romanian army permitted a counterrevolutionary regime under the leadership of Admiral Miklos Horthy to assume power. After the consolidation of this conservative regime by means of a massive bloodletting, stability was restored in 1921 when István Bethlen became premier and established control over the political system through fixed elections and strict direction of his own personal party. When the conservative Bethlen left power in 1931 and Hungary began to suffer the full effects of the depression, its government came increasingly into the hands of men and movements whose policies approached fascism, although extremists achieved power only at the very end of World War II.

No real controversy exists as to why Hungary's political culture was so inhospitable to democracy. Hungarian politics was dominated by the land-owning aristocracy. By the fourteenth century the king and noble estates had become equal partners in sovereignty, and from 1608 a bicameral Diet exercised the rights of the nobility. Locally elected noblemen ran the Hungarian counties, while a relatively large number of free towns were self-governed. In the middle ages, Hungary exported significant amounts of copper and livestock, and imported quality textiles from Western Europe.[23] Paradoxically, when Hungary came under Ottoman rule in the sixteenth century, exports actually increased, especially cattle. In the middle of the sixteenth century Hungary was supplying 100,000 head of oxen or more to the prosperous South German cities through the Viennese market.[24] Imports of textiles, on the other hand, shifted to the Balkans and the Near East, distancing Hungary from Western influence in this key sector. In the seventeenth century, when an increase in Atlantic trade changed the structure of the West European economy and the South German towns began to decline, cattle trade slumped and the Hungarian nobility, which had not abandoned its property rights despite the Ottoman occupation, increasingly had to rely on Austria for its cattle market.[25] Therefore, despite a temporarily favorable moment for capital accumulation in the sixteenth century when cattle exports were prospering, Hungary's isolation from the centers of the new world economic system by the seventeenth century left it unintegrated into that system and permitted the social organization of the aristocracy to remain intact. Unlike in Bohemia, few manufacturing enterprises penetrated into Hungary, so that when the Habsburgs achieved control over Hungary at the end of the seventeenth century the social dominance of the landowning and cattle-raising nobility, with its traditional political practices, was fully reestablished.

Three eighteenth-century processes insured the continued social dominance of the Hungarian aristocracy. The first grew out of economic decline and the policies adopted in Vienna to cope with it. Warfare, the lessening of foreign markets, rapid population growth, and practices designed to protect large landholders all contributed to a decline in the eighteenth century.[26] Maria Theresa's trade policies insured that Hungary would not attempt to solve this problem by turning to manufacturing or industry, which the empress reserved for Austria. In 1756 the crown established a differential tariff for finished goods moving between Austrian and Hungarian lands that favored Austrian finished products and Hungarian agricultural goods. When later in the century Chancellor Kaunitz encouraged the construction of canals and the dredging of waterways to facilitate the export of Hungarian grain to Austria, grain began to overtake cattle, wool, and wine as the main Hungarian agricultural export. In 1783 Hungarian livestock exports still were valued at about 1.6 times grain exports, but by 1834 the ratio had changed to almost four to one in favor of grain.[27] The growth rate in Hungarian cereal production from the 1780s to 1850 approximated 1.2 percent per year, a significant achievement, but precisely because this success removed any need for innovation it was not matched by industrial development, even of the proto-industrial type.[28] Transportation remained poor, town life declined, peasant life stagnated, and the landed aristocracy remained in control.

A second feature of the eighteenth century was the struggle between the ruler and the Hungarian estates for control of the Hungarian political process. In 1687, after his initial victories over the Turks, Leopold I forced the Diet to recognize him as Hungary's hereditary ruler, thus breaking the electoral tradition dating from 1301. It appears that the Habsburgs hoped to Austrianize the Hungarian nobility as they had the Bohemian aristocracy after White Mountain. But the Hungarian nobles resisted, even revolted, and by 1723 Charles VI had to swear to uphold the Hungarian constitution (i.e., to leave the Hungarian nobility alone) in return for the Diet's acceptance of the hereditary right of the Habsburgs, male or female, to rule. Maria Theresa wooed the Hungarians when she needed them to fight Frederick the Great, but she also did her best to weaken them. After 1764 she dispensed with the Diet, simply not calling it into session, and ruled by decree. At the same time, she attracted many of the greatest of the Hungarian nobility to Vienna, where they became closely attached to the crown. Joseph II went even further than his mother in his efforts to emasculate the Hungarian nobility when he attempted to abolish the traditional county governments. Maria Theresa's neglect and Joseph's antipathy provoked a so-called feudal reaction after Joseph's death that succeeded in securing from Leopold II renewed guarantees of the nobility's ancient privileges.

The success of the Hungarian nobleman in retaining his traditional political dominance was matched, especially after the Napoleonic era, by a third development, the subduing of the peasant population. Until about 1750 labor was in short supply in Hungary while abandoned lands were repopulated, and until 1790 a great deal of land clearing and reclamation was carried out, often by independent peasants. In 1767 Maria Theresa issued an urbarial patent defining peasant work obligations. She intended to limit excessive demands on the peasants, but in fact the patent helped the landords in Hungary to extend labor and cash requirements to peasants who formerly did not owe service. In the period 1790 to 1830 the largest Hungarian magnates expropriated tens of thousands of hectares of land cleared in the previous generation by free peasants. The result of the three interrelated processes of the late eighteenth and early nineteenth centuries—the relatively smooth transition to grain production, the nobles' success in defending their political rights, and the subjection of the peasantry—was that at the time Bohemia was changing from proto-industrial patterns to industrialization through the introduction of textile machinery, Hungary was becoming an almost completely agrarian economy under the full control of the landed aristocracy.

Austrian and Bohemian industrialization did not spread to Hungary directly, but the increasing urbanization of the Cisleithenian lands did increase the demand there for agricultural products, which Hungary supplied. There appears to be a direct link, therefore, between Austrian industrialization and the expansion of Hungarian cereal production, which grew in the nineteenth century more or less concomitantly with Austrian industrial development.[29] The growth of the Austrian market, which came about in part because Austria constructed military highways that facilitated grain transport, induced Hungarian landlords, especially the magnates, to improve their agricultural techniques, to establish small local industries such as glassmaking, and to increase their consumption of luxury goods as they sought to keep pace with the wealthy urban populations of Vienna and other European cities they wanted to emulate, but it did not induce them to industrialize. On the contrary: by the middle of the nineteenth century manufacturing equalled only 7 to 8 percent of Hungary's national product.

Contrary to earlier belief, the final liberation of the Hungarian serfs from labor commitments in 1848 and the creation of a customs union between Hungary and Austria in 1850 had little impact on changing the economic and social structure of Hungary.[30] Industrialization began in Hungary after the crash of 1873, when the Hungarian government began floating large state bond issues. Austrian investors, in order to secure a safe and lucrative return, began to pour funds into Hungary. The government turned this capital influx into infrastructure and agricultural improvements, thus fueling an industrial boom. This spurt lasted until the 1890s, when Austrian investment returned to Cisleithenia. Hungarian development leaped forward again after 1906 in concert with a second major influx of Austrian capital.

Hungarian industrialization did not begin in textiles in the classic manner. Instead entrepreneurs took advantage of Hungary's relative strength in grain to make flour its most important manufactured good. By the 1890s Budapest was, along with Minneapolis, the greatest flour milling city in the world.[31] Other successful areas of development included food processing, machine building, electrical and chemical industries, and railroad building.[32] In the period 1870 to 1913 Hungary's industrial product, albeit starting from a very low base, increased at a rate equivalent to that of Germany and substantially exceeded that of France and Italy.[33] By 1913 one quarter of the Hungarian national product was in manufacturing, not a truly developed amount, but enough to have pushed the population of Budapest to "more than a million in the half century preceding World War I."[34]

Hungarian industrialization, therefore, was quite adequate to produce a bourgeoisie capable of entering politics, which in fact it did. But the entry of this new class was conditioned by two fundamental factors: the social structure of Hungarian politics, and the character of the leading stratum of the Hungarian bourgeoisie.

Two main social groups created the modern state in Hungary. The first consisted of the approximately 160 families that made up the great aristocratic clans of Hungary, Croatia-Slavonia, and Transylvania and which in the eighteenth century owned about 40 percent of the seigneurial fiefs in the lands of the Crown of St. Stephen. The second group consisted of a much larger number of well-to-do gentry noblemen, constituting approximately 1 percent of the population (another 5 to 6 percent of the Hungarian population claimed noble status but were too poor to play a major political role). While not fabulously rich, as the great magnates were, members of the gentry were nonetheless usually substantial landholders. Other privileged groups existed, such as the clergy and free townspeople, but the aristocrats were the leaders of Hungarian society, especially in its relations with Vienna, and the gentry dominated county politics and the lower house of the Diet.

Nineteenth-century Hungarian political development can be divided into two general periods: the era during which gentry reformers sought either by action of the Diet or by revolution to establish Hungarian autonomy or even independence, and the era in which this gentry entered government service under the leadership of the magnates, who by the second half of the century had solidified their political control. In neither case, despite the use of liberal rhetoric and the espousal of principles taken from contemporary liberal political theory, did either branch of the Hungarian nobility envisage relinquishing its control of the political machinery.

The first period began with the calling of the Diet of 1825. Despite the crown's promises after the feudal reaction of 1790–1792, during the

Napoleonic period Franz I called the Diet only infrequently, and then mainly to pass appropriation bills. After 1811 he did not call it at all. When the Diet finally reconvened in 1825 a group of young gentry, many of whom were impoverished by their unsuccessful efforts to maintain a life-style the new fashions of industrializing Europe demanded, began to strike out against what they considered Habsburg oppression. Not only did they express an antagonism to Vienna traditional among some elements of the Hungarian nobility, but they also used the new ideas of romantic national-ism generated by the French Revolution. They were modernizers in one sense, since they sought to rework Hungary's laws to be more in accord with nineteenth-century principles, but they were not entrepreneurs or incipient capitalists. Instead they were seeking an arena of public life con-sistent with their dignity that would enable them to achieve power without having to become businessmen. As Andrew Janos put it, they were "a class desperately searching for alternatives to economic entrepreneurship."[35]

The gentry reform movement culminated in the Hungarian Revolu-tion of 1848, which at one point briefly succeeded in creating an indepen-dent Hungarian Republic under gentry leadership. Repression of the revo-lution quieted Hungary temporarily, but by 1867 it proved possible to reach an agreement with Vienna that permitted Hungary to develop its own internal political system. In 1875, after a brief flurry of experimenta-tion with ideas like the Law on Nationalities that might have lessened the influence of the landed class, Kálmán Tisza, a gentry nobleman whose personal wealth and prominent marriage brought him the respect of the highest aristocracy, established his personal control over the political pro-cess and instituted a regime of narrow class domination. Tisza perfected the technique of rigging elections, so that even while the urban vote grew more hostile and opposition parties appeared, control of the countryside through the mechanisms of open voting, indirect elections, and brute force made it possible for the government, which always kept the interests of the aristocratic landed class uppermost in its mind, to dominate Hungarian politics until World War I. Whereas after 1867 local government in Bo-hemia provided a training ground for middle-class politicians, in Hungary local politics either remained in the hands of a fractious but conservative gentry, or came more and more under the control of the central govern-ment, which is to say increasingly into the hands of a more educated and more sophisticated but no less conservative arm of the same gentry.

The salient characteristic of the bourgeoisie that confronted the aristo-cratic political leaders and their gentry government was that in significant measure it was Jewish. In the early nineteenth century Jewish traders, many of them recent immigrants into Hungary, replaced the Greeks who had conducted Hungarian mercantile activities in the eighteenth century. Vir-tually monopolizing the carrying trade in grain, Jews acted as estate man-agers and often were the tavern owners and moneylenders of the provincial towns and villages. From this base Jewish entrepreneurs came, in the second half of the century, to dominate Hungary's largest manufacturing enterprise, flour milling, to control much of the grain trade, and to run the Budapest banks. As McCagg wrote, the most successful Jews became "not only members of Hungary's urban middle class, but . . . the capitalist elite of that class."[36] Unrestricted by the aristocratic or gentry ethic that kept those classes from entrepreneurial success, Jews were at the same time outsiders, non-Hungarians. When the industrialization of the 1870s and later led to the creation of opposition parties, the Jews became vulnerable to the threat of attack by anti-Semitic populists. But Kálmán Tisza, looking for allies in his constant effort to keep his political machine intact, rejected anti-Semitism, even recommending to Franz Josef the ennoblement of a significant number of leading Jewish capitalists.[37] Later, between 1900 and World War I, over two hundred Hungarian Jewish families were ennobled. Alone among the minority peoples of the empire, Jews took to learning Magyar. Some of the new Jewish nobility converted to Christianity in order to join the exclusive clubs of Budapest. Enthusiastic in their support of the government and anxious to put their pariah status behind them, many of the richest Jewish families allied themselves with the great landowning nobility in maintaining the dominance of the aristocracy over the political process, while middle-class Jews showed the strongest tendency toward assimilation of any Jewish community in Eastern Europe.[38]

The tutorial function the landed class maintained over Hungarian industrialization, its domination of capitalist agriculture from the late eighteenth century, and the alliance it forged with a significant element of the bourgeoisie all are characteristics of the process Barrington Moore called "the revolution from above." The Hungarian nobility, both aristocratic and gentry, succeeded in maintaining a repressive labor system into the twentieth century. The formal freeing of the Hungarian serfs in 1848 left 60 percent of them landless. Liberation did eventually pemit a minor consolidation of moderately prosperous Hungarian smallholders by World War I, but this development came relatively late, taking hold only with the industrialization of the 1870s, and was offset by the large number of landless agricultural laborers who remained available for cultivating the landlords' fields and by the enormous increase in the amount of land in the hands of the great magnates.[39]

The revolution that wracked Hungary halfway through the nineteenth century was not a bourgeois revolution, but an effort to exchange Habsburg rule for liberal etatism under the control of the gentry. It changed the legal status both of the nobles, who no longer enjoyed seigneurial rights and were made technically equal to other citizens, and of the peasants, who no longer owed compulsory labor; but it did not abolish nobility as an honor, did not redistribute the land, and did not create a bourgeoisie.[40] Thus, while some reforms of 1848, such as the repeal of the prohibition on mortgaging homesteads, affected Hungarian agricultural development, the main burst of Hungarian industrialization was tied to the industrialization of Austria. Austria provided the market that created a profit-oriented agriculture late in the eighteenth and early in the nineteenth centuries, and in 1870s Austria provided the capital for industrialization. At both moments political power was in the hands of the great landowning magnates, in the second instance supported by a gentry-run state.

The magnates remained in power during the latter phases of this process in part by working out an accommodation with the most successful members of the Jewish bourgeoisie, who traded their pariah status for admission to the ruling elite. Just as in Prussia the Junkers found a way to come to an agreement with certain industrialists in order to preserve both their property and their status, so in Hungary the landed elite found a way to entice a significant number of a pariah bourgeoisie into an alliance by raising them up the the highest social level.[41] Considerable political skill went into this accommodation, which, like those in Germany and Japan, meant establishing a government separate from the people it ruled, but it created a Hungarian political culture in which democracy was considered an inappropriate option. Urban and peasant parties emerged, as did even a social democratic party, but in all segments of society, except perhaps the relatively small working class, acceptance of the aristocratic ideal was widespread. Thus in 1918 the democratic Károlyi stood alone, and even Kun could muster only a fitful spasm of rage. In the interwar years Hungary found itself in the ever more uncomfortable position of drifting toward the fascism that Moore's model predicts for it, even though the most extreme propositions of that faith accorded neither with the noble ethic nor with the interests of its Jewish adherents.

Romanian social structure had a good deal in common with that of Hungary. Romanian landholding at the turn of the twentieth century was at least as concentrated as it was in Hungary;[42] the liberal reformers of the period came from a declining class of gentry boyars;[43] the great Romanian boyars made their fortunes from huge landholdings turned to grain trade; and Jews were an important element in commerce, banking, and industry before World War I. But Romanian political development did not proceed as it did in Hungary. The richest boyars were not able to maintain their position by 1900, being outflanked not only by the Romanian king but also by the bureaucracy of the central government. After World War I, instead of a cosmetic agrarian reform, the Romanians undertook a massive land redistribution that eliminated the great landlords as a class. While Romania was not a model of democracy in the interwar period, it did take genuine steps toward creating a democratic system. In the end, of course, led by a willful king, beset by the economic pressures of the depression, and pressured by the expansionist policies of Hitlerite Germany, Romania drifted into dictatorship.[44]

The origins of the Romanian landowning elite, the boyars, are wrapped in obscurity. Before the coming of the Ottomans, the Romanian lands were not exploited agriculturally by a feudal nobility, but consisted of communal villages making moderate payments to an upper class that made its living from control of the international trade that passed through the principalities.[45] When the Ottoman conquest disrupted and transformed

this trade the boyars could not impose serfdom on the Romanian peasantry because of the low population density and the ability of the peasants
to flee to mountainous regions. The necessity to supply Istanbul with
livestock and grain, however, encouraged boyars to attempt to secure
rights to the agricultural production of villages, and in the seventeenth and
eighteenth centuries a good deal of the plains area came under boyar
control, although not in the form of ownership. Boyars had very little land
that elsewhere would have been called demesne. Instead they were said to
"control" a village, or to be its "master," which meant they had the right to
collect a tithe from those who worked the land. The Romanian peasant
also owed a labor service, but in the eighteenth century it amounted to no
more than six days a year, a very small amount. The fact that a good deal of
the trade of the principalities was in livestock, including sheep that were
raised by transhumance, kept the Romanian peasants in motion and made
it difficult for the boyars to settle them in one place for long. An even more
important hindrance to Romanian enserfment was a demographic decline
of the eighteenth century that resulted from a series of Turkish wars and
from the inability of the weak political system to control the countryside.
The population of the principalities was only about a half million in 1750,
and most of the Wallachian boyars who could afford it moved to Bucharest
for their own safety.

Bucharest was a real city already in the eighteenth century for two
reasons. First, it was the trading center for the significant Romanian exports to Istanbul. Second, it became the center of administration for foreign princes installed by the Ottoman government after 1711. These
phanariot Greeks from Istanbul constituted the top aristocracy of the principalities in the eighteenth century, with the boyars that surrounded them
constituting the next social level. Some of the phanariot families endured
to remain powerful landlords and political figures in the nineteenth century, but the extremely short tenure of most *hospodars* led to chaotic political intrigues in Bucharest and a constant turnover in the composition of
the Romanian elite.

From a low point in the mid-eighteenth century, Romanian population increased rapidly, as did the interest of the boyars in cereal production.
Accordingly, in the last half of the eighteenth century the number of labor
days that could be required of a peasant was raised substantially in Moldavia, and even a modest amount in the more open Wallachia.[46] Shortages
during the Napoleonic period created a demand for cereal products that
encouraged the boyars into further tightening their control over the peasantry. By 1818 settlement on lands controlled by a boyar became a privilege, not a right, and the tithe to be paid for working such land was raised
from one-tenth to one-fifth. At the same time, the eighteenth-century
tendency of the boyars to leave the actual running of their estates to leasing
agents while they themselves resided in Bucharest intensified. When in the
nineteenth century the boyars in Bucharest began to find it necessary to
emulate the ever more wealthy lifestyle of Vienna and, especially, Paris,

their need for income increased.[47] Profit-oriented lessors tended to enforce rules concerning peasant obligations more strictly than had the traditional boyars in the first place, and when the boyars' need for income increased, pressure on the peasantry redoubled.

The peculiar vagueness of the Romanian concept of ownership, which was limited to the right of the boyar to collect both labor (often transmuted into cash) and a tithe, led to the proliferation of sharecropped holdings rather than the consolidation of latifundia. In the middle of the nineteenth century the area directly exploited by the boyars constituted only about 5 percent of cultivated lands.[48] During the second half of the century, however, the tendency was for the portion cultivated directly by the boyars to increase. The global demand for grain exports, including those to the Habsburg lands and to the Mediterranean, pushed more and more of the fertile Moldavian and Wallachian lowlands into cereal production. Concurrently, despite occasional forays into reform and land distribution, the boyars continued to find ways to increase their control over the Romanian peasantry and to increase their own holdings. The reform of 1864, for example, which was intended to relieve peasants of their obligations for servile labor and was bitterly opposed by the boyars, actually increased the landlord's leverage considerably. For the first time the concept of ownership was spelled out in law, with the boyar receiving outright one-third of the property formerly under his stewardship and the peasantry the remaining two-thirds in plots of limited size. By prohibiting peasants from selling their small holdings, the reform prevented the development of a middling peasantry. The new law further restricted the peasant owner by requiring him to pay the state over a fifteen-year period for his liberation from tithe and labor payments. Since the payment usually was set at a level greater than the net income from small holdings, peasants had to work the boyars' land to raise money to pay their debts, which increased steadily nonetheless. The law or 1864 also put outside of the state's concern a type of contract that became very common by the end of the century whereby, in order to be permitted to sign a sharecropping contract for use of a portion of the landlord's land, a peasant had to work another portion for free. By 1900, therefore, the most powerful Romanian boyars controlled huge estates divided into tiny sharecropped holdings plus a growing demesne worked by a peasantry not far removed from serfdom. Despite the size of the holdings of the greatest boyar families, which approximated those of the grandest Hungarian aristocrats, the peculiar history of Romanian agrarian development did not create a rural proletariat, but rather a peasantry of subjugated smallholding sharecroppers.

A few aggressive landlords answered the demand for cereal crops in the nineteenth century by turning to wheat production and by introducing mechanization, but by and large the Romanian boyar remained a *rentier*. Living in Bucharest, the boyar leased his land to a manager for a set fee. The lessor then extended a contract to the peasantry on the most advantageous terms he could, extracted the payments from the sharecropper, and sent the grain on its way into the international market through a network of merchants and traders who often were not Romanian but Greek, Armenian, German, or Jewish. Even though this process constituted a capitalist system of markets, and even though capital accumulation proceeded among those who organized this trade, neither the peasant nor the boyar felt much effect from it. Relying on sharecroppers who usually paid in kind, lessors who insured that income for life in Bucharest would be forthcoming, and a state that made sure this cozy relationship would continue, the Romanian landlords prospered, but they did not mature. Indeed, this system of neo-serfdom was their undoing. Since the great boyars did not enter into the world market as profit-seeking farmers but as tribute-exacting rentiers, they had small interest in creating the revolution from above that Moore identifies as the key modernizing element in the maintenance of landed power into the modern age.

Romania did have its revolution from above in the nineteenth century, but it was conducted by a state dominated by liberal nationalists who emerged from the middling boyars, not by the great landlords. Under pressure like their Hungarian counterparts to maintain new standards of living, but with neither the wealth nor the cultural tools to do so, many middling boyar activists entered public life in the middle third of the nineteenth century. Their first goal in the 1830s and 1840s was simply to make themselves socially equal to the twenty or so great boyar families that dominated political life under the Organic Statutes, but after they had more or less accomplished this goal, the second generation of reformers undertook to make Romania a "modern" state in which they could find employment, dignity, and worth.

Ion Brătianu, the main liberal leader of the independence period, organized the new Romanian state on the basis of the French model, with Bucharest playing the role of Paris. Whereas the landlords controlled the peasantry through their domination of the local communes, after 1878 many other aspects of local administration came into the hands of men appointed by and loyal to Bucharest. At first the centralized state bureaucracy contained a high number of prominent old boyars, but by 1900 the dominant stratum in the state administration consisted of professional bureaucrats whose loyalties were to the state itself and to their careers within it.[49] This did not mean that the state became interested in upsetting the asymmetrical social relations of the countryside. On the contrary, both major political parties, the liberals and the conservatives, the first being the party of the middling gentry and the second being the party of the old boyars, agreed on the necessity of keeping the peasant laboring on his small sharecropped holding. But in contrast to the conservatives, the liberals took up the cause of modernization. Their method was not to introduce capitalism to the countryside, but to introduce it to the towns and cities by industrializing, by encouraging the growth of a Romanian middle class, and by creating a state machinery that would be a loyal arm of liberal policies. Thus, although the liberals had no intention of limiting the rights of the landlords, neither did they see themselves primarily as the landlords' protectors. Instead they were modernizers, national enthusiasts whose support came from the urban professional and official class.[50]

The contrast between Romanian and Hungarian development is nowhere clearer than in the matter of how the modernizing leadership generated electoral support for itself. Hungarian aristocrats entered into capitalist agriculture and used the large number of landless Hungarian peasants to work their lands. Tisza, who represented these landlords, insured his majorities by mobilizing massive pluralities of the landless peasants to offset his weakness in the developing urban areas. In Romania the small sharecroppers were not only difficult to mobilize, but Brătianu did not represent the interests of the large landlords directly. By a law of 1884 he structured his voting system to emphasize the strength of the urban professionals that his policy of modernization and state formation was creating, rather than the mass of subjugated peasants that his developmental plan ignored.

A second difference between the Hungarian and Romanian cases was perhaps even more salient. Control of the state apparatus was vital for the Romanian liberals not only because it could be used to assist modernization, but also because it could be used to channel the fruits of that modernization into the hands of ethnic Romanians. Romanian economic growth in the last third of the nineteenth century and the first years of the twentieth century took place in two parallel currents. First, with state encouragement, ethnic Romanian industry and banking grew to the extent that by World War I a Romanian banking system had been created, and of more than six hundred industrial enterprises in the country, a majority were in Romanian lands. At the same time, however, without help from the state and indeed usually in conflict with it, a naturally evolving Jewish sector of the economy grew up. As of 1800 there were only a few Jews in Moldavia and almost none in Wallachia. But as the century wore on many Jews from the Russian Empire entered the principalities, especially Moldavia. Since they were denied the right of citizenship even if they were born in Romania, denied the right to own land, and denied the right to settle in the countryside, they were forced into the towns and cities, where they became artisans, traders, administrators, and bankers, not to mention peddlers, tailors, and other traditional craftsmen at the low end of the social scale. By 1900 less than 5 percent of Romania's population was Jewish (Moldavia 10.5 percent; Wallachia 1.8 percent), but almost all of that percentage was urban, so that Jews constituted about 50 percent of the population of Iaşi and more than one-third of that of Bucharest.[51] Furthermore, Jews were overwhelmingly employed in the more developed sectors of the economy. Whereas only 13.7 percent of the Romanian work force was employed in industry, trade, and credit, 79.1 percent of the Jewish work force was employed in those areas.[52]

From the beginning of the Romanian national movement liberals struggled against the increasing success of enterprising Jews. When liberals obtained control of the state they made every effort to restrict Jewish activities, even among the vast majority of Romanian Jews who were impoverished artisans and small traders. For example, when complaints were received from villages about competition from Jewish peddlers, the government forbade Jews to pursue this miserable trade, thereby putting some 5,000 itinerant peddlers out of work.[53] On the other hand, a few Jews became very successful, especially in those businesses in which contacts abroad were useful, such as the grain trade and banking.[54] Despite an ingrained anti-Semitism, the large landowning boyars were aware that many of their most efficient lessors were Jewish, that they needed Jewish grain merchants, and that financing was often more secure from Jewish banks. Accordingly, conservative politicians were more restrained than the liberals in their application of anti-Jewish policies.[55] But in contrast to Hungary, the greatest Romanian boyars did not achieve control over the state mechanism and did not produce any leaders of the stature of Kálmán Tisza. The liberals, on the other hand, saw the Jews as serious economic rivals and used the state to give themselves as many fair and foul advantages as they could against their enemy. The complete lack of desire of the liberals to work out a compromise with the Jewish middle class, and the conservatives' inability to do so, left the Romanian body politic splintered and made it impossible for the landlords to control the development of social forces to the same extent as in Hungary.

Another factor that prevented the old boyars from decisively shaping Romanian political culture was the active role played in Romanian politics by King Carol. Carol was Romania's largest landowner and pursued an enlightened policy of agricultural improvement on his lands, including even education for the peasantry. In politics he preferred the liberals, not the conservatives, in part perhaps because of the strong personal influence exercised over him by Ion Brătianu. But Carol was not an ideologue. To insure his dominance over Romanian politics he alternated conservative and liberal governments with only minimal regard to their ostensible ideologies or to public opinion. Hungarian politicians had to deal only with the far-off Franz Josef, who in any event had guaranteed them internal autonomy. The Romanian conservatives had to deal with a king who replaced them with their rivals when he deemed it necessary. Thus, whereas in Hungary a handful of the most prominent landowners exercised ultimate control over the system, in Romania the king did so, and the old boyars were never able to sustain the same confident dominance as their Hungarian counterparts.

The final element that prevented the landowning class from maintaining itself after World War I was the peasantry itself. By bursting into ferocious revolt in 1907 and by making its discontent known while under arms in 1917, the Romanian peasantry convinced even diehards that without agrarian reform an enormous social upheaval would result. Agrarian reform became possible particularly in Moldavia also because the Moldavian upper classes allowed their anti-Russian feelings to make them pro-

German during World War I, thus destroying their credibility and making them fair game after 1918. Therefore, although the postwar land reforms were inadequate because of population growth, and they never went beyond land distribution to achieve agricultural improvement, they did have the remarkable result of destroying the landlords as a class; this was the final price the large boyars paid for their unwillingness, or perhaps their inability, to seize control of the prewar Romanian state.

All of these factors produced in Romania a situation in which a statist middle class dominated politics, at least for the first ten years of the interwar period. The liberals, under Ion C. Brătianu, created the same sort of centralized regime that the elder Brătianu had established in the old kingdom in the 1880s, but two strong parties, the Peasant Party of Transylvania and the National Party of the Regat, provided effective opposition under the protection of a new constitution. The merger of these parties into the National Peasant party led in 1928 to the coming to power of Iuliu Maniu. Despite its name, Maniu's party remained under middle-class leadership, and Maniu himself took important steps toward creating a real constitutional regime in Romania. Maniu's efforts were short-lived, however, because when King Carol II returned from exile in 1930 he gathered more and more power into his own hands, until by 1938 his dictatorship ended Romania's flirtation with democracy.

The Romanian case is less clear than the Czech or Hungarian ones in terms of Moore's model. A landowning class did "use a variety of political and social levers to hold down a labor force on the land,"[56] but the result, at least immediately after World War I, was not fascism. Instead a recognizable, if weak, tendency toward democracy emerged. It is true that a native fascist movement of some importance arose also, but this Legion of Archangel Michael was a mystical movement of regeneration that concentrated in its early phases on mobilizing the neglected peasants rather than on maintaining control over them through a decaying landed elite.[57] The Legionnaires anti-Semitism fed on traditions introduced by the liberals, so that when Romania fell under the shadow of German Nazism the already insecure position of Romanian Jewry turned to catastrophe.

Still, genuine efforts toward democratization were made in the first decade of the interwar years in Romania. In significant measure this modest result was possible because the landlords' social dominance was completely shattered by the postwar agricultural reforms, which in turn came about in part because of pressure from a revolutionary peasantry, exactly the sort of pressure, if not mechanism, predicted by Moore in the case of a landed elite that responds weakly to commercial impulses.[58] This pressure did not result in an actual revolution and the installation of a communist dictatorship, as Moore also predicted, because agrarian reform temporarily mollified the peasantry. But reform itself was possible only because the old boyars had not succeeded in translating their social dominance in the prewar years into control of the state. That control was exercised by the liberals, who, despite their unwillingness to permit full entry into their midst by the powerful Jewish bourgeoisie, represented nonetheless a Romanian urban class in which not only merchants, bankers, and industrialists played a role, but most importantly members of the free professions and state employees. This group, which included even Maniu's peasant party, was not able, as Moore put it, "to cope with the severe problems of the day" and was swept aside by events originating beyond the Romanian borders.[59] Unable or unwilling to find a way to change the peasants into something other than smallholding sharecroppers, the Romanian state bureaucracy simply left them for the post–World War II regime to digest, which it found exceedingly difficult.

It would be charmingly symmetrical at this juncture if we could find that Serbia and Bulgaria represented mature examples of Moore's revolutionary communist type that Romania does not quite achieve. Unfortunately, one of the requirements of Moore's third type of social situation, which he sees exemplified in the cases of Russia and China, is the presence of an old-fashioned landed elite. The salient fact of both Bulgarian and Serbian development, however, is precisely that in both countries the landed elite, which had existed for several centuries, was ejected just before the beginning of the modern era. Both Serbia and Bulgaria had a medieval nobility, but the conquering Ottomans annihilated it. In its place came Ottoman spahis, who held their land and the produce of the peasants on it in return for service, and janissaries, who were at first members of a military elite but by the late eighteenth century degenerated into marauding raiders under the leadership of local strongmen.[60] Disruptive conditions in Serbia prevented the creation of an enserfed peasantry there in the eighteenth century, but the legal right to extract dues and tribute remained firmly in Ottoman hands.

In the first quarter of the nineteenth century, however, the First and Second Serbian Uprisings (1804–1830) forced the Ottoman landowners out of Serbia. During this revolutionary moment the Serbian peasant changed from an encumbered second-class citizen to the free owner of a private holding. During the First Uprising local Serbian military and religious leaders acted as if they might establish themselves as a new Serbian nobility by stepping into the places held by the departing Ottomans, but Miloš Obrenović, the wily leader of the less bloody but more successful Second Uprising, was determined that no one other than himself achieve power over the Serbian peasant. He succeeded to such an extent that he became perhaps the richest man in the Balkans, but at the same time he steadfastly refused to permit the creation of large landed estates or the entry of peasants into servile relations. Therefore, when Miloš was overthrown by a handful of notables, he left a country made up socially of only one class, a highly undifferentiated peasantry. None of the few distinguished individuals who took power in the 1840s owned more than a few hundred acres of land at most, none tried to trace their lineage to noble forebears, none had aristocratic lifestyles, and none were more than barely removed from their peasant backgrounds. Despite the efforts of some

Serbian historians to show class differentiation in Serbia in the 1840s, by the normal standards applied to other European societies we are dealing with an essentially classless system.

In Bulgaria a similar situation obtained, but later and under slightly different circumstances. Bulgarian commercial interests were slightly better developed than those of Serbia. As early as the eighteenth century a small class of successful Bulgarian traders, known as *chorbadjis,* established themselves in the Ottoman Empire, perhaps the most important group of them in Istanbul. Nonetheless, when the Bulgarian renascence began in the middle of the nineteenth century, Bulgaria was a completely rural country, run by Ottoman landlords and their Grecified or Turkified Bulgarian allies. A sense of Bulgarian national consciousness began to emerge among some educated Bulgarians only in the 1850s, taking the form of a struggle for the independence of the Bulgarian Orthodox Church and the promulgation of its liturgy among Bulgarians in Macedonia. But when the Russian victory over the Ottomans in 1878 created an independent Bulgaria, neither the *chorbadjis* nor the churchmen took the lead. Instead a group of liberal intelligentsia dominated the constitutional convention at Turnovo that wrote Bulgaria's new basic law in 1879. It took some time to rid Bulgaria finally of the Ottoman landlords, but the process continued over the next generation in such a way that Bulgaria, like Serbia, became and remained largely a land of smallholding peasants. Not sharecroppers, not a rural proletariat, these independent subsistence producers were only slowly drawn into a minimally complex local system of production and trade.[61]

Both Serbia at the beginning of the 1840s and Bulgaria at the end of the 1870s experienced a situation almost outside our definitional categories: a social vacuum. And in both instances, a class emerged to fill that vacuum: the state. The most coherent institution in both Serbia and Bulgaria, far richer, far more organized, and far better supported by ideological justifications than any other social organizations, the state itself became the dominant class otherwise missing from the experiences of both countries.

By the time of independence in 1878, Serbia already had a state. After the departure of Prince Miloš in 1838 his successors created a strongly hierarchical bureaucracy based on the idea that the educated, those with *znanje,* or knowledge, should administer the state for the benefit of the nation by the use of a strictly controlled bureaucracy. Starting in 1858, however, liberal elements began agitating for a constitutional regime. When the assassination of Prince Michael Obrenović in 1868 brought a fourteen-year-old prince to the throne, the most prominent statist liberal of the era, Jovan Ristić, pushed through a constitutional law that he hoped would permit him and his allies to govern while a docile legislature provided the assent of the nation. By formalizing the institution of a legislature, Ristić laid the groundwork for the emergence of vocal public factions. When in 1880 Ristić fell and a group that favored the creation of formal parties came to power, Serbian politics began to take on the aspect of a rough and ready parliamentary system.

Three competitors vied for control of this system. One remained the bureaucracy, a second became the politicians who achieved prominence through success in the electoral process and in party politics, and the third was the prince. Just as in Romania, but unlike in Hungary and the Czech lands, the prince of Serbia (king after 1882) constantly interfered in the political process, preventing the development of a bona fide democracy. Political parties became important, nevertheless, after the achievement of Serbian independence. The most formidable of these was the Serbian Radical party founded in 1881 and led from that time until 1926 by Nikola Pašić. The Radicals were the first in Serbia to create local clubs linked together by a national organization, the first to enroll peasants with party cards, and the first to mobilize a sizeable electorate on the basis of a program rather than on the basis of police interference.

In the era of independence after 1878, the state over which these three elements struggled was able to extract and spend in its own interest ever-increasing amounts of resources from the productive groups in Serbia, namely the peasantry and a growing urban stratum. This was not simply a history of corrupt, political figures who used the state to feather their own nests, although there was a good deal of that. Instead the state spent the resources it raised on extremely expensive projects that were designed to increase its own wealth, power, and ability to act but were only marginally useful to the peasants. These projects included the creation of a diplomatic service, construction of railroads, expansion of the army, and growth of the bureaucracy.[62] Improving agriculture, an activity that might have bene-fited the numerically overwhelming producing class, was not a priority. In 1908, for example, Serbia boasted only three agricultural schools training 222 students.[63] All the funds spent on agricultural schools, plant breeding experiments, and agricultural stations came to 3 percent of the Ministry of Agriculture's budget for 1910, which itself was only 3 percent of the state budget. The same budget allocated 23 percent for direct military expenditures and 28 percent for debt service, the vast majority of which was interest on loans used to build railroads and improve the army.[64]

The ideology that fit these policies best was nationalism, which justified both the expansion of state activities and the extraction of ever-greater amounts from society to pay for them. One area in which the population at large benefited from state policy was education, by which the state could build support for itself. Those who pushed for an expansion of Serbian education doubtlessly thought in terms of enlightening the nation, but they also designed an educational system that inculcated a point of view from which the state's expenditures would be deemed appropriate.[65] As Charles Jelavich put it in a study of Serbian textbooks, "Right up to the eve of World War I Serbian students were taught Serbian nationalism."[66]

After the assassination of Aleksandar Obrenović in 1903, Serbia actually achieved a working, albeit turbulent, constitutional monarchy. King Petar was by disposition a pacific man who believed in constitutionalism, and this was sufficient to permit it to prosper. At the same time, the political struggle continued to revolve around control of the political mechanism. In the five years preceding the outbreak of World War I, the contenders became the elected party politicians led by Pašić; the state-employee and bureaucratic group, now embodied in dissident military officers led by Dragutin Dimitrijević-Apis; and a crown prince with autocratic ambitions, Aleksandar Karadjordjević. The two branches of the Radical Party retained the loyalty of the peasantry, as did in a certain sense the army, even though in important ways the peasant remained outside the reward structure of Serbian society.

Why was the Serbian peasantry so relatively docile in comparison with the Romanian or even Bulgarian peasantry?[67] The most convincing answer has been put forward by Michael Palairet, who has shown that from the 1860s to about 1910 the main burden of taxation shifted from the peasantry to the nonpeasants.[68] During this period the per capita tax burden of peasants actually decreased relative to income, while the nonpeasants saw their taxes increase in real terms by a factor of almost four. This occurred because the state began to rely more heavily on indirect taxes on goods that the peasants purchased only rarely. Far from being powerless, therefore, the Serbian peasantry was able, either through influence with its advocate the Radical Party or by threats against its opponent the Liberal Party, to prevent the state from unduly oppressing it.

But alongside the economic answer there must be a political answer as well, since the Bulgarian peasantry eventually became much more obstreperous than the Serbian, even though it too found its tax burden declining and its real income increasing in the twentieth century. The key element seems to be the moment at which the peasantry was mobilized politically. In Serbia the Radical Party was successful in presenting itself as the defender of the peasant's interests from the early days of Serbian independence. Basing its program on the semipopulist views of Serbia's first socialist, Svetozar Marković, the Radicals propagated an ideology of antibureaucratism and self-administration that claimed as its goal the lessening of state intervention in the life of the peasantry. On the basis of this program and of vigorous opposition to Milan Obrenović in the early 1800s, the Radicals achieved widespread sympathy among the peasantry. But the Radical Party was not a peasant party. It was created and administered by intellectuals and professional politicians. When it finally gained power in 1889 it continued its normal transition to membership in the state class that had begun a decade before.

During a short tenure in power until 1892, the Radicals pursued a tax-collection policy that Palairet characterized as "positively cavalier" toward the peasantry, in the sense that the party did not push to apply tax rules to the countryside nor to collect arrears. From that moment no government found it politically expedient to enforce the collection of taxes in the countryside, and the burden of supporting the state's expansiveness began to shift rapidly to the nonpeasant sector. Out of power from 1892 to 1900, the Radicals maintained in the eyes of the peasantry their image as the antibureaucratic party. When they finally emerged in the decade before World War I to assume leadership of the state class, albeit in the form of two competing wings, the Radicals had a long record of peasant confidence behind them, so that even though the party now fully entered the state class it was at the same time able to retain the loyalty of the Serbian peasantry. In other words, the Radical Party gained the confidence of the peasantry soon after Serbian independence and retained it into the twentieth century, even as the party itself became more and more state-oriented. The Serbian peasant continued to believe in the party that had helped him in the past, even though the Serbian state run by those Radicals did little to help the peasantry cope with the problems brought on by impinging capitalism.

In Bulgaria, the peasantry was able to prosper moderately in the two decades before World War I by finding ways to retain livestock for its own consumption. But it was only then that the first political party gained the loyalty of the Bulgarian peasantry, long after the formation of Bulgaria's state class. Unlike Serbia, Bulgaria did not have a ready-made state structure available when it achieved its independence in 1878. Instead a congress of the nation's notables dominated by a small national intelligentsia wrote a constitution for the new country. From the beginning there were two main views as to how this new state should work. The conservatives believed the educated or administratively experienced elite should dominate politics and run the state in a patriarchal manner, whereas the liberals believed in "full political equality which, they argued, was only natural for a people which was blessedly free of major social divisions."[69] After a brief flirtation with the latter possibility, Alexander Battenberg, Bulgaria's first prince, established his own personal power in cooperation with the conservatives. In 1885 a war with Serbia and unification with Rumelia led to Alexander's downfall and a turbulent period of instability.

By 1890 the political skills of Stefan Stambulov restored stability, but at the price of completely undermining the liberal provisions of the Tûrnovo Constitution. In the early years of Bulgarian statehood Stambulov used dictatorial methods because threats of assassination, public disorder, international humiliation, and financial disaster had required them. But when these problems diminished Stambulov did not dismantle his oppressive machinery, rather the contrary. He also perfected the familiar system of civil-service bribery and election fraud common to Serbia, Romania, and Hungary, which in Bulgaria is called *partisanstvo*. Right after liberation, as the Bulgarians refer to the establishment of independence in 1878, the new state needed qualified administrators. To get them, it paid excellent salaries, so that by the 1880s educated Bulgarians came to believe that high-paying state jobs were their right, often refusing to serve in lower-ranking jobs. Those among this "civil-service proletariat," as one Bulgarian called them in 1886, who did not get jobs were attracted to opposition parties, so that when a new party achieved power it would sweep all the adherents of the former government out of office and install its own people, whose first job would be to begin insuring the success of the new incumbents in any future elections. Under Stambulov, *partisanstvo* turned Bulgaria's political system into "almost the sole property of a small minority of self-seeking politicians" who were almost totally divorced from the peasantry they governed.[70]

Like its Serbian counterpart, the Bulgarian state pursued expensive projects that enhanced state power but were of little use to the peasantry, paying for these accoutrements of power by taxing the countryside. Not only did peasants pay a great deal more in taxes per capita in the 1890s than did other categories of citizens, especially the privileged civil servants, but those taxes increased dramatically during the Stambulov era. As Stambulov put it, "the peasant can still pay."[71]

Stambulov's success in creating a stable system ruled by a small clique of professional politicians in control of a responsive bureaucracy was itself his downfall, because once Prince Ferdinand stabilized his position he was able to establish supremacy over that highly centralized apparatus. When Stambulov fell in 1894, not only was he disgraced but he was also actually murdered by vengeful Macedonians in retribution for what they interpreted as an accommodating policy toward Turkey and the mistreatment of Macedonians. Elimination of the only other politician of real note in the country permitted Ferdinand to consolidate his personal rule to such an extent that it continued without regard for political parties, governments, peasant unrest, or diplomatic and military defeats right to the end of World War I.

Unlike in Serbia, therefore, the struggle for control of the state reached a definite conclusion in Bulgaria. The prince won. Political parties became nothing more than groups of the educated bickering to gain Ferdinand's favor so that they could get into office and enrich themselves. Just as in Serbia, the general ideology that justified this system was nationalism, although in Bulgaria's case nationalism was directed toward a specific and emotional goal, the acquisition of Macedonia. Originally part of the San Stefano territory of Bulgaria but not included in the Berlin settlement of 1878, Macedonia has remained to this day the touchstone of Bulgarian national policy, even though her greatest politicians, Stambulov and Stamboliski, understood that blind pursuit of that goal was not in the true interest of Bulgaria. Mobilization of national opinion over Macedonia was, however, in the interest of the state class because it justified expenditures that strengthened the state, especially those on the army. In both Bulgaria and Serbia, nationalism was the ideology of the state class's supremacy at least as much as it was the romantic unifying code that nationalists claim it was.

Two important political movements opposed Ferdinand's personal rule and criticized Bulgaria's state class. The first was the Left, which developed in Bulgaria into two sectarian movements of so-called narrows and broads. Eventually they became irrelevant to Bulgarian politics because their fiercely ideological devotion to purity prevented them from making the practical political alliances that might have permitted them to share power after World War I.[72] The other party was the Bulgarian Agrarian National Union, or BANU, which began to organize the Bulgarian peasantry in 1899 in reaction to popular outrage over unfair tax policies. The great leader of the BANU was Alexandûr Stamboliski. This daring "child of the new Bulgaria," as John Bell called him, did not accept the government's view that national policy demanded a strong military, a dictatorial prince, and a heavily taxed peasantry.[73] On the contrary, he believed that Bulgaria should pursue a pacific foreign policy with a view toward Balkan federation, that the army should be cut down to size, that the prince was an irresponsible burden, and that the peasantry was oppressed by the state class. Under Stamboliski's dynamic leadership, the BANU rallied the middling and poorer peasantry to its banner to become by 1909 the strongest nongovernment party in Bulgaria, despite an increase in peasant prosperity after 1900.[74] Advocating neutrality in World War I, Stamboliski accurately predicted that Bulgaria could expect no good result from that conflict. Vindicated by Bulgaria's humiliating defeat, he achieved power in 1919, whereupon he attempted to create a peasantist state, that is, one in which the independent peasant, owner of his small private plot, could prosper without having to shoulder the burdens of overly rapid industrialization, excessive military expenditures, or an extravagant court.

Stamboliski's temporary success in postwar Bulgaria has a curious resonance with Moore's categories. Bulgaria did not have a decaying class of old landlords with weak links to the countryside. It did not have any landlords at all. On the other hand, the state that was created in the absence of a dominant class, and which assumed its role, itself had very weak links to the countryside, running the society simply in its own interest. Thus the door was open to the mobilization of peasant discontent by a radical intelligentsia. In Bulgaria, most of the intelligentsia chose to side with the state class, while socialists and communists who opposed the entire system were too doctrinaire to grasp the utility of mobilizing the peasantry. That left Stamboliski and the BANU. When the war completely discredited Ferdinand's personal rule and briefly brought chaos to Bulgaria, Stamboliski used the moment to come to power on behalf of the peasantry. This is close to the result Moore might predict, but it was not the same result as in Russia and China for two reasons. First, Stamboliski was not a modernizer in the statist mold of Russian and Chinese intellectuals. He did not oppose industrialization, only industrialization at the expense of the peasantry and through the mechanism of a state class. Bulgaria could have both a prosperous peasantry and industrialization, he believed, if it would stop spending a third of its budget on the military, if it would protect the right of the peasant to live a satisfying and fulfilling life on his small holding, and if it would guarantee that exploitation of one estate by another would cease. Neither Chinese nor Russian revolutionaries believed peasant life as it was lived under the old regime could be modern or satisfying. Stamboliski did not care so much about modern; he was willing to settle for satisfying.

Second, Stamboliski's regime was not politically revolutionary. Alone among the defeated powers in World War I, Bulgaria did not change its political structure with defeat. Stamboliski had to try to work his revolution in the framework created by the state class and the prince, and still dominated by them. Unable to break through these restraints, in 1923 he was deposed and murdered like his predecessor Stambulov. Restoration of the state class led Bulgaria into the familiar pathways of nationalism, centralization, militarism, and a mild form of dynastic authoritarianism.

What has been the outcome of this survey of such different East European experiences as the Bulgarian and the Czech? Do Moore's analytic categories describe these small countries? Despite the fact that the typology does not exactly fit any of the experiences, it comes very close to some of them. The Czech history of proto-industry and industrialization does seem to be related to the appearance of a Czech democracy in the interwar years; the dominance of the Hungarian magnates when capitalist agriculture and then industry came to Hungary seems to have led to a conservative result there in the interwar years; and in Bulgaria the separation of the state from the nation offered at least a temporary opportunity for the BANU to attempt the creation of a peasant state. The record in Romania and Serbia is more mixed. In Romania a socially dominant landowning elite found itself outmaneuvered by the gentry and the state class and eliminated after World War I, whereas in Serbia the success of the Serbian Radical Party in securing the loyalty of the Serbian peasantry at approximately the same time it was integrating itself into the state class resulted in a docile peasantry, even though the Serbian state did not act any more in the peasantry's interest than did other East European states.

Moore's analysis leads also to useful speculations on the role of the peasantry. Only in the Czech lands, which became relatively highly industrialized, did the peasantry not play a central political role, even though none of the newly created states saw themselves as advocates of peasant interests. The question was rather in what ways the state managed to subdue or use peasants, and who controlled this state. In Hungary and Serbia the government mastered the peasantry, although by different means and in different socioeconomic circumstances. In Hungary the landed aristocrats maintained control over an agriculture that included a large number of landless peasants and succeeded in imbuing the entire political process with a sense of the rightness of this control. In Serbia, the political professionals mobilized the smallholding peasantry by nationalizing them, that is, by convincing them that the national interests as defined by the state were also the interests of the peasants, although in fact they were not. This produced a rough and ready democracy in Serbia, but not a democracy that threatened the dominance of the state class. In both Romania and Bulgaria, on the other hand, the revolutionary potential of the peasantry came much closer to the surface. The Romanian middle class constrained the peasantry to its own advantage first by permitting it to fall into neoserfdom, and then, when the peasantry's revolutionary potential became all too clear, by eliminating the class of large landowners through an agrarian reform that did not actually increase either peasant productivity or influence, a truly remarkable turn of events. In Bulgaria the state did not nationalize the peasantry as successfully as did the Serbian Radicals, so that when the BANU arose in opposition an agrarian revolution such as Moore predicts was at least possible. Inability of the Bulgarian Left to react to the situation, along with the inertia of the old system, which World War I did not destroy, led however to the victory of the state class.

In at least two areas, however, Moore's analytical hints are not of great help. The first concerns the role of individuals. In each of the countries discussed certain individuals emerged who had an enormous impact on the outcomes. Is it possible to imagine an outcome in Czechoslovakia quite the same without Masaryk? In Bulgaria the BANU was failing until Stamboliski rescued it and drove it to temporary success through his own courage and brilliance. Would not the election of the democratically inclined Petar Karadjordjević to the Serbian throne in 1868 instead of the erratic, insecure spendthrift Milan Obrenović have dramatically changed the course of Serbian development? What if Kálmán Tisza had been a poor gentry politician rather than the wealthy husband of a baroness, or Ion Brătianu a magnate rather than a gentryman? In each instance a key element in the working out of the equation seems to be the personal success of a particular individual. Social historians, while not ignoring the obvious fact that public affairs are conducted by people, not abstractions, are not inclined to grant a truly defining autonomy to individuals, and maybe a closer investigation would sustain that point in Eastern Europe. At this level of generalization it does seem curious that in each country a strong, opinionated, even ruthless individual is associated with the outcome.

The Balkan rulers provide a good linkage point between personal and structural determinants. Coming from, or in the case of Milan aspiring to acceptance by, a dynastic aristocracy not indigenous to the Balkans, these rulers were imbued with a mentality entirely unsuited to the creation of systems consistent with the more or less liberal constitutions with which their new countries presented them.[75] It is not surprising, therefore, that they constantly interfered in the day-to-day operation of politics, sought to create personal regimes they felt were consistent with their aristocratic honor, and favored the military in an effort to create support not offered them by an indigenous social class. In a sense the Balkan rulers were a class in themselves, an anomalous extension of the European aristocracy acting in what they perceived as the interests of that class, but within societies where in actuality the state, not social relations, was the dominant element.

This brings us to Moore's greatest lack, his discounting of the state as an autonomous actor.[76] In all the countries discussed in this article except Czechoslovakia it is how one stands in relation to the state apparatus that constitutes the fundamental social datum. This is true not only in the cases of social vacuum in Serbia and Bulgaria, but in Romania and Hungary as well. At the beginning of this chapter it was suggested that the small countries of Eastern Europe did not differ from the large countries dealt with by Moore, since every country has to confront exogenous forces with the social structure it has at the moment of impact. These exogenous forces normally are summed up as the Industrial Revolution and the French Revolution, or the Dual Revolution as Hobsbawm called it.[77] But what this analysis suggests is that a third exogenous factor is at least as important as the first two—the European state system that was already in existence when both the French and the Industrial revolutions occurred. It is not possible here to go into an exposition of the emergence of this system, or even its main features. But it is a fact that when the East European countries came to political consciousness they had very little choice as to the style of organization their new nations would adopt—it would be the modern state, with its legislature, courts, centralized bureaucracy, and intrusive mentality. By the time the Czechs were able to establish such an entity, their long socioeconomic development had prepared them for bringing the state's power under the control of a pluralist democracy. In Hungary, on the other hand, the magnates accepted the state as their own and used it for their own purposes. In both instances the socioeconomic situation was not entirely different from that of Western Europe, where similar outcomes transpired. In the Balkans, however, introduction of a state on the European model occurred in a social situation that was almost completely unprepared for it.[78] The state, being the most developed institution in Balkan society, became also the dominant element, but whereas it operated using the same forms as its models in the West, the actual content of political activity was more consistent with traditional status societies than with the more legalistic societies from which the state forms were copied. While it is not possible to discuss this point in any detail here, it is clear that these aspects of the turn of Eastern Europe toward modernity are not easily subsumed under Moore's model.

In the social sciences, however, a theory is judged neither by how well it explains data, although it must be able to do that to a significant extent, nor by how universal it is in providing explanations under all circumstances. In good measure, theories are judged by how fruitful they are in suggesting ways to approach problems. If a theory pushes us in the direction of seeing an old situation in a new light, of discerning new concordances or new discords, then it is useful. In Eastern Europe, Barrington Moore's explication of the social origins of dictatorship and democracy well fulfills that function.

II

THE RISE AND FALL OF YUGOSLAVIA

The first article in this section, "Nineteenth Century Serbia: So What?" serves as a bridge between the articles in Part I and those in Part II. It continues to develop the point that the East European state played its role quite separately from socioeconomic development, repeating some of the background from the earlier chapters, but it focuses specifically on Serbia. The rest of Part II continues with other aspects of Serbian and Yugoslav politics.

Despite the peripheral nature of Serbian—and Balkan—history in the eyes of most Europeanists, the Serbian experience provides a telling counterexample to the widely held view that socioeconomic conditions have a decisive impact on political relations. Nineteenth-century Serbia developed political institutions that were similar in form, function, and operation to those created by more developed states elsewhere in Europe, even though its social structure, dominated by a smallholding peasantry, hardly changed at all. Although not many Europeanists have confronted this example of a lack of congruence between social and political change, it nevertheless presents a serious impediment to the social interpretation of politics.[1]

In the 1860s, a vigorous Serbian prince, Michael Obrenović, evolved a scheme to create a large Serbian state (but not a Greater Serbia). He hoped to obtain Bosnia and Herzegovina, which he considered Serbian, and thereby to link up with Montenegro. In his abortive efforts to do so, he worked out a short-lived arrangement with a Croatian leader, Bishop Josip Juraj Strossmayer. In socialist Yugoslavia, some historians attempted to show that this early instance of Serbo-Croatian cooperation indicated a joint Serbo-Croatian aspiration to form a Yugoslav state. In actuality, the negotiations were built on Serbian *Realpolitik* and Croatian weakness, not primarily on Yugoslav sentiments. Michael jettisoned his Croatian partner as soon as he sensed that cooperation with Hungary might achieve his aims. He was equally cold to his Serbian co-nationals in the Vojvodina as he was to his putative Croatian allies.

The weakness of Yugoslavism in the 1860s suggests that differing historical circumstances shaped Serb and Croat national self-definition. For Serbia, a centralized state disposing of a strong military proved functional because during the formative years of its national development it faced a weak and declining power, the Ottoman Empire. Well-organized aggressiveness paid off for the Serbs. They fought a successful "war of national liberation" against the Ottomans in 1877–1878, albeit on the coattails of Russian military success; they seized portions of Macedonia in 1912–1913 by force of arms; and they marched back into the Balkans with the

Salonica expeditionary force in 1918. Serbs therefore had every reason to consider a centralized state employing a respectable military force as the proper way to organize a society.

Military solutions were impossible for Croats. Instead of being able to expand outward from a core region, as the Serbs did from Šumadija, Croats lived under a variety of political arrangements that were all part of a powerful Habsburg state. Some Croats lived in Hungary (Civil Croatia, Slavonia), some in Austria (Dalmatia, Istria), and some in neither (the Military Frontier, Bosnia). It was perfectly rational, therefore, for Croat activists to seek federation within the Habsburg Empire rather than to foment uprisings in search of outright independence.

This different orientation—Serbs successfully creating a centralized state, Croats interested in federal solutions—was visible as early as the negotiations between Prince Michael and Bishop Strossmayer. During World War I it continued to divide Serbs and Croats in the negotiations that led to the creation of the first Yugoslavia. It would be easy to criticize both sides in those negotiations. Nikola Pašić proved too brittle, too set in his Serbophile vision of the new Yugoslavia, to compromise with the Croats, while at the same time the Croat members of the Yugoslav Committee proved short-sighted in their dealings with the Slovenes and stubborn in their unwillingness to concede anything to Italy. In making these criticisms, however, one should keep in mind the atmosphere at the end of World War I. With the exception of Woodrow Wilson, the negotiators in Paris retained a good deal of the narrow self-interest that got them into war in the first place, insuring that the Soviet Union would remain a pariah and that Germany would enter the postwar era bitter and dissatisfied. History has not treated these settlements kindly, but at least we can say that the mistakes made by the creators of the new Yugoslavia did not differ in kind from those made elsewhere.

The question of whether Yugoslavia should be organized centrally or as a federation of equal peoples was never solved. Eventually, in 1991, it led to the collapse of the country and to the vicious wars of Yugoslav succession. Many other factors, of course, contributed to the disaster. In answer to national and ethnic competition, the League of Communists of Yugoslavia decentralized, but it did not open itself to democratic processes. Therefore, when the party collapsed in 1991 and elections took place, political structures in the Yugoslav republics remained weak, permitting nationalist leaders to take over. Communist control over socially owned industries undermined the vigor of the Yugoslav economy. The Yugoslav National Army, in the end the country's only truly Yugoslav organization, proved out of touch with reality and susceptible to Serbian pressures. Finally, the international community pressured Yugoslavia in contradictory ways, and once the fighting began pursued policies that unwittingly exacerbated the conflict.

In my view, however, the single most important factor in the collapse was the execrable leadership both Serbs and Croats endured. In Serbia Slobodan Milošević pursued a nineteenth-century agenda, following an aggressive nationalist policy that had proven successful in creating a Serbian state prior to World War I. Whipping up nationalist enthusiasm, he tried to seize territory that he considered Serbian by force and by inciting revolt among the Serbs in Croatia and Bosnia, much as Michael Obrenović had contemplated in the 1860s. In Croatia, Franjo Tudjman, a historian steeped in traditional views of Croatian aspirations, rejected the Yugoslavism of Strossmayer. He even changed the name of the Yugoslav Academy of Arts and Sciences, which the bishop had founded in 1867, to the Croatian Academy. Tudjman responded to Milošević's threats with a homogenizing nationalism of his own.

In many ways Milošević failed in his aggressive hopes. Slavonia remains in Croatian hands, and the ancient Serb community of Krajina has disintegrated. In terms of lives lost, homes destroyed, and economies ruined, the price of Milošević's ambition has been very high. In one area, however, he may have succeeded. It is not outside the realm of possibility that the Bosnian Republic of Serbia will eventually become part of Serbia proper, much as Eastern Rumelia became part of Bulgaria seven years after the Congress of Berlin. Whatever the outcome, it seems certain, as the last article in this section suggests, that the animosities that Milošević and Tudjman, among others, intentionally brought to the surface for their own purposes will poison relations among the South Slavs for a long time to come.

4

Nineteenth-century Serbia:
So What?

In the nineteenth century, Southeastern Europe turned its orientation from southward-looking to northward-looking. From being culturally peripheral to the Ottoman Empire, the Balkans became culturally peripheral to Europe. The term "peripheral" signals to most readers world system analysis and dependency theory. The former considers the modern history of individual societies explicable only as part of the worldwide system of capitalism that has grown up since the sixteenth century. A small group of core states dominated this system by extracting surplus from a large group of peripheral societies whose social and political characteristics were predicated on their subordinate position in the system. Dependency theory pushes world system theory further by insisting that it is precisely the subordinate role played by the peripheral societies in the capitalist system that prevents them from developing. This "development of underdevelopment" is characterized by the emergence of a class of local economic and political leaders who perceive their own interests more in terms of how they can profit from participation in the system of the core states than in how they can achieve economic development in their own lands, and contrasts with the view of modernization theory, by which development proceeds by a process of diffusion.

From Horst Haselsteiner, ed., *Wirtschafts- und Kulturbeziehungen zwischen dem Donau- und dem Balkanraum seit dem Wiener Kongress* (Graz, Austria: Institut für Geschichte der Universität Graz, Abt. Südosteuropäische Geschichte, 1991), pp. 219–231. Originally entitled "Political Development in Nineteenth Century Serbia." Reprinted by permission.

World system theory and dependency theory were mainstays of radical developmental sociology in the 1970s and 1980s, but they have come under heavy criticism, most tellingly from the Left itself. One analyst summed up the criticisms by declaring that "the dependency position is vitiated by a variable combination of circular reasoning, fallacious inferences from empirical observation, and a weak base in deductive theory."[1] But this devastating judgment does not mean that the notion of dependency is devoid of insights. In fact, if we ignore the need felt by dependency theorists to demonstrate historical necessity and abandon the obligation to root all social and intellectual phenomena in economic relations, instead assigning a certain autonomy to the political and cultural spheres, it is obvious that dependency in the broadest sense has been a ubiquitous phenomenon of human history.[2] It is in this latter sense, rather than in the strict socioeconomic sense called for by dependency theory, that Southeast Europe may be said to have been a dependency area throughout its history.[3]

Early in the Christian era the Balkan peninsula was a marchland of the Roman Empire and, for almost a thousand years after the fall of Rome, Byzantium provided the norms by which Balkan high culture measured itself. Bulgarian and Serbian rulers emulated the rituals, customs and pretensions of the Byzantine emperor, and several of the most powerful of them harbored dreams of seizing the throne of Constantinople for themselves. By the thirteenth and fourteenth centures the Orthodox Commonwealth, as Obolensky has called it, had established a cultural orientation among Serbs, Greeks, and Bulgarians that to a certain extent they still retain.[4] The downfall of Byzantium brought a new and more direct domination to Southeastern Europe, the rule of the Ottoman Empire, which occupied the peninsula and destroyed the byzantophile aristocracy. After hundreds of years under the Ottomans, it was quite natural that Miloš Obrenović, the prince who successfully pushed the Ottoman landlords out of Serbia in the 1820s, slept on rugs and shelves in the Turkish manner, dressed with a turban, ruled with the brutal irresponsibility of an Ottoman Pasha, and was called only half-jokingly by his subjects "the Sultan." But just during Miloš's lifetime Southeastern Europe began its most recent reorientation. By 1900 all the Balkan countries had become independent participants in the European state system, had adopted political systems that in form approximated those of Western Europe, and had adopted Western cultural models as their standard of intellectual respectability.

This sudden transition from Ottoman models to European ones was not a unique event. In the modern era every society has had to find a way to confront the enormous energy produced by industrialism, the integrating and dominating power of capitalism, the corrosive ideal of equality, and the organizing demands of the state system. And no society has been able to choose an optimum way to face the challenge. Each has had to confront unique and overpowering pressures with whatever sociocultural tools it already had at its disposal when the whirlwind struck, even if these were inappropriate for interacting fully with the new forces.

In Southeastern Europe the dynamic of these pressures, which are what forced the turn in orientation from southward-looking to northward-looking, are well illustrated by the case of Serbia. The perspective from which this small country faced the inevitable challenge of European power was singularly inappropriate. In the lands of the Ottoman Empire inhabited by Serbs in 1800 an ethnically non-Serbian landed and military elite, the localized remnant of the no longer powerful Ottoman center, used force to exact tribute from the Serbian peasantry, as well as from the few traders that existed, janissaries and spahis, who by 1800 had been able to assert a considerable amount of independence from Istanbul, ruled Serbian lands that contained few towns, an undeveloped trading system, no educational institutions, and no industry. Serbs had experienced some contact with the Habsburg lands, especially as soldiers and occasionally as traders, but they had not yet felt fully the impact of Europe.

Despite this unpromising situation, the First and Second Serbian Uprisings, which started with rebellion in 1804 and ended with the granting of autonomy by the Sultan in 1830, forced the Ottoman overlords to depart, leaving the land in the hands of the Serbian peasantry. Prince Miloš, the organizer of this success, believed that Serbia should remain a land of smallholders and that the only truly rich man in the realm should be himself. He ruthlessly pursued his own wealth, going so far, for example, as to kill men who refused him loans, but at the same time he prevented his subordinates from carving out their own fiefdoms. He gave away land to immigrating Serbs and established a minimum size of holding that could not be sold for debt. Because the Ottomans had long since eliminated the native Serbian nobility, and since essentialy no commercial infrastructure existed, autonomous Serbia under Miloš experienced a social situation that is almost outside of our definitional categories, a classless, or at least a one-class, society.

This characterization may seem an exaggeration, but it is not. Serbia's population remained primarily rural throughout the nineteenth century. The Statistical Yearbook of 1889 showed, for example, that only approximately 7 percent of the Serbian population lived in towns of 5,000 or more, while another 5 percent lived in towns down to several hundred inhabitants. All the rest lived in the countryside.[5] There the peasantry was remarkably homogeneous. Michael R. Palairet has calculated Gini coefficients of per capita income in Serbia in the 1860s. These coefficients measure the relative equality of incomes, zero being perfectly equal and one being perfectly unequal. The richest regions of Serbia had coefficients of .28, a quite low number, while the poorest regions had coefficients of .07, a remarkably low figure indicating almost perfect income equality. On the basis of these figures Palairet characterizes Serbian income distribution as "unusually egalitarian."[6] Even by the end of the century land remained very evenly distributed in comparison with elsewhere in Eastern Europe.

According to the census of 1897, 79 percent of the population held 68.7 percent of the land in plots ranging in size from 2 to 20 hectares, anything over 20 hectares being considered a "large estate" in Serbian conditions. Only three landowners out of 330,000 families owned estates larger than 300 hectares. This may be compared with Hungary, for example, where a handful of estates over 10,000 hectares constituted almost 20 percent of the land, or with Croatia-Slavonia, where the 209 largest latifundia, those above approximately 600 hectares, controlled 22.5 percent of the landed area.[7] At the beginning of the twentieth century the overwhelming majority of Serbs worked small holdings measuring between 2 and 20 hectares, as they had throughout the nineteenth century, making Serbia one of the least developed but most egalitarian nations in Europe.

The economic backwardness that this egalitarian income distribution and overwhelmingly smallholder agriculture reflected is usually explained in one of two ways, either in terms of a legacy of Ottoman domination or in terms of encroaching capitalism. In the former interpretation the still predominantly peasant character of Serbia as late as World War II is explained as "the economic legacy of centuries of virtual colonial domination by the Ottomans."[8] The second school explains that "by far the most important structural change in the economy of the South Slav lands during the nineteenth century was the penetration of money and credit and of capitalist principles into the existing traditional social and economic system." This destroyed the traditional Serbian extended family, the zadruga, and led to the subjugation of the Serbian countryside to usurers.[9]

Both of these suggestions contain something of the reality of the matter, but neither of them is entirely satisfactory. In the first instance, Ottoman domination is supposed to have created cultural norms that are alien to the ethic of work and productivity necessary for economic advancement. Gregory Clark has argued that low productivity in some parts of early nineteenth-century Europe can be explained by the low intensity of labor, in which people in areas such as Serbia "either worked little or . . . exerted themselves little when at work."[10] In this interpretation, long-term acculturation to Ottoman norms made the Serbs lazy. Many Serbs today still favor this explanation of their economic difficulties, but when such an explanation emanates from a developed country it smacks of condescension, and when the Serbs themselves argue in that way it smacks of self-justification. The Ottoman explanation opens the door to invidious comparisons, provides no sound economic mechanism by which Ottoman customs prevented development, and ignores the fact that during the nineteenth century, in most spheres of public life, Ottoman standards were abandoned, including the laws surrounding landowning and other aspects of economic life.

The second argument seems contradictory on the face of it. How can the penetration of capitalist principles hinder the development of capitalism, as Tomasevich seems to say, especially since the usual explanation of development holds that it is precisely the penetration of trade that leads, semi-automatically, to development?[11] In fact, the explanation is quite commonsensical. The penetration of a money economy forced peasants to raise cash in order to pay their taxes. To obtain this cash, the peasants turned to loans from usurers, which in turn led to crushing debts that kept most peasants from breaking out of the cycle of impoverishment. Tomasevich holds that by prohibiting the peasant from alienating his homestead and garden, while at the same time not providing him with adequate credit facilities, the state both tied the peasant to his land and handed him over to the usurer. This is why Serbia could not develop agriculturally.[12]

Tomasević's explanation has a certain strength to it, and is widely accepted. But it has two faults. First, it assumes that the peasants are a more or less passive element in the equation and that state policy and neglect are the key elements. Second, it fails to take into account that the usurers themselves were usually prosperous peasants, or small townsmen, who could have, on the basis of their profits, accumulated capital and, over the space of a few decades, created substantial estates. It is true that, due to the large reserves of open land in Serbia, the average peasant holding increased from 3.54 hectares in 1863 to 6.4 hectares in 1896, despite an almost doubling of the density of population.[13] But the other side of this coin is that no corresponding landless population emerged. As of about 1900 only about 3 percent of the Serbian peasantry was landless.[14] In other words, the monetization of the Serbian economy in the nineteenth century did not result in either capital accumulation or the creation of a mobile working force.

John Lampe and Marvin Jackson, in their standard economic history of the Balkans, also assign the state a significant role in structuring the Serbian economy in the nineteenth century, but they allow the peasant an autonomous choice in the matter. They begin by pointing out that the decline of the Serbian extended family, the zadruga, which many authors have cited as a sign of the disintegration of the Serbian countryside under the pressure of a money economy, was in fact due primarily to a change in the tax law in 1835 by which taxes were assessed on the basis of individual units rather than households, thus taking away the financial advantage of the very large extended family, and to the law of 1844 that guaranteed private property and thereby insured the development of a market in land. But these observations make it necessary for Lampe and Jackson to explain why, therefore, so little accumulation of larger plots took place by the end of the century. Their explanation is essentially demographic and cultural. Population growth and the lack of primogeniture made land accumulation difficult.[15] What they seem to mean, although they do not state it this way, is that the peasant's predisposition to accumulate land was offset by his propensity to divide lands equally among all eligible family members. Under demographic pressure by the end of the century, the Serbian peasant still chose to distribute land to his family rather than leave them landless.

One of the fundamental problems of all these interpretations of Serbian backwardness is the underlying assumption that the peasant, if left to his own devices, would act in an economically rational way. That is, given an opportunity, peasants would have taken advantage of market opportunities and increased their potential for making a profit.[16] Unless held back by debt, or by failures of the state to offer credit, or by inheritance customs, they would have accepted the challenges of the market. But Palairet has shown that the substantial increase in Serbian exports in the nineteenth century had little impact on the traditional style of peasant life or on Serbian landholding patterns.[17] The Serbian peasant turned only reluctantly to the production of marketable grains, despite the availability of resources and markets, and on average did not greatly increase his holding of arable land in the nineteenth century. Only the poorest and most desperate peasants sold their grain in Belgrade, which had to provision itself with imports from Austria-Hungary. Prosperous peasants enclosed forest in order to preserve forage for their pigs instead of accumulating arable. Such peasants considered growing grain for the market unethical and referred to it as "gypsying." Even when foreign entrepreneurs established and maintained trading networks for the marketing of figs and plums, native Serbs proved uninterested or unable to maintain them when the foreigners abandoned them. In short, Palairet finds that despite an increase in exports and despite the variety of incentives, markets, and opportunities that presented themselves, the landholding and cultivation patterns of the Serbian peasant changed very little during he nineteenth century. The Serbian peasant responded only weakly to the market.

But even Palairet does not present a convincing solution for this failure of development in nineteenth-century Serbia. In my view an answer should be sought neither in the unwillingness of the Serbian state to offer sufficient credit or other incentives in the countryside nor in a perverse unwillingness of the lazy Serbian peasant to do what authors schooled in post–World War II notions of development expect him to do, but rather in the wishes and desires of peasants themselves as shaped by the particular socioeconomic structure in which they found themselves. Robert Brenner has argued that a smallholding peasantry enjoying strong property rights has no incentive to go beyond traditional technology and no need to go beyond local markets, that is, has no incentive to enter into the complex system of capitalist interdependence.[18] Owning the land they customarily have access to, the simple tools they accumulate, and the animals they tend, self-sufficient smallholders are poor candidates for capitalist development. In such a situation, Brenner argues, development will be retarded because the satisfied peasantry will not be forced to enter into problematic market relationships, as they would be if they were being pushed off the land by powerful lords or if they were forced to pay economic rents for the use of their land. They may have to generate enough money to pay taxes, but they are not forced by the economic imperatives of a larger structure to depart significantly from the norms of traditional life, which continue to prove satisfying to them. In direct contact with their means of social reproduction, they have no incentive to enter into the uncertain and indirect mechanisms of the market.

For Brenner, the best example of the inhibition of capitalist development is late medieval and early modern France, where peasants managed to establish strong rights to their property. Since vigorous peasant communities existed to fight for these rights, and since the king saw the peasantry as a source of income in his continuing struggle with a contentious nobility and therefore supported their right to the land, French peasants were able to continue traditional methods of localized production and parcellization right into the nineteenth century. In England, by contrast, a moderate level of cooperation between the king and his landlords made it possible by the seventeenth century for landowners to control something like 70 percent of the land, which they put out to tenants at competitive rents. This meant that, whereas in France the peasantry was simply squeezed by the king through taxation to produce income for the state, in England the tenant farmer was forced into a competitive situation in which the landlords, and coincidentally the state as well, profited through the indirect operation of the economic system rather than through direct coercion. In other words, in England we have the development of capitalism and in France we do not. Stating Brenner's point more generally, it is not capitalism that creates its characteristic class system, but rather the existence of specific class relationships that makes capitalism possible, or, in the case of Serbia, not possible.[19]

Brenner's argument seems perfectly applicable to Serbia's condition in the nineteenth century. Serbia had no noble class because the Ottomans had wiped it out, so when the First and Second Serbian Uprisings cleared the Serbian lands of the Ottomans, the newly autonomous Serbia, under the leadership of a jealous populist, became a one-class society of socially undifferentiated peasants. Serbian authors have called this creation of a smallholding peasantry by the Serbian uprisings a revolution, and in a sense it was, the replacement of a foreign landed and military elite by native smallholders, the substitution of one dominant class of landholders for another.[20] But this outcome was not revolutionary in an economic sense. The substitution of an undifferentiated peasantry for Ottoman feudatories did not push Serbia in the direction of development; quite the opposite. By securing the peasants' rights to their own plots, the defeudalization process, if the Serbian uprisings may be called that, made it unnecessary for the peasantry to seek social reproduction outside of traditional methods. Owning his own land and able more or less to live from it, even if indebted, the Serbian peasant neither accumulated the capital that might be used for investment nor felt an incentive to do so. This meant that Serbian agriculture developed only a few capitalist mechanisms, such as bills of exchange, by 1900.

If nineteenth-century Serbian society consisted of a single smallholding class that did not achieve development, how then are we to explain the emergence there of a state with a cabinet, a prime minister, a legislature, a court system, a legal code, political parties, and competitive elections? In other words, if we want to maintain that political structures have a socio-economic basis, what was the basis of this Serbian state? One possible answer is that the Serbian state in fact did represent the interests of a thin stratum of merchants, government bureaucrats, and well-to-do peasants that perhaps foreshadowed a true bourgeoisie. This might perhaps be the approach of Miroslav Hroch, who argued in his book *Social Preconditions of National Revival in Europe* that even when an actual bourgeoisie cannot be found in national revival movements, early activists should be considered precursors and foreshadowing representatives of that social class.[21] There is something to this argument, for most of the powerful figures of Serbian public life, and many of the less powerful, did come from a stratum of better-off peasants, merchants, and bureaucrats. Specific examples of the state favoring these groups can easily be found, such as the continuing sympathy of the skupština [Serbian legislature] for efforts by town merchants to hinder the development of local village shops.

A second way to retain social determinism in the Serbian situation might be to postulate the subervience of the Serbian mercantile classes to interests outside their nation, to the Austrian market in particular. In this interpretation Serbia, and other members of the periphery, becomes an integral but subservient part of worldwide capitalism and thus can develop a bourgeois state in its clearly noncapitalist situation by finding a real bourgeoisie in Austria whose interests the Serbian state could represent. This argument also has a certain plausibility, since Serbia in the last quarter of the nineteenth century was most certainly subservient to Austria. As John Lampe has shown, however, the data of Serbian economic development do not support an explanation based on dependency theory.[22] And in the end, there is something absurd about wrenching the idea of the bourgeois state around so that it fits a country in which, by the most optimistic estimates, there were, in a population of over two million in the year 1900, only 235 "industrial" enterprises employing a mere 3,262 workers.[23]

If we abandon the possibility of a Serbian bourgeoisie that dominated the state, there remains the possibility that the social basis of the Serbian state was the peasantry. This numerically overwhelming class did indeed exact its political price during the nineteenth century. In 1880, for example, when the Progressives took power from the Liberals, who resigned after a decade in power in protest against an accommodating policy toward Austria-Hungary, this new political party decided on friendship rather than confrontation with Austria precisely in order to assure the Austrian market for Serbian livestock, thereby adopting a policy that benefited the peasantry but did not forward economic development. Palairet has shown that around the turn of the century Serbian tax policy favored the peasantry to the detriment of the urban elements.[24] Furthermore, throughout the nineteenth century the Serbian government undertook few measures that would disturb the traditional peasant lifestyle, and those that it did take, such as the creation of a cabinet position for economic development, or the construction of a railroad, had little impact on the economic life of the peasant.[25] One might argue on the basis of these policies favorable to the peasantry that Serbia was a peasant state, since the state distributed some of the benefits at its disposal to that class and did not force the peasants into more capitalist-style property or labor relations. But such an argument would overlook the overwhelmingly dominant role the state came to play in the Serbian economy and indeed in all aspects of public life, a role in which peasant concerns played an increasingly minor role. Peasant support was necessary to the Serbian state, but the fact of that support is far from sufficient to explain the growth of a European-style state in Serbia in the last third of the nineteenth century.

What sort of description of the Serbian state would be adequate? Liberal political theory sees the state not as a weapon of a given social class at all, but as the guardian of society's powers of coercion, including not only the police and army, but also the educational system, the courts, the administrative agencies, and all the elements of local and mid-range inter-vention in private affairs for public purposes. It regulates these powers by means of a more or less democratic parliamentary system that aggregates the competing interests of a pluralistic society. Conflicts will exist because individuals, associations, and even classes pursue their self-interests, but these conflicts take place within such a broad framework of agreement that in the end compromise is necessary and achievable. In the liberal system, the polity is structured to insure that accommodations will be reached that maintain social stability, which is seen as desirable by most of the articulate participants in public life. Thus the state, despite its ultimate legitimation by the electoral process, must in principle keep its distance from its citizens, no subset of whom should be able to gain preponderant control of its mediating process.

Marxist theory by no means sees the state as neutral, but deciding just how the bourgeoisie exercises its control has proved difficult. Klaus Offe is only one of many who have addressed the issue.[26] He holds that in devel-oped capitalism the state has a specific purpose: the maintenance of the capitalist system itself. But, since the essential relationship of capitalism is private property, and most accumulation ends up in private hands rather than in the hands of agencies of the society at large, the capitalist state faces a fundamental contradiction. It must promote private accumulation through public means. Since the individuals who run the state are not, as a rule, those who achieve power through accumulation but are instead state employees, the state mechanism needs a separate justification other than wealth. This justification is created by claiming that the state represents the general interest. Thus the state presents itself in the same way that it does in the liberal conception, as the agent of the nation or of the people, but rather than reflecting a potentially harmonious social relationship this pre-sentation actually hides the state's class basis, that is, its function as repro-ducer of relations of production that favor those who already have accumu-lated capital. The simplistic view that capitalist states are controlled directly by the bourgeoisie for its own benefit has long since given way to subtler redactions such as Offe's.

The liberal view of the state has its use in understanding the emergence of a functioning state in Serbia in the nineteenth century. For example, the elaboration of electoral processes did give the peasantry a considerably more active ability to articulate its desire to retain its traditional style of life than Prince Michael Obrenović's cold aristocratic rule of the 1860s would have afforded them. If the Marxist view of the state insisits on finding a bourgeoisie, it is less useful. But if we start to think of the state itself as the primary actor, not as a surrogate for a nonexistent bourgeoisie, then it is clear that the Serbian state did exercise a hegemonic influence on its own behalf throughout the last third of the nineteenth century. Despite its appearance of liberalism, the Serbian state was so much more powerful than any other institution in society, so much richer, so much more a resource for employment, and so much more technologically advanced, that it was not simply an arena for balancing competing interests, but it-self the dominant interest. Given the undeveloped character of the Serbian economy, the state did not redistribute wealth primarily through the indirect operation of the market. Despite its surface similarity with Western bourgeois forms, in the absence of capitalist development the Serbian state had little choice but to operate in a way analogous to the way absolutist predecessors to the capitalist state operated, simply taking from society what it could squeeze out and spending it in its own interest. The best way to understand the unfolding of the Serbian experience in the nineteenth century, therefore, is to think of the state not as a mediator in the struggle between social entities, or as a surrogate for one of these entities, but as an actor in its own right, one that behaved a good deal like a dominant class.[27] In other words, the creation of an institution that looked like a bourgeois state but acted like a precapitalist one is the primary event of sociopolitical interest in nineteenth-century Serbia and, by extension, in Southeastern Europe in general.

5

Yugoslavism in the 1860s?

The motto of historians who attempt to uncover historical roots might be "Seek and ye shall find." Since we believe in causation, the very existence of a phenomenon guarantees that persistent research will uncover the forces that made it possible, even inevitable. And, if we believe the final result is a good thing, we may judge its roots accordingly, even at the risk of anachronism. Some such process seems to have been at work in the case of the Yugoslav idea. It appears self-evident that historical forces which could be called "Yugoslav" must have existed in the nineteenth century because the state of Yugoslavia actually existed for more than seventy years in the twentieth century. And indeed, historians found the Yugoslav idea a major theme. One scholar even suggested that Yugoslav unity was "the best solution" to the conflicts between Serbs and Croats in the 1860s, "the most natural possibility,"[1] and another was chided for trying to graft the good term "Yugoslav" onto the bad phenomenon, Serbian nationalism.[2]

The remarkable thing when one considers the enthusiasm with which Yugoslav ideas were uncovered in the late 1960s and early 1970s is the almost utter lack of community-building forces at work among the South Slavs during the nineteenth century. During the 1860s no social structures existed that held hope of drawing the South Slavic peoples together. Economic development, the strongest force for breaking up the traditional isolation of peasant societies, had not achieved the implacable force it attained in the twentieth century; literacy was extremely low; communica-

From *Southeastern Europe*, 1 (1974), pp. 126–135. Reprinted by permission.

tions, even within national groups, were halting and difficult; and linguistic assimilation was not occurring within minority groups.

This is not to say that the notion of South Slav cultural unity did not exist in the nineteenth century, because of course it did. In the 1860s, the strongest and most farseeing manifestation of this sort of Yugoslavism was found among the Croats. Franjo Rački and Josip Juraj Strossmayer were the leaders, inspiration, and support of the movement. In contrast to their Serbian contemporary Vuk Karadžić, who believed that everyone who spoke štokavian was a Serb, and their Croatian contemporary Ante Starčević, who believed that Serbs as such did not exist, Strossmayer and Rački understood the common linguistic heritage of the South Slavs, appreciated their historical proximity, and believed that it would be possible through historical research and cultural links to build a bridge among these people that would establish their cultural and, perhaps eventually, their political unity.

The subordinate position of Croatia in the Habsburg Empire made it natural that ideas of Yugoslav unity should grow up there at the same time the more ordinary nineteenth-century idea of nationalism appeared.[3] As their sense of national identity grew Croats began to seek out ways of establishing their autonomy and independence. The historical and geographical facts made three solutions possible: autonomy within the Habsburg Empire, independence as a nation state, and independence as part of a larger Balkan state of some kind, perhaps Yugoslav. None of these solutions was inevitable, but given the lack of integrating forces at work in the nineteenth century, perhaps the most far-fetched of all was the Yugoslav solution. In time, it is conceivable that concerted and coordinated efforts at creating cultural unity might have led to the growth of a sense of Yugoslav nationalism among the South Slav peoples, but one thing the Yugoslav idea did not have was time. The accelerated maturation of political events in the fifty years between the establishment of the Yugoslav Academy in Zagreb in 1867 and the end of World War I in 1918, a space of less than two generations, did not give Yugoslavism a chance to sink deep roots. The only shortcut to unity lay in the political sphere, and here the Yugoslav idea of the Croats had to contend with the successful nationalism of the Serbs.

Instead of finding themselves in a still vigorous European empire, the Serbs had the good fortune in the nineteenth century to be located in the faltering Ottoman Empire.[4] Success in establishing their autonomy in this empire gave the Serbs little reason to doubt that their nationalism was a viable ideology and no reason to turn to other unifying notions, such as the Yugoslav idea. It is ironic therefore that Prince Michael Obrenović of Serbia made the only moderately serious attempt to create a Yugoslav state in the nineteenth century. The state Michael hoped to create was not a federation of equal nationalities, however, although many of his subordinates and opponents talked at great length about the possibilities of Balkan federation.[5] Michael sought to unify all Serbs into one independent state.

In pursuit of his goal Michael followed the foreign policy advocated by his foreign minister, Ilija Garašanin. When Michael ascended to the throne in 1860 Serbia was still a province of the Ottoman Empire. Garašanin believed, however, that the main obstacle to Serbian independence was not this empire, which most Europeans believed was a dying state, but the Habsburg monarchy. Since uniting the Serbs living outside the principality would mean cutting off Austria from southward expansion, Garašanin sought the official and unofficial support of Austria's chief rival for Balkan influence, Russia. Depending on Russia diplomatically, Prince Michael also was prepared to use force to achieve his goal. He authorized Garašanin to establish a network of underground agents in the Balkans and sought to strengthen his army so that if the occasion arose he would be able to expel the Ottomans from the Balkans.

When Michael and Garašanin spoke of uniting all Serbs, however, they did not really mean all ethnic or linguistic Serbs. They showed only a passing interest in the fate of the Serbs lining in the Vojvodina, for example. On the other hand, they did not mean to exclude non-Serbs either. Their main practical goal was to achieve control over Bosnia and Herzegovina, which were ethnically mixed.[6] Neither Michael nor Garašanin favored the Yugoslav idea in the way Strossmayer did. Michael told Lajos Kossuth in 1859, for example, that Serbia was "appointed to form the nucleus of" a Slavic state and that Croatia was only on the periphery,[7] and in 1844 Garašanin had stricken all references to Croats from the original draft of his *načertanije*. Garašanin had been suspicious of Strossmayer personally since 1854, when he had opposed Strossmayer's efforts to have an Austrian Catholic appointed spiritual leader of the few Catholics in Serbia, and in 1859 he characterized Strossmayer as an Austrian agent.[8] Because of Michael's and Garašanin's views, no formal contacts with Croatian politicians matured during the early years of Michael's reign. Individual Serbs contacted Croatian leaders in the late 1850s and early 1860s in an effort to begin a movement toward a larger Yugoslav state, notably Matija Ban in 1860–1861, but these efforts were both unofficial and unsuccessful.[9]

Serbian disinterest in political cooperation was reciprocated by the Croats. In the early 1860s Croatian politicians did not think in terms of joint political action with Serbia. At this time Dalmatia and the Military Frontier, both ethnically Croatian, were under separate administrations. The first goal of Croatian patriots was to unite these provinces as one part of the Habsburg Monachy, which they hoped would be reorganized on a federal basis.[10] The Croatian leaders, suspicious of Vienna because of the centralizing excesses of the Bach period, looked to Hungary, not to Serbia, for help in achieving this goal. Unfortunately for Serbo-Croatian relations even in 1860, many Croats also believed strongly that historical precedent gave them hope of some day incorporating Bosnia "once again" into Croatia. Even though some hopeful statements concerning cultural or linguistic unity appeared in the early 1860s, the Croatian legislature (*sabor*), passed a resolution supporting Croatia's "virtual right" to Bosnia in 1861, causing the Serbs to respond angrily. In 1866 a polemic broke out between two organs of the liberal movement, *Zastava* (Novi Sad) and *Pozor* (Zagreb), over the same question. In sum, during the first half of the 1860s there were no significant political contacts between the Serbs and the Croats.

The events of the year 1866 changed the international situation drastically, however, and led to a brief period of joint efforts to achieve a larger Yugoslav state. The Austrian defeat by the Prussians at Königgratz in the summer of 1866 forced Emperor Franz Josef to the conclusion that he had to reach an agreement with the dissident Hungarians if he was to reestablish the strength and unity of his realm. For several years the leaders of the Croatian National party, as the informal grouping of intellectuals and liberal politicians surrounding Strossmayer has become known, had looked to the Hungarians as allies in the struggle with Vienna. Now they suddenly faced the likelihood that Hungary would conclude an agreement with Austria at Croatian expense. This imminent dualist compromise ruled out federalism, the Croatian hope, and put Croatia in the difficult position of having to reach agreement with a satisfied Hungary.

For the Serbs, the strategic implications of the Austrian defeat were also significant. Now that the Austrians could no longer consider Southern Germany as their area of hegemony, their thoughts, the Serbs feared, shortly would turn to Bosnia and Herzegovina. If Serbia was to obtain those provinces from the Ottomans, it would have to do so at once, before Austria began to move. At the same time, a Greek uprising on Crete seemed to offer the Serbs an opportunity for action against a disorganized and defensive Ottoman Empire. The uprising on Crete not only distracted the Ottomans, but it intensified the interest of the Great Powers in the Eastern Question as well. The Serbs sensed that an opportunity was at hand for striking at a weakened Ottoman Empire at a moment when the Great Powers might be in a mood to accept a settlement at Ottoman expense. In 1866, therefore, the problem of how to seize Bosnia became acute for the Serbs.

The simultaneous disillusionment of the Croatian National Party leaders with their possibilities within the Habsburg Empire and the intensification of the Serbian interest in Bosnia brought the leaders of the two peoples together. Following several months of preliminary contacts by secret emissaries, in August 1866 Strossmayer and Garašanin agreed to "common work between the Triune Kingdom and Serbia to found a Yugoslav state independent from both Austria and Turkey."[11]

It is unclear precisely what common work was envisioned by this agreement, but undoubtedly the Serbs hoped to receive Croatian assistance in arming and organizing bands of volunteers in Bosnia, whereas the Croats sought support from Serbia in their efforts to reach a satisfactory accommodation with the Hungarians. From the Serbian side there is another possibility, more devious perhaps, but not unlikely. Prince Michael's plan for uniting Serbia was not simply to start a war against the Ottomans, a strategy his liberal opponents advocated. He and Garašanin realized that the diplomatic ground needed preparation. As part of a diverse burst of diplomatic activity during the second half of 1866, the Serbian government sought to embarrass the Ottomans by demanding that the Ottoman troops that still occupied various strongpoints in Serbia be withdrawn. Garašanin believed, even hoped, that the Ottomans would reject this demand, thereby giving Serbia a legitimate grievance to take before the powers. As this diplomatic question matured, Michael and Garašanin set the machinery in motion that would lead to the outbreak of the long-discussed uprising in Bosnia in the summer of 1867. They expected that the Ottomans would not be able to suppress the uprising easily. When this became clear, Serbia, already aggrieved by Ottoman unwillingness to withdraw its troops from the fortresses, could join in and expel the Ottomans forcibly. The powers would be disgusted by this time and would not intervene.

At least the Serbs hoped the powers would not intervene. This proviso was the most crucial condition for the success of Serbia's strategy. If the great powers decided to enter any Balkan conflict militarily, they, and not Serbia, would be the beneficiaries. In fact, the result of such intervention would probably be Austrian seizure of Bosnia and Herzegovina, precisely the thing Garašanin and Michael sought to avoid, and just what actually happened in 1878. Serbia's main diplomatic effort in the 1860s had been, therefore, to encourage the powers to adopt a policy of nonintervention in Balkan affairs. In the case of France, it was necessary to allay fears that Serbia was an agent of panslavic Russia, scheming to establish an Orthodox hegemony over the Balkans. Since Napoleon III had shown some sympathy for Balkan nationalism in the past, it seemed to the Serbs that favorable French policy might be possible if Napoleon could be convinced that the Balkan liberation movement was not a Russian conspiracy, but rather a noble effort to establish a Yugoslav nation in which Catholics as well as Orthodox would be included. In this way a policy of nonintervention might be pressed on France and, in turn, on other powers. The Serbophile Frenchman, Jean Ubicini, actually approached Napoleon III on Serbia's behalf in September 1866, but nothing would have been more impressive than the direct support of Serbian policy by Josip Strossmayer, Catholic Bishop of Croatia. No direct evidence exists that this line of thought motivated Garašanin to overcome his personal antipathy and approach Strossmayer in 1866, but shortly thereafter Strossmayer agreed to cooperate with Serbia. Garašanin asked him to write a statement for presentation to the French expressing his support for the Serbian movement. Strossmayer did so, although in such noncommittal terms that it was never used.[12]

Whatever ulterior purpose Garašanin had in mind in contacting the Croatian leadership in 1866, the fact remains that in the last months of 1866 the Serbian government and the leaders of the Croatian National party considered themselves verbally committed to a joint effort to create a Yugoslav state. Early in 1867 the Serbian government prepared a proposal specifying the extent of cooperation in the uprising scheduled for summer 1867 and outlining general plans for the future. However, just as these plans were forwarded to the Croats for their approval, the Ottomans, under pressure from the powers, cut the diplomatic ground out from under Prince Michael by suddenly granting the Serbian demand that the Ottoman troops be withdrawn from their fortresses. Garašanin was surprised and confused by this unexpected development. Instead of being presented with a grievance, Serbia unwittingly found itself the satisfied party, no longer able to justify vigorous action on the basis of Ottoman intransigence. At the same time Prince Michael was coming under increasingly serious pressure from the great powers. Count Friedrich Beust, Austrian foreign minister, fearing the possibility of the creation of a large Slavic state to the south of the Monarchy, sent his personal emissary to inform Michael that Austria firmly opposed any Serbian adventures in Bosnia.[13] To give his message force Beust eventually mobilized troops in the southern military frontier. Russia's foreign minister Prince Alexander Gorchakov gave public assurances that Russia had no intention of supporting dismemberment of the Ottoman Empire. Finally, Michael's sober reevaluation of Serbia's strength showed that it was far too weak to hope to defeat the Ottomans in a war.[14] As a result of these factors, early in March 1867 Michael postponed the summer uprising in Bosnia.

These sudden and drastic changes made the cooperation of the Croats much less useful to Garašanin, who had been none too enthusiastic about cooperating with them in the first place, and he allowed contacts with them through his secret emissaries to wither. The Croatian leaders did not realize at once what had happened. It appeared to them from the vocal support Belgrade newspapers gave them early in 1867 that Serbia was living up to its part of the agreement. When relations seemed to cool, they ascribed it not to a change in Serbian policy but to Prince Michael's lack of confidence in the emissaries, something which the Croats could easily believe since they did not have much confidence in them either.

Prince Michael went further than simply putting off the 1867 uprising, however. Intrigued by overtures from the Hungarians, pleased with what now appeared to be his diplomatic success in achieving the withdrawal of troops, and disappointed in the weakness of his military forces and the fickleness of Russian support, Michael began to consider turning to Hungary for diplomatic support against Austria. Already in February 1867 Michael's representative had suggested to Gyula Andrássy, head of the new Hungarian government formed as a result of the *Ausgleich,* that Serbia might administer Bosnia and Herzegovina as the Sultan's vassal.[15] In that way Serbia could exercise *de facto* control over the two provinces, but the *de jure* integrity of the Ottoman Empire would be upheld. The Austrians flatly opposed such a plan, as did Napoleon III and the Ottomans themselves. But the Hungarians hinted that they might favor a diplomatic solution to the Bosnian problem in Serbia's favor. In August, 1867, these hints led to a meeting between Prince Michael and Count Andrássy at Ivanka, Michael's family estate in Slovakia.[16]

At the Ivanka meeting Andrássy apparently offered Michael Hungary's diplomatic support in a campaign to obtain Bosnia for Serbia in return for Michael's promise to cease supporting Strossmayer's Croatian National party and to forego further nationalist agitation among the Serbs in the Vojvodina. By this offer Andrássy hoped to accomplish several things. First, by planting the idea that there was a difference of opinion between Count Beust and him on the Bosnian question, he encouraged Michael to believe he could play off the Germans and the Hungarians to his own benefit. Second, he hoped to drive a wedge between the Serbs and the Croats.[17] Not only would such a split have long-term advantages for both the Hungarians and the Austrians, but Andrássy also hoped it would weaken Croatian resolve in the political struggle that had arisen between Croatia and Hungary in the wake of the *Ausgleich*. Third, a Serbian alliance with Hungary would turn Michael away from dependence on Russia, whose intentions in the Balkans Andrássy feared. Finally, if Serbia would keep the Balkans quiet, Austrian energies would be released for the policy of *revanche* that Beust hoped to follow toward Prussia.

The advantages of the agreement were not all on Andrássy's side, however. Michael never was convinced of the value of the Croats to the liberation struggle he thought would come. Furthermore, the Croats had a claim to Bosnia that would become embarrassing if the two peoples were allied in its liberation. Neither did he trust the Serbs of the Vojvodina, the most vocal part of whom were liberals opposed to his regime. The events of early 1867 had shown that not even Russia was unequivocally prepared to support the decisive action he and Garašanin wanted to take in Bosnia. Moreover, Michael had become aware of the importance of railroads to the modern state, and he realized that friendship with Hungary was crucial to a rational program of railroad building for Serbia. Therefore, it doubtless seemed to Michael that he would give up very little by agreeing with Andrássy. For abandoning allies he did not trust and a policy that had already been a failure, he received in return a new chance to obtain Bosnia. He accepted Andrássy's offer. Two months later he dismissed his Russophile Foreign Minister, Garašanin, and completely abandoned the underground organization in Bosnia. Michael's new alignment ended for several decades all possibility of political cooperation between Serbia and Croatia for the purpose of establishing a Yugoslav state.

The Croats were very poorly served by Prince Michael in this brief period of contact from 1866 to 1868, but not because of the cultural, religious, or linguistic differences which separated the two peoples. The Serbian government acted with equal cold blood toward the Serbian minority in the Vojvodina. For the decade of the 1860s, the history of this minority is similar in many ways to that of the Croats. With the downfall of Bach in 1860 a vigorous Serbian political movement grew up in the

Vojvodina under the leadership of Svetozar Miletić. These Serbs looked toward Budapest for help in achieving their national autonomy, just as the Croats did in the same period.[18] After difficult times in 1864, the movement revived in 1865 when Franz Josef began to seek an accommodation with the Hungarians. In 1866 Svetozar Miletić founded his famous liberal newspaper *Zastava* (The Banner) and in the same year other Serbian liberals, some of them in exile from the principality, conceived the idea of creating a broad nationalistic society. Early in June, 1866, *Zora* (Dawn), a Serbian student society in Vienna, called upon all Serbs who were "young at heart" to unite in a society dedicated to "throwing off the invisible and visible chains of darkness which have bound us."[19]

In August 1866 four hundred Serbs, most of them from the Vojvodina, but some from the principality as well, met in Novi Sad and organized the United Serbian Youth, or Omladina.[20] The fundamental idea of the Omladina, one that it never abandoned and which eventually led to its downfall, was that it was a society for all Serbs everywhere, not only Serbs in the Vojvodina. At each congress of the society, from 1866 until the last one in 1871, this principle was reaffirmed. Although these same congresses also expressed concern for the other South Slavic groups and specifically included Croats within the family of the Omladina, the basic thrust of the society was Serbian, not Yugoslav. Nonetheless, for the Serbs in the Vojvodina, the Omladina served a similar function as the Yugoslav idea did for Croats. During the first year of the Omladina's existence they, like the Croats, become acutely aware that their hope in Hungarian help had been misplaced. As soon as the Hungarians saw that a dualist solution to the monarchy's nationality problem was imminent, a solution which favored Hungary, they lost interest in maintaining relations with the Vojvodina Serbs. This abandonment by Hungary had the same effect on liberal Serbs as Hungarian hostility toward Croatia did on liberal Croats. It forced them to consider political alternatives. The alternative that was immediately available in the Vojvodina was the Omladina, which supported the unification of all Serbs into one independent state. Therefore, in the years 1866 through 1870, the Omladina flourished as a cultural and political organization among the Vojvodina Serbs.

When the Omladina was founded in 1866, and during its first year of existence, Prince Michael welcomed its unifying ideology. He contributed to the society's treasury and granted permission for the society to hold its second annual congress in Belgrade. Michael was preparing for the summer uprising of 1867, an effort which required the utmost moral and physical support from all Balkan Slavs. Once Michael abandoned the uprising in Bosnia, however, and began considering cooperation with Hungary, the Omladina, with its large following among the Serbs in Hungary, became an embarrassment to him. He warned the Omladina congress which met in Belgrade in the summer of 1867 not to raise any political issues. When it did, his ministers sent the delegates home. Shortly thereafter Michael met with Andrássy at Ivanka. In pursuit of the policy decided at that meeting, Michael dropped all pretense of supporting the Omladina and the Vojvodina Serbs.

It seems clear, then, that Prince Michael and his main minister, Ilija Garašanin, had no interest in either the Croats or the Serbs in the Vojvodina as such, but simply treated them as the larger strategy of obtaining Bosnia dictated. This was an understandable policy. By obtaining Bosnia and Herzegovina, Serbia would link up directly with Montenegro, where Prince Nikola had agreed to abdicate in favor of Michael if success crowned their joint efforts against the Ottomans. Had such a success created a large South Slavic state, it would have been overwhelmingly Serbian in population and there would have been no practical reason for Serbia to take account of the problems of either the Serbs or the Croats in the Austrian Monarchy. Quite the contrary, it would have been in their interest to mollify Austria and Hungary by abandoning their former friends there. When Michael came to his agreement with Andrássy, this is in effect what he did.

The Croats were in a different and extraordinarily difficult position. The National party looked to Serbia in 1866 simply out of desperation. The Croats correctly saw that they were about to suffer from an Austro-Hungarian agreement. They were searching for some alternative, even a remote one. Unfortunately, the agreement they made with Garašanin had an adverse effect on their chances for preventing the outcome they feared. The National party was curiously inactive and conciliatory in the sabor of 1867, the last chance the liberal nationalists had to influence the *nagodba* (the Croat-Hungarian Compromise of 1868), as it turned out. Their inaction grew in part out of their false hope, encouraged by their agreement with Garašanin, that a more general solution to the Eastern Question was in the offing. Thus, not only were the Croats misled by the Serbs, but they were misled at a particularly unfortunate moment. By the time the Croats realized that it was useless to rely on Serbia, now the ally of the main Croatian enemy, Hungary, it was too late. The *nagodba,* which nationalists came to consider a fatal blow to Croat aspirations, was an accomplished fact.[21]

The Serbs in the Vojvodina were in an even more impossible position after 1866. They did not possess the powerful historical arguments on which Croatia based its claims for special consideration, but simply were part of Hungary. Therefore, when Serbia abandoned them, and when Hungary achieved its compromise with Austria, they were unable to sustain a movement that looked outside of the Monarchy for fulfillment of their political aspirations. The symbolic last act of their efforts to do so came at the Omladina congress in 1871. The Hungarians closed the congress and banned the Omladina when it refused to pass a resolution limiting membership to Serbs living in Hungary.

Serbia operated at an enormous advantage in these interchanges, as it did throughout the nineteenth century, because it was a quasi-independent state. Free to act in their own interests, Serbian politicians of the 1860s did not have to think in terms of larger issues such as Yugoslavism, nor did their success in establishing themselves as a state encourage them to do so. The Croats and the Serbs in the Vojvodina were minority peoples in one of the great empires of Europe. Their subordinate position led them to elaborate all sorts of solutions and hopes, realistic and otherwise. In the Vojvodina the main hope after 1867 centered on the creation of a large Serbian state, perhaps by a great uprising. In Croatia many ideas appeared: trialism, federalism, independence, even Yugoslavism. All of them, and maybe especially Yugoslavism, were idealistic reflections of impotence more than they were realistic plans for action.

The inability of Serbian and Croatian politicians to cooperate in the 1860s was symptomatic of the fact that community-building forces were not at work among the South Slavs one hundred and thirty years ago. Croatian Yugoslavism and Serbian nationalism were appropriate reactions to different situations and do not attain their significance from the later creation of Yugoslavia. For that reason it is unhistorical to describe Croatian Yugoslavism as a particularly good or correct idea, or Serbian nationalism as a bad, non-Yugoslav policy, as some Croats did in socialist Yugoslavia. It is equally futile to describe either the aspirations of the Omladina or Serbia's Great Serbian policies as "really" Yugoslavism. Such evaluations do not grow naturally out of the circumstances of the nineteenth century.

6

The Role of the
Yugoslav Committee in the
Formation of Yugoslavia

The breakup of Austria-Hungary in the name of national self-determination brought about the creation of an equally multinational new state, Yugoslavia.[1] It is paradoxical that the idea of Yugoslavism, emphasizing as it did the subordination of historical peoples to an ideal of brotherly unity, should have triumphed at a moment of nationalist exaltation, especially since Yugoslavism was popular only among the youth and a few intellectuals at the outbreak of World War I. This outcome may be attributed, in part at least, to the activities of a group of politicians and intellectuals from the Habsburg lands who escaped into Western Europe at the beginning of the war and organized themselves into a political action group called the Yugoslav Committee. By 1917 this committee had become a quasi-independent body with a headquarters in London and private financial support. Members of the committee had close connections with the French and British governments, and emigrants who supported the committee in the United States even had some influence on American policy.[2] In 1917 the committee reached an agreement with the Serbian government that a new Yugoslav state would be founded after the war, so that when separate peace talks with Austria-Hungary failed for the last time in 1918 the committee was in position to push for the complete dismemberment of that ancient state. When the war ended, the committee's efforts had helped create an atmosphere in which the establishment of a Yugoslav state be-

From Dimitrije Djordjević, ed., *The Creation of Yugoslavia* (Santa Barbara, CA: Clio Press, 1980), pp. 51–72. Reprinted by permission.

came not only an acceptable policy for the allies, but a desirable postwar goal.

The Yugoslav Committee, therefore, has with justice been considered an important element in the history of the formation of Yugoslavia.[3] It would perhaps be an exaggeration to say that without this committee no Yugoslavia would have emerged, but its significance is unquestionable. And yet, there is another side to the story, a more ominous side whose history is still being written, because the Kingdom of the Serbs, Croats, and Slovenes did not turn out to be the sort of state the Yugoslav Committee had hoped.

Frustrated by German and Hungarian domination in the Habsburg Monarchy, the Croatian and Slovenian members of the Yugoslav Committee had sought to create a state in which no people would dominate or feel dominated. Aware of the dangers of imbalance in a multinational state, Croatian and Slovenian emigrés insisted throughout World War I that postwar Yugoslavia would have to be a fusion of peoples, an equal partnership or organic union, not a Slavic Habsburg empire in which certain national groups were favored. Despite their understanding of this danger, their insistence that it must not happen, and their work to avoid it, committee members could not prevent the creation of a Yugoslavia that was dominated by Serbs. The costs of this failure were incalculable. Politics in interwar Yugoslavia never functioned normally, because the only real issue was the national one. Hitler's easy success in 1941 was partially attributable to widespread disaffection with Belgrade, and the victory of Tito's Partisans during World War II was in important measure the result of the promise to put into practice the ideal of equality among the Yugoslav peoples.

The history of the Yugoslav Committee, then, is one of many important successes and one fundamental failure. The purpose of this chapter is not to enumerate or praise the successes, which has been done often enough, but to analyze the failure. The basic reason the Yugoslav Committee did not find it possible to create the state of equal peoples it sought was that the committee only worked within the limitations of its situation and never transcended them, so that in the end its success was limited as well. To achieve the equitable Yugoslavia it desired, the committee would have had to overcome four liabilities: its emigré nature, its vulnerability to Serbian initiatives, the incompatibility of its territorial aims with Italian aspirations, and its Croatian, even Dalmatian, composition.

The emigré nature of the committee was its most obvious and problematical feature. Just before and just after the beginning of actual warfare in 1914, several prominent Croatian politicians from Dalmatia succeeded either in leaving the Habsburg lands or in not returning. Ante Trumbić, Frano Supilo and Ivan Meštrović established a nucleus around which later emigrés could gather. But no matter how well balanced this nucleus strove to become by additions from inside Croatia and Slovenia, no matter how much support it generated among South Slavic immigrants in the new world, and no matter how favorably inclined friendly individuals close to allied governments became, the committee remained an emigré organization, unrecognized by the law of any state, and without official sanction to represent the people for whom it claimed to speak. In the early stages of the war this did not matter. The committee could conduct its propaganda easily enough as a private interest group. But later, its only hope of influencing the character of the new Yugoslav state was to be formally recognized by the Great Powers as the legal representative of an allied people. To achieve diplomatic recognition, however, the Yugoslav Committee needed the acquiescence of the two allied powers already interested in South Slavic lands, Serbia and Italy.

The small likelihood that Serbia would permit the Yugoslav Committee to achieve legal status was implicit in the assumptions under which its Premier, Nikola Pašić, helped the committee form in 1914 and 1915. Pašić's immediate fear in 1914, besides collapse, was that an early peace would be signed before Serbia could formulate comprehensive war aims.[4] Very early, therefore, the Serbs laid out a maximum program calling for the creation of a large South Slavic state. On September 21, 1914, Pašić formally suggested borders for a postwar state that stretched well into Habsburg lands, split Istria with Italy, and claimed all of Dalmatia. These proposed borders conflicted with Italian ambitions in the Adriatic and would necessitate the destruction of the Habsburg Empire.[5]

At the same time, the Dalmatian emigrés in Italy had begun to discuss their situation. They concluded that the best hope for the future of Croatia and Slovenia lay in the creation of a new Slavic state on the Adriatic. This state would have to include Serbia, so that it could act as a Slavic barrier to German penetration into the Balkans, but, more important, it would provide a chance for Croatia and Slovenia to become independent of Austrian and Hungarian domination. These conclusions led to specific goals that were remarkably similar to those of Pašić: dismemberment of the Habsburg Empire and acquisition of lands on the Adriatic. Already in October Frano Supilo was in France trying to interest French politicians in adopting the destruction of Austria-Hungary as a war aim.

When Pašić heard of Supilo's campaign in France and realized that Serbian and Croatian goals coincided, he quickly grasped that the Croatian emigrés, who had excellent contacts, could be helpful in popularizing Serbian war aims in Western Europe. Accordingly, he sent two special emissaries to Italy to offer the emigrés financial support in their common effort. On November 22, 1914, these representatives concluded an agreement with Ante Trumbić in Florence to establish a Yugoslav Committee consisting of leading emigré politicians from the three major South Slavic peoples. The purpose of the committee would be "to assist in the creation of a united Yugoslav (possibly Serbo-Croatian) state by informing leading circles and by publicity activity."[6] As this wording indicated, the committee was to assist Serbia through a propaganda effort. As far as Pašić was concerned, this was the extent of its purpose and authority.[7]

Pašić unquestionably sought the creation of a Yugoslav state.[8] The position papers worked out for him in the fall of 1914 demonstrate this, as does the Niš Declaration of December 7, 1914, by which the wartime Serbian government committed itself to a Yugoslav goal.[9] But quite naturally, Pašić did not think of Serbia as merely a partner of the other South Slavs in the struggle to create this new state. He thought of Serbia as a liberator. Since he considered the Macedonians and Montenegrins as Serbs that should be united with the motherland, he had no thought of allowing them any special status. The Croats and Slovenes were clearly not Serbs, so he was willing to allow them their national symbols, alphabet, religion, and even their traditional political organs. But the new Yugoslavia was not going to be an amalgam of these peoples. It was going to be a state in which the victorious Serbs would grant their new acquisitions equal rights as Serbs or as associated peoples. Pašić's supporters found this prospect emotionally satisfying, but they also had a good legal argument, since Serbia was recognized as an independent state and therefore could expand legitimately without a revolutionary European settlement.[10]

The Croats and Slovenes did not find the idea of liberation by the Serbs a congenial prospect. The example of Macedonia worried them. When Serbia seized Macedonia from the Ottoman Empire in the two Balkan wars, it did not extend normal constitutional rights to the newly acquired territory, even though it insisted that the Macedonians fulfill the regular obligations of citizens, including taxation and conscription. The Croatian emigrés in Italy who agreed to propagandize for a Yugoslav state had no desire for Croatia to become another Macedonia.[11] They were willing to begin cooperating, even if at first the Yugoslav Committee was subordinate to the Serbian government, because they believed there could be no Yugoslavia without Serbia. But they firmly believed that the logic of events would eventually transform the Yugoslav Committee into an equal partner.

Doubtful of Serbian intentions but assured of Serbian financial support, the committee members began to work. They laid plans for Yugoslav legions composed of volunteers from allied prisoner-of-war camps, invited politicians from Croatia proper and from Slovenia to join the emigration, and sent their representative to America, where he met with an enthusiastic welcome. But fearing that their interest in the Adriatic would spark a reaction from Italian nationalists, they did not make the committee's work public.

As one of the primary organizers and most prominent figures of the Yugoslav Committee, Frano Supilo spent the early months of 1915 attempting to work out a clearer understanding with Serbia and the Allies of what Croatia's future might be.[12] In the early spring this effort took him to Niš, the wartime capital of Serbia, where he found it very difficult to discover from Pašić what sort of terms the Croats could expect if they were to unite with Serbia. From Aleksandar Belić's semi-official *Srbija i južnoslovensko pitanje* [Serbia and the South Slav Question], he learned that the Serbs believed no special compact was needed. Belić claimed that Serbs and Croats were simply the same people with two names, so that any sort of autonomy that divided them would go against the national consciousness.[13] The dangers for the less numerous Croats of uniting with the Serbs before achieving agreement on the terms of unification were obvious to Supilo, but he was not able to find much sympathy for his point of view.

Unsuccessful in Niš, Supilo traveled on to Petersburg to seek assurances from the Tsarist government. Instead of assurances he found disaster. Late in March, Sergei Sazonov, Russian Foreign Minister, let slip to Supilo that the Allies were about to promise Italy Dalmatia in return for her declaration of war. Supilo immediately informed both Pašić and Trumbić of this finding, but despite a month of frenzied activity by all three men, they were not able to head off the debacle. On April 26, 1915, Italy and the Allies signed the Treaty of London, by which lands claimed by the Yugoslavs on the Adriatic were assigned to Italy.[14] Stunned by this provocation, on April 30 Trumbić hastily assembled Croatian and Slovenian emigrés in Paris and brought the Yugoslav Committee out into the open. Designating London as its headquarters and electing Trumbić president, the now public committee sent a delegation the very next day to French foreign minister Théophile Delcassé to complain about the concessions to Italy, and within a few days it produced a policy memorandum setting out aims that directly conflicted with Italian goals.

Territorially, the committee's memorandum of May 1915 went beyond Pašić's memo of September 21.[15] Besides Dalmatia, it claimed for the Yugoslavs all of Istria, Gorica and Koruška, allowing to the Italians less territorial gain in the case of victory over Austria than Austria herself had offered as a reward for staying neutral. This emphasis on Slovenian and Croatian claims in the Adriatic was only natural for the Yugoslav Committee, since its composition was heavily Croatian, and its leadership Dalmatian. Just as the Serbs considered Macedonia inviolate, and the Italians came to see the Treaty of London as unchangeable, so the Yugoslav Committee became intransigent concerning lands to which it was emotionally attached.

The committee's obduracy cannot be considered solely a matter of principle, such as self-determination, or nationality, although this is no doubt how many saw it. On occasion, for example, members of the Yugoslav Committee suggested that Serbia give up part of Macedonia and concentrate on creating an outlet to the sea. This position was fully comparable to the Serbian view that Macedonia was untouchable, but compromises on the Adriatic might be possible. And, just as Serbia gave up too little too late in Macedonia to prevent Bulgaria from attacking, so eventually Trumbić conceded too little too late on the Adriatic to obtain Italian support. From the first moments of the committee's public existence this strong Adriatic orientation hindered the evolution of a realistic policy.

By the time the Yugoslav Committee began the public phase of its work in May 1915, then, the restraints within which it worked for the rest of the war were established. It was an emigré committee with a special interest in the Adriatic and Dalmatia, it was an uneasy junior partner of Serbia, and it was in conflict with Italy. Its goal, beyond the day-to-day demands and programs, was the creation, with Serbia, of an equitable Yugoslav state on the ruins of the Habsburg Empire.

This requirement that a Yugoslavia could exist only if Austria-Hungary ceased to exist had an important effect on the work of the committee. Until the spring of 1918 the likelihood that the Allies would seek the breakup of Austria-Hungary was small. The remoteness of the possibility of a Yugoslav state meant that committee members felt only the relatively light pressure of working out ideal plans, not the inexorable urgency associated with immediate and actual possibilities. With so much else uncertain, there seemed to be no compelling reason to break with Serbia even though the committee was not achieving equality, or to accommodate Italian wishes in the Adriatic, even though Italy continued to oppose Yugoslav aspirations there. In 1916 and 1917, therefore, the committee took two crucial steps that confirmed its original relationship to Serbia, thereby helping to ensure that the committee would not achieve its ultimate goal.

By 1916 relations between the Serbian government and the Yugoslav Committee had become strained. In trying to convince Bulgaria to enter the war against the Central Powers, the Allies had offered Serbia several territorial gains in the West in return for concessions to Bulgaria. Quite naturally, when rumors of these possibilities leaked out the Croats and Slovenes felt that they were being callously parceled out as compensations, not treated as peoples with their own aspirations. At one point, in an effort to work out a solution, Supilo endorsed a compromise suggestion made by Sir Edward Grey that Bosnia and Herzegovina, Southern Dalmatia, Slavonia, and Croatia be allowed to choose their future by plebiscite after the war. This formula only worsened the situation. The Serbian government interpreted this initiative to mean that Supilo was preparing the ground for the creation of an independent Croatia, while members of the Yugoslav Committee objected that Supilo had made this important compromise without consulting them. Supilo responded vigorously.[16] He hoped, he said, that successful prosecution of the war would produce a state that would be the "harmonious product of all our national strengths, a fusion of spirits, traditions, and hopes." But for this to happen, Serbia would have to accomplish fundamental political, constitutional, and cultural reforms that would prevent what he called a serbo-orthodox exclusivism from destroying Yugoslav unity. If Serbia did not change, Supilo warned, unification would have to await a more opportune moment. In the meantime, in the absence of reform, all those Yugoslav lands in which a majority of people wanted to be united with Croatia should be granted that desire.

Supilo's outright threat to seek a separate Croatian state did not achieve the support of the Yugoslav Committee. Naturally, the Serbian members of the committee, as informal representatives of Pašić's government, opposed it, but so did the Slovenes. One of Supilo's blind spots was that he thought of Slovenes much in the same way that he complained Serbs thought of Croats. He considered Zagreb the center of Croatian-Slovenian activity, and did not understand that the Slovenes found this offensive. Naturally, therefore, he could not count on their support of his Croatian-centered idea. Even some Croats opposed Supilo. Still, at a plenary meeting of the committee in February 1916, the crisis was patched over. The committee formally reaffirmed its commitment to a broad unification, but placed many of Supilo's views in a policy memorandum to the French government on March 13. This was only a temporary solution, however.

The situation of the Serbian government had changed dramatically for the worse by 1916. Thoroughly defeated by the Austrians under German leadership and hounded by the Bulgarians from the south, the Serbian army had conducted a heroic but costly retreat through the winter of 1915–1916 that took it finally to the island of Corfu. In the spring of 1916 Pašić was bearing the political consequences of this defeat, threatened on the one side by the machinations of Regent Aleksandar Karadjordjević, and on the other by disloyalty of an important segment of the military under the leadership of Colonel Dimitrijević-Apis.[17] In an effort to improve his fortunes at home by success abroad, Pašić traveled to Paris, London, and Petrograd in May 1916. Under great pressure, not certain of the outcome of the war, and none too confident of the purposes of the Croatian emigration, Pašić stated in an interview to the Russian press that he was ready to recognize Italy's predominant interest in the Adriatic.

Pašić's statement outraged the Yugoslav Committee, particularly Supilo, for whom it simply demonstrated the impossibility of trusting the Serbs to protect Croatian and Slovenian interests.[18] Supilo demanded the Yugoslav Committee break its relations with Serbia. But, once again, an emergency session of the full committee did not agree.[19] Harmony with Serbia was considered so vital that the committee simply asked its president, Trumbić, to speak privately with Pašić. To restrain Supilo from using his great personal influence to promote a break with Serbia, the committee prohibited any member from making personal contacts and statements without approval from Trumbić. Supilo responded to this gag rule by resigning from the committee, leaving it firmly under Trumbić's leadership until the end of the war.[20]

Supilo had accurately assessed the underlying attitude of Pašić and his government. Not only was Pašić a superb politician, a magician of appearance and nuance, and a dogged pursuer of personal power, he also was a true representative of the faith of all Serbian politicians in Serbia's destiny as the liberator of the Balkans. Supilo grasped that in something as basic as the structure of a future Yugoslavia, Pašić could never yield, either politically or temperamentally. Some others saw this, but none were hard-headed enough to follow the logic of the realization to its unpalatable conclusion: a break with Serbia. So Supilo was isolated, and despite its doubts, the committee tied itself even closer to Serbia.

A year later, conclusion of the Corfu Agreement seemed to indicate that the decision of 1916 had been correct. This agreement, which was achieved by lengthy and difficult negotiations between the representatives of the Yugoslav Committee and the Serbian government, was signed by Pašić and Trumbić July 20, 1917.[21] It called for the creation of a democratic, constitutional Kingdom of Serbs, Croats, and Slovenes under the Karadjordjević dynasty in which the cultural and religious rights of all three peoples would be preserved. A constitutional assembly to be held after liberation would determine the internal organization of the state.

The two signatories interpreted the Corfu Declaration quite differently, however. The Yugoslav Committee believed it had achieved basic agreement with Serbia. Even Supilo's pessimism was momentarily overcome. Despite the failure of the conferees to agree on the organization of the new state, it seemed that a great step forward for Yugoslavism had been achieved, and many still hold that this was the case.

Today, however, one may doubt that this positive interpretation is the whole truth. Pašić did not come to the negotiations because of any desire to plan for the future Yugoslav state. He called for discussions only under severe pressure, and after the agreement had been signed he ignored it except as a device for silencing those who accused him of ignoring the committee. Internally, Pašić's government was under attack for accepting Regent Aleksandar's scheme to rid the army of disloyal elements. By this plan Colonel Dimitrijević-Apis and his closest collaborators had been condemned to death for treason and attempted assassination. There is considerable doubt that these charges could have been sustained in a fair trial, but no doubt whatsoever that Apis and his organization, Union or Death, were a center of independent power that had disrupted Serbian public life for years. Union or Death had been involved in the assassination of Franz Ferdinand, and its machinations had resulted in the fall of Pašić's government in June 1914. The basic question was who would be the final authority in Serbia, the prince, the army, or the government. Because of his opposition to Pašić, Apis had close links with the opposition parties. Therefore, when Pašić decided to go along with the regent's plan to remove Apis he lost the support of these parties, with whom he had been allied in a coalition government since 1914.[22] Apis's trial also hurt Serbia's reputation abroad, because Pašić's enemies represented it not as an effort to establish the authority of the civilian government, but as an act of political revenge.

Pašić faced other uncertainties. In May 1917, the South Slavic political parties remaining inside Austria-Hungary proclaimed their desire for unification "under the sceptre of the Habsburg-Lorraine dynasty."[23] It appeared possible that the new Emperor Charles might be on the verge of forestalling Serbian gains by granting the Croats and Slovenes some sort of autonomy within the empire. Rumors of peace feelers further indicated that Serbian war aims might be in danger. Furthermore, Pašić was worried that the Yugoslav Committee, which he still considered simply an arm of Serbian propaganda, was slipping away from him. Not only did the committee constantly have its own views on affairs, but by 1917 it had become financially independent due to the generous support of the Croatian community in South America.

Rapprochement with the Yugoslav Committee would have a positive effect on all these problems. It would provide an antidote to the bad press Pašić was receiving abroad over the Apis case by pleasing the foreign supporters of the committee; it would mollify the opposition, which tended to favor accommodation; it would reaffirm Serbian claims to represent the Habsburg South Slavs in spite of the May Declaration; and it would draw the committee into closer cooperation with Serbia.

Having called for the meeting to serve these clear short-term ends, Pašić almost ignored the agreement after it was made. Before the ink on his signature was dry, he left Corfu to attend the conference on Balkan problems being held at Versailles. Rather than present the agreement officially to the Powers, as the Yugoslav Committee hoped, he contented himself with belatedly and reluctantly making it known to them orally.

In a way, of course, the standard interpretation of the Corfu Agreement as a positive step for Yugoslavism is correct. The agreement put both the Serbian government and the Yugoslav Committee on record as pursuing the same broad goal. But unfortunately for the Yugoslav Committee, it was not realized at the time, nor has it been clearly seen since, that the agreement was also a masterful diplomatic success for Pašić.[24] In return for acceptance of the Karadjordjević dynasty, with its clear implication of Serbian continuity, Pašić agreed to the principles of democracy, civil rights, and constitutionalism. This was not any sort of concession for him, since all of these were features of prewar Serbia and matched well the policy he had enunciated in 1914. Beyond that, however, Pašić conceded nothing. He did not change his view that Serbia should be the liberating power, nor did he make any agreement that would hinder his ability to organize the state after the war. In a typically brilliant maneuver, he achieved several short-term goals while putting the committee in his debt by giving it something it wanted, all the time retaining full initiative for himself in those things he considered most important. Without giving up anything fundamental, he severely limited the Yugoslav Committee's freedom of action by linking it more closely to Serbia than it had ever been before.

Committed now to cooperating with Serbia in the creation of a new state rather than going it alone, as Supilo had suggested, Trumbić had reason to hope in 1918 that progress in modifying Italian policy might also be possible. The solid rock of that policy was foreign minister Sidney Sonnino.[25] Sonnino had negotiated Italy's entrance into the Great War in return for South Tirol, Trentino, Istria, and central Dalmatia with its islands. Sonnino considered the acquisitions in the north the final stage of

Italian unification, and those on the Adriatic necessary for Italian security. Since the treaty also provided that the Great Powers could eventually assign some of the Adriatic lands to Slavic states, he believed that the treaty was a "working formula" from which all could profit.[26] The Slavs did not believe him. They saw the treaty only as a threat to their unification, not as a starting point for negotiations. And in fact, from the moment Sonnino secretly negotiated the treaty until his death in 1922 he resolutely held out for every last inch of territory promised him. As a result, even though some influential Italians favored a modified policy of cooperation with the South Slavs, Italian foreign policy remained until the end of the war extremely hostile to both Serbia and the Yugoslav Committee.

Late in 1917 British supporters of the Yugoslav cause began trying to do something about the deep differences betwen the Italians and the Yugoslavs.[27] Several meetings ensued, including one between Trumbić and the head of the Italian government, Vittorio Orlando. The eventual outcome was the Torre-Trumbić Agreement of March 1918.[28] Andrea Torre was the chairman of an *ad hoc* committee of the Italian parliament that was trying to organize a public meeting of the leaders of the Habsburg nationalities in exile for propaganda purposes. He had come to London to get the agreement of the Yugoslav Committee that was needed if the meeting was to be held. Trumbić was not enthusiastic. He refused to discuss border issues with Torre, and by insisting that the Italians renounce the Treaty of London he pushed their discussions to an impasse. Only when Henry Wickham Steed, foreign editor of *The Times* and a staunch supporter of Yugoslavism, frankly told Trumbić that his attitude would forfeit the support of Steed and his friends did Trumbić consent at the last minute to a statement of rather general principles. The Yugoslavs recognized the legitimacy of Italy's policy of national unity and the Italians recognized the Yugoslav goals of unification and independence. No specific territories were mentioned because "national unity" for the Italians included the same lands the Yugoslavs meant when they used the term "independence." Accordingly, and just as impossibly, it was agreed that territorial disputes would be decided after the war on the basis of the principle of nationality but in a way that would not injure the vital interests of either people. Rather than deciding anything, the Torre-Trumbić agreement simply recognized the two parties had incompatible goals: "nationality" for the Yugoslavs, and "vital interests" for the Italians.

But this was enough, and the Congress of Oppressed Nationalities was duly held in Rome in April 1918, bringing together not only the Yugoslavs, but Poles, Czechs, and Romanians as well. Orlando, along with other Italians more or less sympathetic to the South Slavs, attended the two-day meeting, but the intense feelings and rivalries precluded meaningful negotiations. The only communiqué adopted by the congress was simply a verbatim rendering of the Torre-Trumbić agreement.

Despite the superficial nature of this accomplishment, it appeared to many that the Pact of Rome, as it was called, implied that the Italians were willing to renounce Dalmatia and the Yugoslavs Trieste and Istria. For this reason it created considerable enthusiasm among the subject nationalities and was a great propaganda success. Leo Valiani has even gone so far as to say that the congress "represented a mortal blow to Austria-Hungary."[29] But for the Yugoslav Committee the ratification of the Pact of Rome was the Italian counterpart of the Corfu Declaration, with Sonnino playing the part of Pašić. Just as Pašić had drawn the committee closer to Serbia by concessions that did not forfeit his own initiative, so Sonnino allowed the Pact of Rome to achieve a propaganda success for the Italians without budging an inch on the Treaty of London. Sonnino did not approve of Torre's initiatives except in so far as they might help an Italian propaganda effort, did not attend the Rome Congress, and did not turn away from his obsession with the Treaty of London. Having committed himself to cooperation with the obdurate Pašić in 1916 and 1917, Trumbić committed himself to finding a compromise with the unyielding Sonnino in 1918.

These commitments proved to be the committee's downfall. When the war began to draw to a close, Trumbić realized ever more clearly that unless the committee could achieve formal recognition as the representative of the Habsburg South Slavs it would not be able to influence the shape of the postwar state. The last few months of the war were taken up with this fruitless task. None of the Powers would recognize the committee, even though they recognized the Czechoslovak National Committee and expressed increasing sympathy with the Yugoslav aims, unless Serbia and Italy also agreed. Agreement with Italy meant agreement with Sonnino, who continued to ignore the South Slavs and to consider the Treaty of London inviolate. The last possibility of a modification of his position occurred in August 1918, when Leonida Bissolati, the socialist Minister without portfolio, convinced Orlando to call the first full meeting of the Italian cabinet in two years to discuss foreign policy. One of his main motives was to achieve a more balanced Italian policy toward the Yugoslavs. The importance of this opportunity was so obvious that for the first time Trumbić was moved to modify the committee's maximum territorial claims, originally established in reaction to the London Treaty in 1915. But when his compromise offer fell far short of total acceptance of the London Treaty, Bissolati could only get the cabinet to agree to an offical statement recognizing the existence of "the movement of the Yugoslav peoples."[30]

This result was not encouraging, but it was enough to make it seem that progress was being made. It was not. The Italian government did not publish its mild statement, which fell far short of recognition, until September 25, and more important, Sonnino did not change. He intended to occupy the Yugoslav lands promised Italy by the Treaty of London as enemy territory. Recognition of the Yugoslav Committee would make those lands friendly territory, preventing their occupation. The futility of the committee's campaign received its final confirmation at the meeting of the Supreme Allied War Council at Versailles on November 1, at which time the Italians easily brushed aside the Yugoslav demands for recognition and received permission to occupy territory up to the line of the 1915 agreement.

Pašić too was intransigent. Responding to a request from Trumbić that Serbia support formal recognition of the committee, he claimed that the Serbs, Croats, and Slovenes were already adequately represented by the Serbian government, and that it would be a mistake to have two centers of power. This policy took enormous personal strength on Pašić's part. He was ruling without a majority in a rump parliament. An intense opposition criticized his every move, and most of this opposition favored an accommodation with the Yugoslav Committee. His potential friends in the West, in both France and England, were becoming estranged by his unwillingness to negotiate. Robert W. Seton-Watson, England's foremost authority on Eastern Europe, publicly attacked him, and when he visited London in early October 1918, British Foreign Minister Balfour warned him in person that no positive outcome for the Yugoslavs could be expected if he continued his adamant attitude.[31] And yet he stood firm against recognition.

By the end of October, as the Central Powers neared collapse, a new element entered the picture. Throughout the war the politicians who had remained in Austria-Hungary had been constrained to follow policies that were more or less loyal to the crown. But this did not prevent some of them from expressing their desire for unification and recognition, as the May Declaration demonstrated. In the difficult year of 1918, those parties that were inclined toward the creation of a larger Yugoslavia gained in strength. When it was obvious that the days of the monarchy were numbered, intense activity by these parties led to the creation in Zagreb of a government of the Serbs, Croats, and Slovenes in the Habsburg lands on October 29, 1918. With the formal approval of the Croatian sabor and shortly of Emperor Charles himself, the *narodno vijeće,* as this government was styled, proclaimed itself sovereign. Immediately its president, the Slovenian Anton Korošec, set off to Geneva to seek recognition from the Allies and to establish relations with the Serbian government and Yugoslav Committee. Korošec immediately contacted both Pašić and Trumbić, and when he learned that the Allies were meeting in Versailles during the first few days of November to discuss armistice terms for Austria, he designated the Yugoslav Committee in the person of Trumbić as the official representative there of the *narodno vijeće.*

The Yugoslavs were not able to influence the Versailles meetings, but the allied powers did recognize that something had to be done about the existence of two, now three, groups that claimed to represent portions of the Yugoslav peoples. The French government in particular summarily directed Pašić to meet with Trumbić and settle their differences. Accordingly, these two met in Paris on November 4. On Korošec's invitation, however, they immediately adjourned to Geneva to attempt to achieve agreement on the composition of a joint government, as demanded by the

Allies. The Serbian opposition was also represented at this meeting, which took place from November 6 to November 9.[32]

Trumbić appeared to have the strongest hand at Geneva, since the Serbian opposition parties opposed Pašić intransigence, as did Korošec. Pašić realized that he would have to come to a distasteful compromise, and on November 9, 1918, he signed the Geneva Agreement, even though it did not accord with his views. By this compromise, put forward by Trumbić, a dual government reminiscent of the Dual Monarchy that it was in part replacing would be formed. This new government would regulate the joint activities of the South Slavs, but the *narodno vijeće* and the Serbian government each would retain sovereignty over their own local affairs. The members of the joint government would take their oaths to their own sovereigns, Alexander Karadjordjević in the case of the Serbs, and the *narodno vijeće* in the case of the Habsburg Slavs. A more lasting constitutional arrangement would be worked out later.

This agreement, had it lasted, meant unification on the equal basis the Yugoslav Committee had sought. It appeared that Trumbić and the Yugoslav Committee had succeeded. But once again, and for the last time, appearances were deceiving. When Pašić first notified his government on Corfu of his signature, Stojan Protić, his closest political associate, accepted the decision. But the next day, November 10, Pašić sent a telegram to Protić in which he broadly hinted that if the Regent wished another sort of arrangement he could accept the government's resignation. On November 11, Protić changed his mind and repudiated the Geneva Agreement. The government resigned. Within a few days Pašić destroyed the support of the Yugoslav Committee among Serbs by asking the political parties that had opposed him for so long to join in a coalition government. Accepting the opportunity to participate in the making of a new Serbia, these parties lost much of their interest in the Yugoslav Committee, and the Geneva Agreement was forgotten.

Meanwhile, the Yugoslav Committee was being undermined in Zagreb as well. Prince Aleksandar did not favor the Geneva Agreement since it did not require all of the persons in the new state to take an oath of allegiance to him. This obviously influenced Protić's rejection. But another important reason for Protić's step was that he discovered on November 10 that the balance of forces in the *narodno vijeće* was shifting away from the Yugoslav Committee. The main South Slavic political force in the Habsburg Monarchy for the decade preceding 1918 had been the Serbo-Croatian Coalition. Although originally founded by men such as Supilo and Trumbić, during World War I it had remained passive toward the efforts of others to bring forth a new Yugoslav state. Only with difficulty and at the last minute was the Coalition enticed into the *narodno vijeće*. Its acceptance of the national program was considered the final step that would insure the creation of a new Yugoslavia. However, when the Coalition entered the *narodno vijeće* it immediately became the dominant force and its leader, Svetozar Pribićević, the strongest figure. Pribićević was a Serb who favored unification along the lines suggested by Pašić and Protić, not those favored by Korošec and Trumbić. Fortuitously, Protić had received word on this favorable situation on November 10 from Prince Alexander, who was not in Corfu, but in Belgrade, having entered the Serbian capital only the day before with his victorious army. Protić was able to repudiate the Geneva Agreement in the knowledge that the *narodno vijeće* was likely to do so also under Pribićević's leadership. In fact, on November 25, this is just what happened.

In November the rapidly changing course of events moved completely out of the control of the Yugoslav Committee. The Serbian army occupied Belgrade on November 1. By November 13 a military representative of the high command was in Zagreb, encouraging Pribićević. By the end of the month the *narodno vijeće,* without consulting Trumbić or Korošec, decided to join Serbia immediately and without conditions. On December 1, 1918, Alexander received the petitioners of the *narodno vijeće,* as well as representatives of other bodies from Montenegro, Bosnia and Herzegovina, and the Vojvodina, and announced the formation of the new Kingdom of the Serbs, Croats, and Slovenes.[33] The Croats and Slovenes had done just what Supilo had feared in 1915 and what Pašić all along had hoped they would do: they had agreed to unification with Serbia without first working out the terms.

There is probably only one way the Yugoslav Committee could have improved upon this result. If it had understood how accurately Pašić represented the deep feeling of most Serbs that Serbia should be the liberator of the South Slavs, its only course of action would have been to break with Serbia. If the committee had appreciated the impossibility of agreeing with Sonnino on any terms less than full acceptance of the Treaty of London, its only solution would have been to accept that treaty. But these were impossible choices. Not only did the Serbian government have its representatives on the Yugoslav Committee, but even among the Croats there was no agreement that Pašić's way was wrong. The Slovenes could not accept Supilo's proposal to break with Serbia because Supilo treated the Slovenes as merely adjuncts to Croatia. Furthermore, none of them would have agreed to give up the Adriatic lands Italy craved. The Yugoslav Committee was in a similar position to that of the Polish government in exile during World War II. The only way the Poles could have reached an accommodation with Stalin would have been to recognize the 1941 borders. But the very reason the Poles went into exile in the first place was to protect 1939 Poland. For both the Poles and the Yugoslavs, the one thing they most needed to do was the one thing to which they would never consent.[34]

Politics may be the art of the possible, but in this case the only way the Yugoslav Committee could have succeeded would have been to practice the art of the impossible. The committee needed to accept the Treaty of London and break with the Serbs. Had the Yugoslavs accepted the Italian claims they would not have lost much more territory than they did anyway, but they would have opened up enormous positive possibilities. One of the constant and unsuccessful struggles of the committee, for example, was to create a Yugoslav Legion from Habsburg prisoners of war in Italy.[35] The experience of the Czech Committee in exile showed how important it was to have such a force in being. In the spring of 1918, when the manpower shortage was critical on the western front, the Czechs had been able to extract concessions from the Allies because they controlled Czech legions that could be assigned to the front. Sonnino did not want the Yugoslavs to have such legions because he feared they would be used on behalf of the South Slavs in the lands Italy had been promised in 1915. But if the committee had accepted the Treaty of London, this fear would have been allayed and perhaps Sonnino would have let the Yugoslavs form their legions. With these forces at their back, the committee might have been recognized in mid-1918 at the same time the Czechs were.

This is all the more likely because of a second result that acceptance of the London Treaty would have produced. From the beginning, the fact that many Slavs lived in the territories the Italians claimed by the Treaty of London threatened the Italian aims. They needed some group that spoke for these Slavs to agree to Italian rule. The Yugoslav Committee was such a group. But acceptance of the Italian territorial demands by the committee would gain legal significance only if it were a legal entity, not just an emigré group. It is almost certain, therefore, that if the committee had accepted the London Treaty the Italians would have favored recognition, because in that way any possible ethnic stain on the Italian claims would have been wiped clean.

Naturally, acceptance of the Treaty of London would have meant breaking with Serbia, as Supilo suggested. Difficult though this would have been, it too would have had positive effects. For example, Pašić's opposition to recognition would have been much less effective if the committee was not seen as subordinate to the Serbian government. As the war drew to a close and the *narodno vijeće* came into being, the Yugoslav Committee could have offered the new state its assets: military forces and formal recognition, a combination that would have been hard to resist. Two possibilities would have opened up. Either two South Slavic states would have been established at the end of the war, or Serbia would have had to meet the Yugoslav Committee and *narodno vijeće* on equal terms and work out a mutually satisfactory agreement. In either case, the chances that Serbia could dominate Croatia and Slovenia in a postwar state would have been greatly lessened, and the goal of the Yugoslav Committee would have come much closer to realization.

In fact, of course, none of this happened. Frano Supilo was willing to break with Serbia and even to make concessions to Italy, but most of his colleagues, including Ante Trumbić, were not. Trumbić believed that the exclusion of Serbia from a South Slavic movement would eviscerate the entire idea of Yugoslavism. Therefore, he was always willing to make one more effort to work out an agreement with Pašić. The irony of this position was that precisely his belief that Serbia was necessary to a new Yugoslavia made it impossible for Trumbić to make the cold-blooded decision that could have made an equal partnership possible. This, coupled with his inability to negotiate realistically with Italy, prevented the committee from transcending its emigré status and reduced its historical role to that of a propaganda agent for Yugoslavism.

In this capacity, the Yugoslav Committee was extremely successful. But in its political goal, it was not. One's evaluation of this outcome depends a good deal on whether one is a pessimist or an optimist. The pessimists will say that Trumbić failed because he did not have the greatness to correctly evaluate the situation and lead his committee to the extremely difficult decisions that hindsight shows were necessary. The optimists will point out that Trumbić always kept before his eyes the ultimate goal of a unified Yugoslavia, successfully created a climate of opinion in Europe favorable to that idea, and had the charity and vision to refuse to consider a new Yugoslavia without Serbia. Both evaluations are correct, but in either case, the result did not turn out as Trumbić had hoped.

7

The Devil's Finger: The Disintegration of Yugoslavia

Yugoslavia had neither a velvet revolution nor a velvet divorce. Midway through 1991 two of its six constituent republics, Slovenia and Croatia, declared their independence, provoking a vicious civil war that spread in 1992 to Bosnia and Herzegovina. Ethnic emotions run deep throughout Eastern Europe, but nowhere did they reach the level of bestiality that they did in Yugoslavia. As one observer put it, the devil must have pointed his finger at this country.[1] Grotesque atrocities, ethnic cleansing, bombardment of priceless cultural artifacts, hundreds of thousands of refugees, cities destroyed, obsessive propaganda and disinformation—these were the realities in many parts of Yugoslavia at a time when other East European countries were holding elections, negotiating with the European Community, writing constitutions, privatizing industry, and otherwise trying to find their way back to Europe. What happened? How did Yugoslavia, the first communist state to break with the Soviet Union and the most open communist state in the world in the 1960s, come to this depressing impasse?

The answer is not simple, but it revolves around the inherent weakness of Yugoslavism itself. The concept emerged first in the nineteenth century, when Slavic peoples in Russia and Eastern Europe were beginning to understand that they spoke related languages.[2] In a day of powerful empires, Panslavism suggested that the Slavs might form the basis of a power-

From *The Walls Came Tumbling Down: The Collapse of Communism in Eastern Europe* by Gale Stokes. (New York: Oxford University Press, 1993). Reprinted by permission.

ful empire of their own some day. Among the Yugoslavs (the term means "South Slavs"), the idea came to expression in the 1840s in the work of Ljudevit Gaj, a Croat who argued in his journal *Danica* (Morning Star) that all the south Slavic peoples were branches of the same Illyrian tribe. In the 1860s Illyrianism gave way to the Yugoslavism of the Catholic bishop of Croatia, Josip Juraj Strossmayer, who also believed in the cultural unity of the South Slavs. When he founded an Academy of Arts and Sciences in Zagreb in 1867, he did not name it the Croatian Academy but rather the Yugoslav Academy. Serbs in the 1860s also had a program for uniting the South Slavs in a single state, the ideal of a Balkan federation propagated by Prince Michael Obrenović. But Prince Michael, despite some desultory negotiations with Bishop Strossmayer, believed unification should take place under Serbian leadership. From the earliest days of the idea of Yugoslavism, therefore, the orientation of Serbian and Croatian Yugoslavists differed, the latter thinking in broad cultural terms and the former thinking in practical terms of a state under Serbian leadership.

Serbs and Croats living in the Austrian half of the Habsburg Empire found ways to cooperate politically prior to World War I, and a number of Croatian and Serbian intellectuals in Zagreb and Belgrade, especially students, were enthusiastic about Yugoslavism in the years before World War I. But it could not be said that the idea had struck very deep roots by 1914. Much stronger was the idea of nationalism. This is the issue over which World War I began. Austria-Hungary attacked Serbia not for any clear-cut economic or strategic aims but because of the belief that the independent state of Serbia represented the national principle of governance, which, if accepted, would destroy the Habsburg state. Since medieval times *Kaisertreue,* or "loyalty to the emperor," had been the principle that held the varied Habsburg lands together. If all the peoples of that multinational empire were to adopt the notion championed by Serbia—that each ethnic group had the right to its own sovereign state—the empire was doomed.

From the beginning of the war many South Slavs were thinking about what the postwar arrangements would be. As early as September 4, 1914, Nikola Pašić, prime minister of Serbia, informed the Allied Powers (Russia, France, and Great Britain) that the best way to assure the containment of Germany would be to create a strong national state in the Balkans that would consist of all Serbs, Croats, and Slovenes.[3] In December 1914 the Serbian government officially adopted a set of war aims calling for "the liberation and unification of all our unliberated brothers: Serbs, Croats, and Slovenes." The non-Serbs in this state were not to be partners exactly, but in victory the Serbs intended to grant them equal rights as Serbs or as associated peoples.

On the Slovenian and Croatian side, some Dalmatian and other Croatian emigrés created the Yugoslav Committee, which lobbied in London for the recognition of a new postwar state, much in the way that Tomaš Masaryk did in America on behalf of Czechoslovakia. In 1917 leaders of the Yugoslav Committee and of the Serbian government met on the island of Corfu and agreed to establish a democratic, constitutional Kingdom of Serbs, Croats, and Slovenes under the Serbian dynasty. The cultural and religious rights of all three peoples were to be preserved in this new state, although Albanians, Bosnians, Macedonians, and other minorities were not mentioned. But the Corfu Agreement left one major question unsettled: Would Yugoslavia be a centralized state as the Serbs wanted (and still wanted in 1991) or a federation of equal and sovereign peoples as the Croats wanted (and still wanted in 1991)?

The actual founding of the new state took place just after the last days of the war in conditions of utmost confusion. The Austro-Hungarian state collapsed; an allied army, which included a significant number of Serbian divisions, pushed into the Balkans from Salonica and spread out toward the Adriatic, where it encountered a hostile Italy; and demobilized soldiers returning from Russia created "green armies," quasi-revolutionary movements whose members often were little better than bandits.[4] Independent committees and councils arose in many South Slavic areas, but the only realistic option they had was to gravitate toward Serbia, which was the only entity among them (except tiny Montenegro) that European powers already accepted as a sovereign state.[5] Representatives of the Montenegrins, the Bosnians, and the Hungarians and Serbs from the Vojvodina all decided to link up with Serbia in a new Balkan state.[6] In Zagreb, the National Council of Slovenes, Croats, and Serbs, newly formed by politicians who until shortly before had been more or less loyal to the Habsburgs, decided to follow suit on behalf of the Croats and Slovenes. The council had little choice, since the alternative was to create an independent country, which would have faced powerful Italian claims, a victorious Serbian army, and none-too-sympathetic Great Powers. Only one member of the council, Stjepan Radić, leader of the Croatian Peasant party, favored independence, and even he acquiesced temporarily in the decision to join with the others.[7] Late in November delegates from the various councils gathered in Belgrade, and on December 1, 1918, King Aleksandar of Serbia announced the formation of the Kingdom of Serbs, Croats, and Slovenes.[8]

Even though the constituent peoples voluntarily entered into the new state, which Woodrow Wilson and the other wartime leaders blessed in Paris in 1919, the question left unsettled at Corfu immediately provoked bitter political controversy. The Serbs, having fought heroically in the Balkan Wars of 1912–1913, having suffered greatly during World War I, and having won in 1918, quite naturally expected that the new state would be an extension of the old Serbia. The Croats, noting the overbearing way in which the Serbs had incorporated Macedonia in 1913 and anticipating that the Orthodox Serbs would not be sympathetic to their Catholic World War I adversaries, feared a centralized state with its capitol in Belgrade. Unfortunately, rather than fight this fundamental issue out in the constituent assembly elected for that purpose, the Croatian Peasant party, which under Radić held the loyalty of the overwhelming majority of the Croatian peasantry, chose to boycott the constitution-writing process. The constitution promulgated in 1921, therefore, was essentially a Serbian document that could never be satisfactory to the Croats, although the Serbs did find ways to placate Slovenian and Bosnian political figures. From the very beginning, the actualization of the never-too-widely-accepted idea of a single South Slavic state, a Yugoslavia, was seriously, probably fatally, flawed.

Politics during the 1920s in the Kingdom of the Serbs, Croats, and Slovenes were extremely volatile, to the extent that in 1928 a disgruntled Montenegrin member of Parliament shot five Croatian representatives on the floor of the assembly itself, killing three of them, including Stjepan Radić. In 1929 King Aleksandar, fed up with the constant squabbling, seized power on his own, suspended the legislature and the constitution, reorganized the country into provinces based on river valleys, and changed the name of the state to Yugoslavia.

Aleksandar did his best to turn his diverse collection of peoples into a nation, but his efforts to impose Yugoslavism by force only discredited the idea. Yugoslavism became associated in the minds of non-Serbs with Serbian oppression, and in the minds of the many leftist Serbs Aleksandar sent to prison, simply with oppression. After Aleksandar's assassination in 1934 by a Macedonian terrorist, the Croats were able to distance themselves from Yugoslavia by extracting an agreement from Belgrade in August 1939 that granted Croatia autonomous status. The agreement also granted the Croats territorial gains around Mostar in Herzegovina and in northeast Bosnia that closely approximated the territories the Croats seized in 1992. But the agreement came far too late to permit Yugoslavia to prepare for Hitler's onslaught. When the Wehrmacht took less than two weeks to crush Yugoslavia in April 1941, the first experiment in creating a multinational Yugoslav state came to an ignominious and, for some, unlamented end.

The second Yugoslav experiment began in the depths of World War II. From the beginning, the communist resistance under Josip Broz Tito, fighting for its life in the vastness of Bosnia and Herzegovina, intended to create a revolutionary Marxist state, but at the same time Tito understood that a new Yugoslavia would have to be based on a more evenhanded treatment of the various Yugoslav nationalities. From the first meeting in 1942 of the Anti-Fascist Council for the National Liberation of Yugoslavia, as the precursor to the postwar government was called, the Communists advocated a Yugoslavia that would be "a voluntary union of separate peoples" and began using the slogan "Brotherhood and Unity." When they recreated Yugoslavia in 1945, it was as a federal state consisting of six equal republics and two autonomous regions within the Republic of Serbia. The new republics were Slovenia, a relatively prosperous South Slavic people in the northwest; Croatia, a Catholic people living along the Adriatic coast as well as along the Sava River; Bosnia and Herzegovina, an ethnically mixed republic with a strong Muslim tradition; Montenegro, a small mountainous entity with a proud tradition as mountaineer fighters; Macedonia, an entirely new entity that set about creating a Macedonian language and national culture; and Serbia, Orthodox Christians who were the largest group in Yugoslavia, but not a majority.[9] Serbia also contained two autonomous provinces: Vojvodina to the north with a significant Hungarian minority, and Kosovë to the south, which ethnically was predominantly Albanian.[10] This new federal republic of equal peoples was probably as good a solution as the inextricably mixed ethnic character of the region permitted.

The Yugoslav Communists were brutal in imposing their revolutionary programs, but their position on ethnic equality shone in sparkling contrast to the bestiality of World War II in Yugoslavia. In the Independent state of Croatia, for example, a fanatical band of fascist enthusiasts, called the Ustasha, was so ardent in its massacres and forced removals of Serbs, Communists, Roma, Muslims, and others that even the Germans were shocked.[11] Serbian Chetniks in Bosnia and fascist collaborators in Serbia proper often matched Croatian brutality with cruelty of their own, and the Germans themselves contributed their share of massacres. To many, the communist program of brotherhood and unity also offered a superior choice to the one offered by the Chetniks, the official resistance force of the Yugoslav government in exile under the leadership of Draža Mihailović, which also committed atrocities during the war and whose Serbian orientation was obvious.

The Partisans, as the Communists called themselves, had one other advantage: They won the three-cornered civil war (Chetnik, Ustasha, Partisan—Serb, Croat, Communist) that went on simultaneously with Yugoslav resistance to fascism. This gave them the power to impose their vision of a communist Yugoslavia by force. In 1945 they rid themselves of the Ustasha problem by killing tens of thousands of Croats, not all of them guilty of crimes, and in 1946 they captured and executed Mihailović. They also cleared the field of thousands of other potential political opponents by the less dramatic but no less effective means of arrest, imprisonment, and intimidation.

These traditional methods were eminently successful in creating a communist state in Yugoslavia, but they had a serious long-term negative effect, especially in Croatia. The wartime experience in Croatia was as far beyond the ordinary experience of Croats as the Holocaust experience was beyond the ordinary experience of Germans. And yet it happened. In Germany the question of responsibility for the Nazi period has been debated, discussed, refined, and talked about for forty years. As a result, most adult Germans are sensitive to their historical experience and determined that it should not happen again. A real democracy has become established in Germany in good measure because Germans have faced their unpleasant past squarely.

In Croatia, by contrast, and in fact throughout Yugoslavia, the wartime horrors were never openly confronted. Hundreds, perhaps thousands, of researchers investigated every aspect of the partisan struggle, but basic questions about the relationship between the Independent State of Croatia and Croatian culture and history, or between the Chetniks and Serbian history, were never asked. Every society, perhaps every person, contains a dark element that, in the right circumstances, can burst through the normal crust of civility in an explosion of murder and plunder. But Serbs and Croats were not premitted to face that experience in their own past, to atone for it, to understand it, and to commit themselves to not repeating it. Instead of permitting the Yugoslavs to face this unpleasant past, the Communists simply condemned the horrors of the wartime experience as an extreme outburst of bourgeois society and proclaimed that such things could not happen in the new order. Any effort to confront the issues directly was forbidden. This failure to provide for remembrance and reconciliation, not only in Croatia but in other parts of Yugoslavia as well, was one of the most significant negative aspects of the imposition of Communist rule in Yugoslavia. The wounds of World War II were covered over, but they never healed.

The Yugoslav Communists possessed three unifying elements that lifted their effort to build a multinational Yugoslavia above earlier ethnic conflicts, at least potentially. These were their Marxism, which provided an ideology of internationalism; their partisan experience, which bonded the leadership together with powerful feelings of purpose and commitment; and their leader, Josip Broz Tito, whose authority was unquestioned during his lifetime. These advantages did not mean that no ethnic controversies erupted in the second Yugoslavia. Ivo Banac has shown how pervasive and divisive these struggles were even in the early postwar days.[12] But in contrast to their predecessors in the first Yugoslavia, the main communist leaders had a vision of a socialist Yugoslavia in which nationality problems would wither away if they were suppressed long enough. Tito himself hoped that someday a sense of Yugoslavism would supplant the sense of individual nations, and the party platform of 1958 spoke of a "Yugoslav socialist consciousness." But the linkage of "Yugoslav" and "socialist" contained a critical weakness that Tito and his colleagues could never have imagined. As long as the communist movement remained strong, Yugoslavism was not in danger. If nationalism reared its head the party could and did push it back under the surface. If the League of Communists of Yugoslavia should disintegrate, however, then the Yugoslavism it championed would disintegrate too.

And the party did disintegrate, not in the sudden and dramatic way that the parties of Hungary and Czechoslovakia did, but over a long period of time through an incremental process of decentralization. The most original innovation of the Yugoslav Communists was their attempt to structure their economy, and eventually their entire public life, on the principle of self-administration (also called self-management). At first the idea was simply that workers should manage the socially owned factories in which they worked. But self-administration is inherently disaggregating. If each enterprise should manage itself, why not each republic, each city, or each village? If self-management was good for factory workers, why not for hospital workers, university employees, or even government employees? Indeed, why not for the party itself?

Yugoslav experimentation with market mechanisms reinforced the decentralizing character of self-management. The market is by definition decentralized. In its search for economic mechanisms more viable than the Stalinist ones it had installed from 1945 to 1948, the Belgrade regime began to dismantle its absolute economic authority as early as 1954 by giving enterprises some leeway in making business decisions and by devolving a small but significant amount of power over enterprises to local governments. Once begun, the process of devolution continued for thirty-five years, until in 1991 the center lost control completely.

Both economic and political disagreements drove the decentralization process, with the ethnic factor always lurking close beneath the surface. By the 1960s the republics of the northwest, because of their advantageous location on the Adriatic coast, were earning considerable foreign exchange from tourists. How much of that should they keep and how much should go to the federation for countrywide use? Croatia and Slovenia argued that the center took too much, while the other republics complained that Croatia and Slovenia kept too much. A similar controversy raged over the allocation of investment resources. Was it better to invest funds in the developed republics, which once again were Slovenia and Croatia, where one reasonably could hope the monies would be used effectively to increase productivity, or in the poorest parts of Yugoslavia, which desperately needed development but where a good portion of the funding probably would be wasted?

These tough economic issues would have been difficult to arbitrate even in an ethnically homogeneous environment. But Yugoslavia was far from homogeneous. All sides perceived controversies over economic efficiency, investment allocation, and convertible currency rules in ethnic terms. Therefore the arguments were always more intense than they otherwise might have been. Constant efforts by the communist leadership at the center could control the debates and downplay their ethnic elements, but they could not solve the basic conflicts of interest.

The economic debates of the 1960s and 1970s, were not as disruptive as they might have been because Yugoslavia prospered during those decades. The modest marketizing reforms the Yugoslavs undertook in the 1960s led to significant growth that not only benefited industry but trickled down to ordinary people as well. Dennison Rusinow summed up the results with the comment that in the mid-1960s Belgrade was "the only communist capital with a parking problem."[13] This palpable economic improvement convinced Tito, always the final arbiter in any controversy in which he took an interest, to side with those who favored a more open economy. In 1965 the economic reform known as the "New Measures" revalued the currency, opened up foreign trade regulations, and gave enterprises more autonomy. With Tito's blessing, Yugoslavia became the most open communist state in the world. Its citizens could freely travel—over a million of them were working as guest workers in Germany by the end of the 1960s—and they could even emigrate. Despite contemporary reports about how badly the Yugoslav economy worked and despite continual tinkering, the influx of foreign loans during the 1970s made that decade the most prosperous time ordinary Yugoslavs have ever known.

The Politics of Decentralization, 1966–1976

The political concomitant to the economic reforms was decentralization of the party and of the federal political processes.[14] Two tendencies characterized the party during its early years in power: a centralizing one associated with the Serbian head of the federal security services, Aleksandar Ranković, and a decentralizing one associated with the Slovenian theorist of self-management, Edvard Kardelj. The struggle reached its climax in 1966 with the removal of Ranković, considered at that time second only to Tito himself, for "factional activity." Although Ranković's downfall was always discussed publicly in terms of the deformation of self-management and similar acceptable rubrics, popularly his demise was seen as a defeat for the Serbs. Such a simplified interpretation overlooked the diversity of opinion within each ethnic group and undervalued the views and influence of the smaller republics, but it was widely held nonetheless.[15] Revelations of Ranković's brutal policies against the Albanians in Kosovë and the Hungarians in the Vojvodina provided grist for the mill of those who saw in Ranković a rebirth of Serbian hegemonism.

The defeat of the centralizing Ranković led to an assertion of authority by party organs in each republic and the confirmation by the Ninth Party Congress of March 1969 that the League of Communists of Yugoslavia comprised eight constituent bodies, one each for the republics and one each for the two autonomous provinces. As Steven Burg put it, the Ninth Party Congress "institutionalized the existence of eight distinct blocs in the Yugoslav political system. . . . Conflict between the blocs became dominated by the national cleavages that divided them."[16] The Yugoslav Communists had no intention of dissolving their party in the late 1960s, but the actual decentralization put in train by Ranković's fall began the process anyway.

Decentralization came to formal government structures at the same time. The passage in 1971 of twenty-three constitutional amendments led to the adoption in 1974 of a new constitution and in 1976 to a new "Law on Associated Labor," all suffused with the spirit of self-administration. The amendments of 1971 and the constitution of 1974 established a complex system of delegates and consultations at all levels of government, while the law on associated labor divided all economic enterprises, even hospitals and charitable organizations, into what the Yugoslavs called "Basic Organizations of Associated Labor," which were to be the fundamental negotiating units in each self-managing enterprise. Edvard Kardelj, the architect of the 1974 constitution, characterized the complex new system as a "pluralism of self-managing interests." This sounded good, but in practice the new laws made it almost impossible for the federal government to pursue a coherent economic program, since each republic now held a suspensive veto of federal legislation, and very difficult for enterprises to run themselves efficiently, since each Basic Organization of Associated Labor held what amounted to its own miniveto of enterprise operations.

The most important political provision of the new constitution was the raising of the autonomous regions of Kosovë and Vojvodina to a status equivalent to that of the republics by giving them a voice equal to the republics in the newly created nine-person presidency and by giving them an equal ability to hamstring federal legislation. Only after a lengthy series of steps could the federal government override the objections of a republic or an autonomous region to a particular piece of legislation, and then only when it was declared vital to the interest of the entire federation.

Giving the autonomous regions equal status with the republics was particularly repugnant to some Serbs. They looked back to Serbia's history as an independent state; its victories in both the Balkan wars and World War I; its domination in the interwar years of Macedonia and Kosovë, which were then integral parts of Serbia; and the inclusion of Vojvodina after 1945. After World War II Macedonia became one of the six constituent republics, and after 1974 Kosovë and Vojvodina became almost equal to the republics. Was this the fruit of all their struggles—to win the wars and lose the peace?

The more radical of the critics went further, pointing out that many Serbs lived outside the Republic of Serbia and hinting that border changes in Croatia and Bosnia were needed to create a Greater Serbia. In one particularly interesting complaint, which rehearsed the arguments Slobodan Milošević used in 1991 to justify his war on Croatia, Mihailo Djurić argued in 1971 that Serbia was

> already in an unequal position with respect to the other nations in Yugoslavia, such that the proposed constitutional changes, in the final analysis, are directed against its deepest vital interest. The final consequence of the change will be its complete disintegration. It is obvious that the borders of the present Socialist Republic of Serbia are neither the national nor the historical borders of the Serb nation. As is well known, outside the borders of Serbia the Serbian nation lives in four of the five other republics, but not in one of these republics can it live its own life. . . . The Serbian nation must turn to its own devices, it must begin to fight for its dangerously threatened national identity and integrity.[17]

The mainstream of Serbian communism in 1971 harshly condemned Djurić's arguments, and he spect time in prison for voicing them. More moderate Serbian Communists found another, less ethnically charged way to criticize the decentralizing thrust of the constitutional changes. These critics argued that it was not possible to have a united state without efficient, independent, and strong central governmental organs. In particular they argued that it was absolutely crucial to Yugoslav economic well-being that the center control banking, fiscal matters such as the currency, and international trade rules.

Croatian leaders dismissed these not unreasonable arguments as camouflage for the real Serbian desires. Savka Dabčević-Kučar, a leading advocate of the Croatian position, suggested that behind the economic arguments for a strong center lurked Mihailo Djurić's pleas for a Greater Serbia. Calls for unity at the federal level, in Dabčević-Kučar's view, were only "a mask behind which [Serbian] hegemonism hides its face." She considered even Yugoslavism an "unacceptable phenomenon" denoting "some superior supranational phenomenon."[18]

In the most important area, the adoption of the new constitution in 1974, the Croats essentially sustained their position. Federal powers were weakened and republican powers strengthened, both in the party and in government, and Vojvodina and Kosovë received greater authority, thus reining in the Serbs. But Croats could not savor their victory because of a controversy over Croatian nationalism in 1971. After the fall of Ranković it became easier, although not officially condoned, to express nationalist viewpoints throughout Yugoslavia. In Zagreb, late in the 1960s, *Matica hrvatska* (Croatian Home), a Croatian cultural society dating from the 1840s, came into the hands of nationalists, including the future president of Croatia, Franjo Tudjman.[19] Undertaking an aggressive publicity campaign to create local clubs on the basis of a nationalist program, Matica raised its membership from about two thousand to just over forty thousand by the end of 1971.

Meanwhile, a trio of Croatian party leaders (Mika Tripalo, Pero Pirker, and Savka Kabčević-Kučar) were pressing Tito for a radical reform of the Yugoslav currency system that would give Croatia more control over its foreign currency assets. During 1970 the Croatian party split between the old hands, who wanted to clamp down on nationalism, and this trio of younger leaders who began using nationalist arguments. Tripalo and his colleagues rejected complaints from other republics that nationalism was starting to get out of hand in Croatia with the remarkable argument that in Croatia nation and class had become identical, so that pursuit of Croatian national aims was the same thing as pursuing the interests of the working class. As the year wore on, the political climate in Zagreb became heated, both inside the party and among the supporters of Matica hrvatska. This Croatian group now openly pursued what Dennison Rusinow reluctantly characterized as the policies of a "nineteenth-century National-Liberal party . . . with roots deep in the intellectual and political history of the Habsburg Monarchy." The result, as Rusinow tortuously put it, "is something that belongs in that part of a typology of political and ideological systems which is loosely and sometimes misleadingly called fascist."[20]

In November 1971 the nationalist newspaper *Hrvatski tjednik* (Croatian Weekly) brought things to a head by publishing a proposal from Matica hrvatska for a new Croatian constitution. It provided that Croatia was "the sovereign national state of the Croatian nation," that it had the right to secession, that Croatian would be the sole official language, that Croatian authorities would have full control of all tax revenues collected in Croatia, and that there would be a Croatian territorial army.[21] The suggestion was even made that Croatia should have its own representative at the United Nations. These proposals, which Franjo Tudjman's Croatian Democratic Union successfully put forward again twenty years later (in 1992 Croatia became a member of the United Nations), were completely unacceptable to the rest of Yugoslavia, so radical at the time as to be beyond discussion.

The climax to this volatile situation came late in November, when students at Zagreb University went on strike over the foreign currency issue. Dennison Rusinow suggested that the strikers may have "reckoned that if even just a few factories joined them, the triumvirate and their Party following would have to [join them also], facing Tito with a civil war if he called in the army."[22] But that calculation was twenty years too early. In 1971 the population at large did not join in.

When Tito finally realized the seriousness of the situation, it was he who stepped in, bringing all the important party leaders to his hunting lodge at Karadjordjevo near Belgrade, where he imposed a solution. Matica hrvatska was closed and its leaders, including Tudjman, imprisoned; many student activists were arrested; the Croatian triumvirate resigned; and the party itself was "cleansed." To be evenhanded, in 1972 Tito purged the Serbian party too, so that by the time the constitution of 1974 was adopted he and his center of old partisan leaders had reasserted their dominance.

The restructurings from 1966 through 1976 and the nationalist confrontations of the same period satisfied no one. The Serbs felt aggrieved because they had lost the battle to prevent decentralization and resented Tito's sacking of their relatively moderate leaders. The Croats were frustrated that the center had crushed what they considered their legitimate ambitions for national identity. Tito had reasserted the center's authority explicitly on the basis of revolutionary power, but at the same time he had permitted the creation of a decentralized constitutional arrangement that made it very difficult for that center to conduct ordinary business. Order had been restored by the special intervention of the only person in Yugoslavia with authority commensurate to the task, Tito himself. But in the day-to-day life of the federation impasse and controversy became endemic.

The Economy Turns Down

In 1980 Tito performed his last service to Yugoslavia—he took a long time dying. He entered the hospital early in January for a blood clot and had his leg amputated; after declining physically over the next four months, he died. When somber martial music interrupted the normal television programming on the afternoon of May 4, 1980, the Yugoslavs, who had been a bit panicky in January and February, were more or less prepared, at least for the short run. Tito's death was not just the end of the personal rule of a pleasure-loving but not unloved dictator. It also marked the end of the entire postwar generation whose commitment to Marxism, to the partisan experience, and to Tito himself had provided the glue that kept Yugoslavia together. Persons aged forty and under, as well as many older people, found the endless celebrations of the partisan movement, which was in fact a thrilling and inspirational struggle against terrible odds, simply boring. And self-management proved to be a fraud. Workers had almost no say in how their enterprises were run, despite spending sometimes as much as 30 percent of their time in meetings of their Basic Organizations of Associated Labor. In many of the less successful firms, networks of party officials maintained their control through local party connections, republican governments, and the Socialist Alliance. By the time of Tito's death many Yugoslavs had come to the same conclusion about socialism as had the citizens of the other East European states: it was a sham.

To make matters worse, just before Tito's death the economy took a downward turn. During the 1950s rapid Yugoslav growth had been fueled by American aid.[23] In the 1970s, much as in Poland and elsewhere, growth was fueled by foreign loans. But, as in Poland, instead of igniting export-driven growth, the loans of the 1970s either ended up in the pockets of the workers in the form of increased consumption and a higher standard of living or were wasted in inefficient investments undertaken for political reasons. Efficiency did not increase, but debt grew rapidly. In 1979, when the second oil crisis hit and the loans slowed down, the Yugoslav miracle was over. As an editorial in Socialist Alliance's newspaper *Borba* (Struggle) put it, "The present hardships are in great measure due to rising domestic consumption being fostered on the basis of foreign loans."[24]

Economic difficulties were also due to the same soft budget constraints and political interference that characterized every socialist economy.[25] Despite Yugoslavia's favorable reputation in the 1970s as a hybrid of both the planned and the market economy, Yugoslav Communists were just as enamored of metal-eating industries as Communists anywhere. Instances of incredible waste were perhaps even more commonplace in Yugoslavia than in the other socialist economies, since eight political entities all felt they had to have their own "modern" industries, however irrational their operation might be. For example, the giant iron ore-processing plant at Kavadarci in Macedonia, started in the 1960s, gobbled up almost one-half billion dollars in convertible currency loans and an equivalent amount of domestic investment before being scrapped in the 1980s because the available local ore was too deficient in iron to make the plant feasible, a fact known before the project was begun. In Serbia the steel plant at Smederevo on the Danube, started in 1963 and not yet finished in 1987, cost $1.5 billion in hard currency plus the equivalent of $1 billion in dinars. It was losing so much money in 1987 that all enterprises in Serbia were forced to contribute an amount equivalent to one-half of one percent of their production to keep it going, since, after all, it employed eleven thousand workers.[26]

Heavily in debt, hamstrung at the center, and with a dispirited work-force, in the 1980s the Yugoslav economy declined precipitously. Almost every measure went into reverse—social product dipped, efficiency dropped, real income went down, and investment declined. One of the few indicators that went up was inflation, making ordinary citizens acutely aware that their standard of living was falling. Yugoslav governments spent most of the 1980s stumbling from austerity programs to currency devaluations to restructuring plans to price and wage freezes to bridging loans in a fruitless search for stabilization. One author counted twenty price freezes implemented and dropped between 1965 and 1985.[27] Constant stop-and-go stabilization programs produced the worst of both worlds, a result known elsewhere in the 1980s as stagflation. On the one hand, real wages and the standard of living dropped—the price of the reforms that were tried—but on the other hand, efficiency did not improve, inflation wors-ened, and growth rates stayed low. Under these unstable conditions the very term "stabilization," introduced in the reforms of 1979 and used throughout the 1980s, became so devalued that its mere mention brought wry smiles to Yugoslav faces.

Serbia and Kosovë

The significant political activity of the 1980s did not take place at the federal level, which was the focus of most foreign attention. During the 1980s the future of Yugoslavia was being decided in the republics, par-ticularly in Serbia and Slovenia, but also to a certain extent in Croatia. The road to civil war began in March 1981 when Albanian students took their demands for better conditions at the University of Prishtinë to the streets in the time-honored tradition of students everywhere. Their demonstra-tion touched a nerve of Albanian patriotic feeling, and over the next month anti-Serbian demonstrations demanding that Kosovë become a Yugoslav republic became so massive that the federal government sent in troops.[28]

Serbs have been hostile to Albanians at least since the nineteenth century. This hostility is in part a function of the Serbian origin myth created in the nineteenth century and available since then to nationalist demagogues. Because the medieval Serbian empire was located in what is today Kosovë, many of the most important Serbian cultural monuments can be found there, including the patriarchate of Peć, the center of Serbian Orthodoxy during the Ottoman period, and many Serbian Orthodox monasteries and churches containing late Byzantine frescoes of exceptional quality. The Serbian national mythology holds that the Orthodox church preserved Serbian national consciousness over the centuries of Ottoman domination, endowing these monuments with highly charged emotional significance. *Kosovo polje* (The Field of Blackbirds), not far from Prishtinë, was the site of the Serbs' epochal battle with the Ottomans on June 28, 1389.[29] The cycles of oral poetry that preserved the story of that battle (and of Serbian medieval experiences), along with the Byzantine frescoes, are the most important Serbian contributions to European culture.

The importance of the Kosovo myth to Serbian politics lies not in these actual historical qualities but in its selection by the nationalists as the appropriate symbolic universe of Serbianness. It provides a vocabulary of experiences outside of time, so to speak. For example, the contrast between the mythically heroic battle fought by the brave Serbian warriors at Kosovo and the final outcome, which was Ottoman domination, can be understood as the "normal fate of Serbs"—to die for freedom in war and yet to be denied the fruit of victory, that is, to win World War I and yet "lose" in 1945 and 1974. To refer to a rival as a modern Vuk Branković, who in the epics is understood to be a traitor, is to smear that rival with a morally devastating accusation that is beyond appeal. Slogans attractive to the ear can be written in the decasyllabic style of the folk poetry and Slobodan Milošević can be described in terms reminiscent of the folk epics.[30]

This style of discourse isolated only one strand of the Serbian experience, the religio-romantic strand, and shut out others, such as the liberal strand. At Serbian political rallies in 1988 one saw many pictures of Vuk Karadžić, the nineteenth-century gatherer of the folk epics, and of Petar Petrović Njegoš, the great epic poet of the same period, but few of Dositej Obradović, the early nineteenth-century advocate of Enlightenment rationalism. One of the accomplishments of the Serbian nationalists has been to fill the public space with the Kosovo strand of Serbian history that suits their mobilizational strategies and to downplay the rationalist strand that stands in mute criticism of those strategies. "In comparison to myth," said one critic, "history is fatiguing."[31]

Many Serbs feel emotional about Kosovë, but few Serbs actually live there. The proportion of Serbs living in Kosovë dropped from 24 percent in 1953 to less than 10 percent in 1990.[32] This does not bother the most extreme nationalists, who claim that Kosovë remains Serbian even if not a single Serb lives there.[33] The more common nationalist argument is that the Serbian population has declined precipitously because of harassment by lawless, irredentist, racist Albanians. More likely reasons are the high birth rate of the Albanians (more than thirty-two per thousand) and the poor economic prospects in the region (unemployment was about 25 percent in 1980), which has led to Albanian as well as Serbian emigration.

Kosovë is poor, but not for lack of resources devoted to its economic development. Up to 1980, about half of the federal monies allocated for underdeveloped Yugoslav regions went to Kosovë. But these funds tended to go into loss-producing, capital-intensive industries such as mining and power generation, rather than into labor-intensive industries like consumer production, so they did not alleviate unemployment. Worse, a significant amount of the money ended up increasing the number of administrators in the social sector, so that instead of improving efficiency, the investment funds probably decreased it. Whereas in 1954 per capita income in Kosovë was 48 percent of the Yugoslav average, in 1980 it had dropped to only 28 percent of the national average.[34] Prishtinë University was one institution that received investment funds. Nonexistent in 1960, by 1980 it had thirty-five thousand students. The idea was noble: provide Kosovë with the human capital it would need to develop. But with few suitable jobs available, Prishtinë University was not preparing a new class of managers so much as it was producing thousands of educated, unemployed, and very frustrated young men, an almost perfect formula for unrest.

When the unrest came in 1981 the Serbs and the federal government both denied that they bore any fault for the serious problems the region faced, calling the outbreak a counterrevolution led by outside agitators who were trying to unite Kosovë with Albania. There was a certain superficial plausibility to this argument, since in the 1960s Kosovë had adopted the literary language used in Albania rather than one based on its own dialect, and at least half of the books used in Prishtinë University originated in Albania. But from the initial riots in 1968, through the second wave of demonstrations in 1981, right up to the civil war of 1991, the leaders of every major Albanian movement in Kosovë stoutly denied any interest in joining Albania and demanded only that Kosovë become a republic in Yugoslavia.

The battle lines were clearly set. On the one side Albanians, who constituted 90 percent of the population of Kosovë and wanted to have their own republic in the Yugoslav confederation; on the other side Serbs, to whom Kosovo was an emotional homeland that they wanted to control more fully than the 1974 constitution permitted them. With such incompatible aims, the level of agitation and conflict grew through the 1980s. The Serbian media blamed all problems on the Albanians, refusing to recognize that Serbian repressive acts had any relationship to the problems. Between 1981 and 1985 the predominantly Serbian police arrested over three thousand Albanians and killed more than one hundred Albanian protesters. On their side, the Albanians firebombed the ancient patriarchate at Peć and harassed Serbs into leaving the province (although the many stories of Albanian rapes of Serbian women seem to have been manufactured by the Serbs).

Slobodan Milošević

After Tito's death it took several years for Serbian resentments over Kosovë to reach a public level of expression. In the late 1970s Serbian president Dragoslav Marković produced a confidential "Blue Book" criticizing the constitutional arrangements of 1974, but it never was publicly discussed. During the early 1980s Serbian historians, novelists and poets found it not only increasingly easy to publish works with explicitly Serbian national themes but they found that these works sold very well. Taking cognizance of the increased interest in Serbian patriotism, in May 1985 the Serbian Academy of Sciences undertook to produce a memorandum on the Yugoslav condition. When in September 1986 a version of the document was leaked to the press, it created a sensation. The SANU Memorandum, as it became known, criticized Tito and his successors for discrimination against the Serbs.[35] Serbia's poor economic condition, the academicians argued, was due to Serbia's inability to control its own destiny. By raising the autonomous regions to almost republican level in 1974, non-Serbian Communists such as Tito and Kardelj had denied Serbs the right to their own state. Not only were Serbs suffering "physical, political, legal, and cultural genocide" in Kosovë, but many Serbs in other republics were threatened by the same fate.[36] "The economic subjugation of Serbia," the memorandum concluded, "can be understood only if one understands its political inferiority."[37]

The SANU Memorandum became public not long after Slobodan Milošević became head of the Serbian League of Communists.[38] Slobodan Milošević is not an attractive man. He is reclusive, stubborn, vindictive, narrow-minded, and covetous of absolute power. Born just after the start of World War II (in August 1941) of an activist Communist mother and a Montenegrin Orthodox priest, both of whom later committed suicide, Milošević was a good law student at Belgrade University but a narrow and driven one not given to extracurricular activities. Hitching his star to his university friend Ivan Stambolić, the nephew of an important partisan leader, he rose along with Stambolić. Until 1986 little distinguished Milošević from other successful apparatchiks. His enthusiasm for Marxism seemed perhaps excessive, but otherwise he was simply one of hundreds of Yugoslav careerists who had made their way through the system because it was the system in which they found themselves. When Stambolić moved up to the Serbian presidency in May 1986 and Milošević took his place as head of the party, no one in the West, except a handful of specialists, took particular notice.

Milošević's breakthrough came on April 24, 1987. On that day an excited crowd of ten thousand agitated Serbs and Montenegrins had gathered in front of a building in Kosovo polje, where a meeting to discuss their complaints against the Albanian pressures was underway. When the crowd became unruly, police used rubber truncheons to force them back. Milošević, who was attending the meeting, heard the ruckus and stepped outside to calm the crowd. "I want to tell you," he said, "that you should stay here. Here is your land, here are your houses, your fields and gardens, your memories. . . . [By leaving] you would betray your ancestors and disappoint your descendants. But I do not propose that in staying you continue to endure a situation with which you are not satisfied. On the contrary. We have to change it. . . . Don't tell me that you can't do it alone. Of course you can't do it alone. We will change it together, we in Serbia and everyone in Yugoslavia."[39] Various versions exist of the key phrase he uttered in the heat of this moment, such as "No one will ever beat a Serb again" or "No one has the right to beat the people!" Whatever his exact words, ordinary people throughout Serbia responded to the image of Milošević "standing up for Serbs." When he returned to Belgrade, a friend reported, "he was like a heated stove. He was full of emotions. He could not control his feelings. He could not calm down."[40] Milošević had discovered he possessed the heady power to move people.

The more liberal party leadership headed by Milošević's old friend and mentor, Ivan Stambolić, had been a calming influence in the tensions between Serbs and Albanians over control of Kosovë. Stambolić believed that Serbs were treated unfairly in the 1974 constitution, but he argued that Serbia's relations with Kosovë were a Yugoslav problem, not a narrowly Serbian one. He had been negotiating in a relatively patient way with the other republics to change the constitution to bring Kosovë into closer alignment with Serbia. In contrast to Milošević, Stambolić believed that the party should allow differences of opinion, and he brought along younger persons with an engaging openness.

Milošević, on the other hand, believed in the Stalinist party model—abject loyalty to every aspect of the leader's position. He thought Kosovë was a Serbian problem, not a Yugoslav one, and he was not a patient man. Rallying support among former Ranković supporters, academicians at Belgrade University, and mid-ranking party functionaries who found the idea of a strong leader appealing in the post-Tito vacuum, Milošević promised that the Kosovë problem could be solved quickly and unilaterally, by force if necessary.

At the key eighth session of the Serbian central committee held in September 1987, a surprised Stambolić, who had heard warnings about his old friend's intentions but chose to ignore them, found himself confronting a solid phalanx of local party delegates prepared with speeches calling for a new and more aggressive leadership. Defeated, Stambolić soon was recalled from the presidency and replaced by an old partisan general.

Stambolić's sudden defeat marked the beginning of a new order for Serbia. In the next three months, in a process he termed "differentiation," Milošević purged the Serbian party of those who would not give prompt assurances of total loyalty. From their new positions in control of the state television station and of what was once Serbia's best newspaper, *Politika* (Politics), Milošević's cronies attacked anyone who would not abjectly support him, branding them as opposed to party unity and, worse, as anti-Serb. In Kosovë itself Milošević thoroughly purged party members too lenient toward what the Serbs now routinely but inaccurately called Albanian irredentism.[41] By early 1988 Milošević had become the most dynamic, visible, and frightening politician in Yugoslavia.

Milošević thinks in nineteenth-century terms. He is completely insensitive to other ethnic groups and knows nothing of the give-and-take of democratic politics. He simply wants to make the Serbs the strongest and most united people in his part of the world, at whatever cost. Initially he probably thought that he could achieve control of the Yugoslav federal system through taking command of the League of Communists of Yugoslavia. When the party disintegrated, he tried to get control of the federal government, particularly the presidency and the army. Finally, when the federation collapsed, he turned to a more direct method of achieving his nationalist aims: the creation of a Greater Serbia dominating the center of the Balkans by armed force.

His first step was to rewrite the constitutional arrangements of 1974. By accusing everyone who opposed him of being involved in an unprincipled alliance against Serbia, Milošević bullied the other republics into accepting Serbia's right to change its constitution and thereby to limit the rights of Kosovë and the Vojvodina. He packed the Kosovë assembly, found a way to replace the leadership of the province of Vojvodina with his own people, and pushed his amendment through.

His most powerful tool in achieving this goal was mass rallies. In the rest of Eastern Europe people power, as it was called after huge popular demonstrations brought Corazon Aquino to power in the Philippines in 1986, was a force for democracy and pluralism. In Serbia, however, Milošević mobilized people power to destroy Yugoslavia and to create the conditions for civil war. In September and October 1988 thirty thousand, fifty thousand, one hundred thousand, even one million people gathered in Serbian cities to shout their approval of Milošević's effort to subdue Kosovë. When Albanians tried rallies of their own or conducted strikes in the important mining industry, as they did in November 1988, Milošević sent in the riot police and arrested their leaders. In February 1989 the most dramatic protest broke out when Albanian miners barricaded themselves underground and went on hunger strikes. Milošević eventually tricked the miners into coming up, whereupon he arrested their leaders for "counter-revolutionary activities." In the rest of Eastern Europe people power toppled the old Communist regimes in the name of democracy. In Serbia, Milošević manipulated the same force by racist appeals in order to legitimate his transformation of the League of Communists of Serbia into a nationalist party organized on neo-Stalinist principles.

The Serbian Assembly, along with the assemblies of Kosovë and Vojvodina that Milošević now dominated, approved the new constitutional arrangements, putting the autonomous regions firmly under the control of the Serbian central government in March 1989. Acceptance of the constitutional provisions produced six days of rioting in Kosovë, which Milošević subdued with substantial loss of life (estimates ranged from 20 to 140), but many Serbs rejoiced over the restoration of Serbian unity, as they thought of it. "Sovereignty returned to Serbia," crowed the headline in *Politika*. "What was more natural, more humane, more democratic, for the Serbian people," said Borisav Jović, Serbian representative to the federal presidency, "than, in accordance with their peace-loving traditions, to again enter upon the stage of history and make a demand in the form of the simplest, the most noble formula of justice and equality. . . . [Serbs are] the people who in the modern history of the Balkans made the greatest sacrifices and demonstrated the greatest scope and evidence of its love for freedom and democracy. . . . Serbia is equal now."[42]

But Milošević's successful subjugation of Kosovë was a disaster for Yugoslavia and, perhaps, in the long run, for Serbia too. By running roughshod over the democratic elements in both Serbia and Kosovë, Milošević confirmed the worst fears of the other members of the Yugoslav federation, especially the Slovenes and the Croats. The likelihood that they would sympathize with any future Serbian calls for Yugoslav unity dropped nearly to zero.

Slovenia and Croatia React

Slovenes, as close neighbors of Italy and Austria, had long considered themselves somewhat removed from the passions of Balkan politics. They also took pride in being the most prosperous Yugoslav republic.[43] More open economic policies and considerable experience with Western business practices permitted Slovenes to produce roughly 20 percent of Yugoslavia's domestic product and 25 percent of the country's hard currency exports while constituting only 8 percent of the Yugoslav population. Slovenia did not suffer much repression in the fallout from the 1971 crisis in Croatia, and during the 1970s Slovenian intellectuals adopted an antipolitical stance. When Tito died Slovenia boasted perhaps the most independent minded intelligentsia in Yugoslavia. By the mid-1980s its capital city Ljubljana could boast of an influential student press, a strong group of intellectuals surrounding the avant-garde journal *Nova revija* (New Review), and the first stirrings of alternative movements of feminists, gays, peace activists, and environmentalists.[44]

These modest beginnings sprang to public life in the spring of 1988, when the journal of the Socialist Youth League, *Mladina* (Youth), published an article claiming that the army was planning a lightning arrest of important Slovene political figures in order to stop the growing Slovenian nationalism. *Mladina* had already annoyed the army by calling the Yugoslav chief of staff a "merchant of death" for selling arms to Ethiopia, and it followed with an article showing how Yugoslavia had conspired with Sweden to ship arms to Libya. Angry army officials hauled three journalists and one noncomissioned officer into military court and convicted them of revealing military secrets. The enormous hostility against the army that this event and its outcome evoked was not only a sign of antimilitarism among Slovenian youth, although it was that. It signified also a rejection of Communist Yugoslavia as typified by the partisan generation and a rejection of Serbian centralism, because Slovenes perceived the army to be dominated by predominantly Serbian generals.

The *Mladina* trial galvanized the Slovenian democratic opposition. Supporters of the accused formed a defense committee, which they quickly turned into a Committee for the Defense of Human Rights that demanded and got an investigation of the army. In the fall of 1988 members of this committee went on to create four political parties, technically under the mantle of the Socialist Alliance but actually new formations.[45] In May 1989 these parties, along with the Slovenian Writers Union, produced a political program advocating political pluralism and expressing the desire "to live in a sovereign state of the Slovene people."[46] Shortly thereafter they proposed making the next election, scheduled long before for spring 1990, open and multiparty. In the meanwhile, a group of leftist intellectuals, students, workers, and even some party members formed the Social Democratic Alliance of Slovenia, which advocated a Western-style democratic socialism, while a group of nonsocialists created the Slovenian Democratic Alliance, dedicated to the establishment of parliamentary democracy.[47] By February 1989 Radio Free Europe analyst Milan Andrejevich could report that about one hundred grass roots organizations and ten independent political groups were active in Slovenia.[48]

Far from condemning these pluralist endeavors, Slovenian Communists found ways to accommodate themselves to them, first by suggesting that the new movements remain part of the Socialist Alliance and then by moving in the direction of pluralism themselves. Early in 1989 Milan Kučan, the head of the League of Communists of Slovenia, welcomed what he called "the opening up of political space." "There is no real democracy without political pluralism," he said.[49] In April 1989 the Communists ran a direct, secret, and contested election, the first of its kind in Yugoslavia, to elect the Slovene representative to the federal presidency. And in September of the same year, using the precedent set by Milošević's successful effort to change Serbia's constitution, the party pushed constitutional changes through the Slovenian assembly that declared Slovenia a "sovereign and independent state." The assembly asserted Slovenia's right to secede, claimed the authority to veto the use of armed force in its territory, and deleted the provision that the League of Communists should play the leading role in society.

Creeping pluralization in Slovenia outraged Slobodan Milošević. He accused the Slovenes of endangering Yugoslavia by threatening secession, which invited civil war. The Slovenes did not look upon it this way. Their strategy, which evolved in the doing rather than in any programmatic statement, was to put a clear choice before Milošević: negotiate with us for a viable kind of federated Yugoslavia or we will leave. The Slovenes denied they were advocating the breakup of Yugoslavia. "This is not secession," the speaker of the Slovene assembly said blandly. "We want to remain part of Yugoslavia."[50] We want a third Yugoslavia, the Slovenes were saying, not one dominated by Serbia and one organized by Communists, but one based on truly voluntary association.

The Slovenes were Milošević's most active critics in Yugoslavia, particularly of Serbian actions in Kosovë. In March 1989, for example, one million persons out of a total population of only about two million signed a declaration protesting the Serbian treatment of Albanian miners and criticizing the long-standing state of emergency in Kosovë. Milošević, always on the attack, criticized the Slovenes for their "fascist hatred" of Serbia and accused them of an "unscrupulous coalition" with the Croats to denigrate Serbs. Slovene leaders responded by characterizing the Serbs as "irrational" and "arrogant." In December 1989 Milošević attempted to take his version of people power to Ljubljana by organizing a mass meeting there of Serbs similar to the successful rallies he had held in Serbian towns and cities in 1988. When the Slovenian authorities forbade the meeting, an angered Milošević asked Serbs to boycott Slovenian goods. It became distinctly unpleasant to ask for a Slovenian product in a Belgrade store. In retribution for the boycott, which affected about 7 percent of its trade, Slovenia began to hold back its payment to the federal fund for the undeveloped regions, which lessened the monies Serbia would have available for Kosovë. Convinced that Milošević was a nationalist tyrant and increasingly certain that each Yugoslav republic would have to make its own political arrangements, the Slovenian legislature agreed in December 1989 to hold open, multiparty elections, which it set for April 1990.

Croatia was not as open intellectually or politically as Slovenia, and, while its economy was in better condition than those of the southern republics, its prosperity was not uniform. Some regions, such as the one northwest of Zagreb where Tito had been born or the mountainous regions inland from the Adriatic and heavily populated by Serbs, were very poor. Others, such as the beautiful and popular Dalmatian Coast or the industrial region around Zagreb, were quite prosperous. Croatia's main problem, however, was not economic. It was ethnic. About 12 percent of the populatin of Croatia were Serbs, a significant portion of whom were concentrated in the poor Karst region of southwest Croatia. In that area bitter fighting between Serbs and Croats had taken place during World War II, and in 1971 some of the most active nationalists on both sides had reemerged there.

In the increasingly tense situation provoked by Milošević and by the general crisis of Communism, the nationalists could not be silenced, although the communist regime tried to do so. For example, it imprisoned opposition leader Franjo Tudjman in the early 1980s and upon his release forbade him to speak in public. But in January 1989 Tudjman read a draft program for a political party he proposed founding at a meeting of the Croatian Writer's Union, and in June 1989, after a request for a public meeting had been denied, he and a few others gathered in what they called a "non-public place" to create the Croatian Democratic Union (Hrvatska demokratska zajednica—HDZ). By the end of the year some sixteen independent groups had formed in Croatia and the reform Communists, who were now in the ascendancy in the party, agreed that Croatia too would have to strike out in its own direction. Early in February 1990 the Croatian assembly passed broad political reforms that scheduled open, multiparty elections for April and May 1990.

The Collapse of the Center

With political decisions made at the republican level pushing Yugoslavia in two different directions, a centralizing Serbian one and a pluralizing Croatian-Slovenian one, the federal government found itself hamstrung by political impasse and economic decline. During the 1980s no Yugoslav government proved able to work the complex Yugoslav system of delegations and consultations effectively. Overall debt did not increase, because of a series of last-minute reprieves from the international banking community based on unfulfilled promises of reform, but inflation began to run at 100 percent per year and more. The climax came in December 1988 when, for the first time in socialist Yugoslavia, a government lost a vote of confidence in the federal assembly and resigned. The political crisis this unprecedented resignation touched off gave Yugoslavia one final chance for survival, because the man who emerged as prime minister in March 1989, Ante Marković, proved able to take control of the federal mechanisms and to push through substantial economic reform.

Marković's strategy was to outflank the republics and the party. Former prime minister Branko Mikulić had put forward five reform plans, but all failed because they had to be vetted by the republican presidencies and party leaders. Marković minimized these negotiating steps and went straight to the legislature. He promised that his new ministers, whom he appointed by ability and not primarily by party connections, would henceforth be responsible to the federal assembly, and he used the assembly's committee structure to promote his plans. In parliamentary countries this is the normal way governments pursue their legislative programs, but in Yugoslavia Marković's maneuvering was a daring—and difficult—innovation. It took the new prime minister most of 1989 to get approval for his plans, but in December of that year the federal parliament passed the most comprehensive and hopeful economic reform Yugoslavia had ever seen.

Marković was a market-oriented Communist who stressed deregulation, elimination of laws that hindered entry into the market, privatization of small businesses, and creation of capital markets. But in order to put these ideas into effect, Marković, like others in Eastern Europe, first had to get control of the macroeconomic situation, primarily by stopping inflation. Despite a succession of austerity measures, price freezes, and currency manipulations throughout the 1980s, when Marković took office in March 1989 the rate of inflation was several hundred percent a year and climbing. By the end of 1989 it reached over two hundred percent a month.

Marković's reform, which went into effect on January 1, 1990, wrote off all the contaminated debts produced by the worthless promissory notes that Yugoslav firms had been giving each other, thus taking a long step toward getting control of the money supply.[51] Marković made the new "heavy" dinar convertible at seven to the deutschmark, introduced a balanced budget, inaugurated restrictive monetary policies, froze wages for six months, and freed all prices except about 20 percent of the retail prices and 25 percent of industrial production. The results of this shock therapy were spectacular. Inflation dropped precipitously, reaching close to zero after a few months, foreign exchange reserves rose dramatically, and foreign debt declined. Encouraged, foreign investors flocked to Yugoslavia. During 1990 and the first few months of 1991 almost three thousand foreign firms initialed agreements calling for about $1.2 billon of investment in the Yugoslav economy (although little of the money had actually arrived by the time the civil war began).[52]

From the foreign point of view, Marković was a miracle man, clearly the hope of the future for Yugoslavia. As Yugoslavia began to pull apart late in 1990 and early in 1991, almost every foreign leader from George Bush through Mikhail Gorbachev to Pope John Paul II indicated his support for Marković's government. As late as June 21, 1991, only a few days before civil war broke out, United States Secretary of State James Baker visited Belgrade to encourage Marković and to advocate the maintenance of federal Yugoslavia in its old form.

Inside Yugoslavia, however, Marković was increasingly unpopular. Non-Serbs saw him as a centrist Communist trying to impose rules from Belgrade, whereas Milošević's supporters reviled him with populist slogans as a man undermining socialism and ruining Yugoslavia on behalf of foreign bankers. Borisav Jović, a member of the federal presidency and a close ally of Milošević, called Marković "a foreign agent" who advocated the "uncontrolled transfer of social ownership into private hands" and the "sale of property to foreigners for next to nothing." Joze Pučnik, head of the oppositional DEMOS alliance in Slovenia, understood that Marković would never be able to get the feuding republics to agree. He called Marković "one of the biggest bluffers that ever managed to obtain Europe's support."[53]

Despite the apparent initial success of his economic reforms, Marković's fatal disability was the same as that of every other federal leader in post-Tito Yugoslavia. He showed great skill in conceiving his program and in finding a way to get it approved, but no amount of skill was adequate to overcome the unwillingness of some, even all, of the constituent republics to continue an economic program that required restraint. As soon as the six-month freeze on wages expired, workers everywhere demanded increases—and got them. The federal bank's inability to keep track of the money supply reached a climax in December 1990, when Milošević found a way to divert $1.8 billion, which was half of the entire amount available for the increase in money supply scheduled for 1991, to Serbia's use. He simply passed this enormous amount out in bonuses, wage increases, subsidies, and interest-free loans in a classic vote-buying spree during the month before Serbia's elections in December 1990.

Many observers in the West believed that, despite the political skirmishing, economic rationality eventually would bring Yugoslavs to their senses. After all, the World Bank and the IMF were prepared to release

funds that would free up over $4 billion in investment resources for Yugo-
slavia, and foreign investors were prepared to add more if Yugoslavia
remained stable. With Milošević and the other republics raiding the federal
treasury (both Slovenia and Croatia also siphoned off significant amounts
late in 1990) and with inflation starting up again, early in 1991 the IMF
and the World Bank told the Yugoslavs they would release the funds
scheduled for that year only if the republics agreed to implement economic
discipline. But the confidence that Yugoslavs would respond to economic
stimuli proved to be misplaced. By early 1990 emotions in Yugoslavia had
reached the point at which economic arguments ceased to have an impact.
Marković failed not for economic reasons but for political and emotional
ones. His country was collapsing.

The glue that had held Yugoslavia together, the League of Communists of Yugoslavia, led the way toward this collapse by disintegrating early
in 1990.[54] Yugoslav Communists were not immune to the forces of change
sweeping Eastern Europe, as the changes in Slovenia and Croatia testify.
Yet, understandably, many party members could not bring themselves to
turn their backs entirely on the past. Thus the draft resolution placed
before the special party congress that convened at Milošević's insistence on
January 20, 1990, was a muddled document unsuited to the needs of the
day. It supported Marković's economic reforms but called only for a mixed
economy, not for the creation of a market system. It proposed that the
League of Communists of Yugoslavia (LCY) achieve political legitimacy in
the future through free elections, but it did not mention multiparty elections. And it confirmed the Serbian constitutional changes of 1989. These
proposals were far too cautious for the Slovenes. They proposed a substitute motion that explicitly advocated a multiparty system, secret ballots,
"asymmetric federalism," and a federal League of Communists made up of
separate, independent parties. To make it precisely clear where the Slovenes stood, their proposal pointedly called for the introduction of democracy in Kosovë and the abolition of "democratic centralism," the code
word for Milošević's neo-Stalinist methods.

Milošević rejected the Slovenian amendments out of hand, calling
them an invitation to "internecine warfare in the party and the country,"
and on the same day the congress voted them down by a wide margin.[55]
Frustrated and sensing the futility of participating in a party unable to
resist Milošević, the Slovenes walked out. Two weeks later in Ljubljana
they announced the formation of an independent party based on the principles of social democracy (the Party of Democratic Renewal) and with-
drew from the LCY.

Milošević tried to turn the walkout to his advantage by proposing the
congress continue without the Slovenes, but the delegations from Croatia,
Macedonia, and Bosnia-Herzegovina refused, so the congress suspended
its meeting without even electing a new leadership. *Borba* correctly
analyzed the significance of these events in its headline the next morning:
"The League of Communists No Longer Exists."[56] Ante Marković bravely

maintained that "Yugoslavia continues to function with or without the League of Communists," but he was wrong. The League of Communists had been what held Yugoslavia together. When it disappeared Yugoslavia could not be far behind.

Free Elections in the Republics

Slovenia and Croatia were prepared for the disappearance of the League of Communists of Yugoslavia because they had already scheduled elections to create new governments. These first free parliamentary elections in Yugoslavia since before World War II took place at the same time elections were going on in the rest of Eastern Europe—April and May 1990. The details are complex, since each country has a tricameral legislature and the presidents were elected differently, but the results in each place were clear. In Slovenia the parties that grew out of the *Mladina* controversy of 1988 had banded together with several others, such as the Greens and the Tradesman's party, to form the oppositional alliance called DEMOS (Demokratska opozicija Slovenije—Democratic Opposition of Slovenia). Their main opponent was the Party of Democratic Renewal (Stranka demokratične prenove—SDP), or old Communists. Both parties had superficially similar platforms, which included marketizing reforms and more independence of action for Slovenia in Yugoslavia, but the Party of Democratic Renewal was slightly less insistent on these planks and had the sizeable disadvantage of having been in power for forty years. Accordingly, the DEMOS took a clear majority of seats in two of the three houses of the legislature and the largest block of seats in the third house. Lojze Peterle, head of the Slovene Christian Democrats, the party that obtained the largest number of votes among those parties that made up the DEMOS coalition, became prime minister on May 16, 1990.

In the direct elections for president, however, the former leader of the Communist party, Milan Kučan, took the runoff with almost 60 percent of the vote. Most observers did not perceive this as a victory for the Communists but rather as a personal victory for Kučan, whose popularity had peaked after his confrontation with Milošević at the special party congress in January. All in all, it seemed that the Slovenian voters picked the most democratic-sounding of the available choices without completely rejecting the progressive communist leadership that had been defending Slovenia's separate path for the past several years. The new government contained a mix of radical nationalists, moderate nationalists, and liberal economic reformers, most of them politically unseasoned intellectuals.

The outcome in Croatia was quite different. There the Croatian Democratic Union, led by Franjo Tudjman, waged an overtly nationalistic campaign against the Communist party, now renamed the Party of Democratic Changes (Stranka demokratskih promjena—SDP), which for many years had opposed Tudjman's brand of xenophobia as dangerous and destructive. It was no contest. Praising the Independent State of Croatia, the degenerate fascist state of World War II, as an "expression of the historical aspirations of the Croation nation for its independent state," Tudjman called for a Croatia within its "historic and natural boundaries," advocated the "economic, spiritual and cultural union of Croatia and Bosnia-Herze-govina, which form a natural, indivisible political unit and are historically destined to be together," and asserted, in a manner reminiscent of Todor Zhivkov's claim about Turks in Bulgaria, that many of Bosnia's Muslims were in fact ethnic Croats. At the same time he was staking out these claims to a Greater Croatia, Tudjman railed against "Great Serbian hegemonistic desires" and promised to rectify what he called the overrepresentation by Serbs in the government, the police, and the media.[57]

The Party of Democratic Changes, on the other hand, supported pluralism ("We are serious" was its slogan), backed Marković's painful economic reforms, and campaigned against nationalism and for the maintenance of Yugoslavia. One of its candidates, Zdravko Tomac, put it this way: "Yugoslavia has to be a federation because 2.2 million Serbs live outside Serbia in other Yugoslav republics. About 1.1 million Croats live outside Croatia. This means that the national question cannot be settled within a single republic, but within Yugoslavia as a federation." Creation of anything other than a true federation, Tomac said, would mean civil war.[58] Rejecting Tomac's accurate prediction, Croatian voters gave the Croatian Democratic Union 60 percent of the seats in the sabor, and at the end of May 1990 Franjo Tudjman became president of Croatia. In his first few weeks in office Tudjman distanced himself from his more radical colleagues, but few doubted that he intended to conduct his regime with little sympathy for non-Croats.

The other four republics in Yugoslavia joined the electoral bandwagon six months later. In Serbia, Milošević had conducted a suddenly called election late in 1989 in which he permitted only his own candidates to run. The quality of this election may be indicated by the fact that just after the polls closed one Belgrade district reported that 102 percent of the registered voters had voted, 92 percent of them for Milošević.[59] Still, the genuineness of Milošević's popularity, especially in the countryside, could scarcely be doubted. Some thought that the elections to the Serbian National Assembly one year later—they took place in December 1990—might provide an opportunity for an opposition to form and conceivably even to challenge Milošević's Communists. The main opposition late in 1990 came from the Serbian Renewal Movement (Srpski pokret obnove—SPO), led by an eccentric writer named Vuk Drašković, who affected a full beard reminiscent of the Chetniks of World War II, flourished a dramatic cape, and tried to be more nationalistic than Milošević. At the last minute, ten democratic opposition parties formed a United Serbian Opposition, attempting to do for Serbia what the DEMOS did for Slovenia, but it was too little too late. Whereas both the DEMOS and the Croatian Democratic Union profited from their nationalism, in Serbia, Milošević had already appropriated that sphere beyond recall. Many educated young people ridiculed and ignored the election and Milošević's Socialist party did poorly in Belgrade and some other urban areas; but in the country at large the socialists took 77 percent of the vote while Milošević himself swept into the presidency again with 65 percent.

Elections took place in the other three republics in December 1990 also. In Montenegro the League of Communists of Montenegro took 66 percent of the vote and its leader, Momir Bulatović, became president. Bulatović was a young and potentially reform-minded Communist, but for the time being he threw Montenegro's weight fully behind Milošević. In Bosnia-Herzegovina, on the other hand, the three parties representing the three main ethnic groups received a number of votes and a number of seats roughly comparable to their population size. This meant that the Bosnian Muslim party (Party for Democratic Action) got 32 percent of the seats (lower than their approximately 44 percent of the population but still a plurality), the Serbian Democratic party got 26 percent, and the Croatian Democratic Community got 15 percent. The Communists trailed badly with 10 percent and evaporated as a force in Bosnian politics. Despite serious tensions and divisions, the new Bosnian parliament selected Alija Izetbegović, a Muslim moderate, as president.[60]

In Macedonia the victor was the Democratic party of Macedonian National Unity/IMRO. The additon of "IMRO" sent a chill through the Balkans, since it was the acronym of the Internal Macedonian Revolutionary Organization, an ultranationalist, terrorist organization active in the first half of the twentieth century. In the first round of the Macedonian elections, IMRO had not fared as well as the Albanian party of Democratic Prosperity, which eventually ended up with 21 percent of the seats in the Macedonian legislature. Whereas most of the attention on Albanians in Yugoslavia justifiably centered on Kosovë, a large Albanian minority lives in a compact area of northwestern Macedonia, where they suffered repression at the hands of the Macedonians in the 1980s analogous to that suffered by the Albanians at the hands of Serbs in Kosovë. Their good performance on the first round of elections generated a sudden interest among Macedonian voters in the IMRO, which ended up with 31 percent of the seats after the second electoral round. The League of Communists of Macedonia, now the Party for Democratic Transformation, took second place, gathering 26 percent of the seats. The new assembly elected Kiro Gligorov, a reform Communist, as the president of Macedonia.

By the end of 1990, therefore, all of the six Yugoslav republics had elected, in more or less free elections, new legislatures and new presidents. Ironically, all of the presidents were former Communists, including even Franjo Tudjman, but only two of them, Milošević and Bulatović, continued to rule in the manner of their predecessors. The only important figures in the country who had not been elected were at the federal level. There the federal assembly, the presidency, and of course Ante Marković himself had all come to office on the basis of the constitution of 1974. Their inability to claim the legitimacy of popular election was a fatal liability in the post-1989 world.

The Road to Civil War

From the first free elections in the spring of 1990 it took a little more than a year for war to begin. Three events that took place in July 1990 hinted at the direction in which Yugoslavia was headed. In Serbia, Milošević remained unsatisfied with the constitutional changes he had rammed through in 1989. Even though his security forces occupied Kosovë, forty thousand Albanians still demonstrated in Prishtinë in January 1990 for free elections, and in February the army had to be sent in to quell riots. Milošević's response was to propose a completely rewritten constitution. This one would permit multiparty elections, which he correctly believed he would win, thus outflanking the new but weak democratic opposition, and would tie the autonomous regions, Kosovë and Vojvodina, more firmly to the Belgrade center. His first step in this strategy was to call a referendum on two weeks' notice asking for popular approval to write a new constitution before the December elections.

In reality, Milošević was asking for approval to crush Kosovë and to pursue his nationalist arguments with Slovenia and Croatia. Just before the vote, he forcibly disbanded the Kosovë legislature, which still contained a majority of ethnically Albanian members, ostensibly in response to strikes and other disturbances but actually to inflame the electorate. On July 2, 1990, the overwhelming majority of Serbs approved Milošević's strategy. On the same day 114 members of the Kosovë legislature—all the Albanian representatives who had been locked out of their offices—met and declared that Kosovë was now fully independent of Serbia and should be considered a constituent republic of Yugoslavia. Within days the Serbian assembly not only rejected the Kosovë declaration of independence but "permanently" abolished the Kosovë legislature and transferred all its functions to the Serbian assembly in Belgrade. Not to be outdone, the fugitive Albanian legislators convened secretly in September and produced a Constitution of the Republic of Kosovë, which, while remaining a dead letter under the new Serbian laws, remained the basis for the continued assertion by Albanian activists that the will of Kosovë was to be a republic like the other republics of Yugoslavia. The situation in Kosovë remained at an impasse: a small minority of self-righteous Serbs fully in control by force of arms, the large majority of frustrated Albanians dispossessed and hostile.

On the same day the Serbian voters approved Milošević's xenophobic policies, the Slovenian Assembly in Ljubljana formally declared Slovenia to be fully sovereign, thus taking the measures already adopted in September 1989 one step further. Slovenia now asserted that its laws took precedence over those of the federation, that it could control the armed forces on its soil, and that it intended to conduct its own foreign and trade policy. At this point, these actions by the Slovenes remained assertions rather than actualities, but they could now be understood as part of a systematic Slovenian strategy of incremental and orderly dissociation from Yugoslavia.

The third group of July events surrounded constitutional changes approved by the Tudjman government in Croatia on July 25, 1990. Since his electoral victory in May, Tudjman, instead of finding ways to calm the fears of the large Serbian minority in Croatia, had done just the opposite. He proved unwilling to talk seriously with their representatives while at the same time purging police forces of Serbian members and provoking confrontations by disarming police forces in predominantly Serbian towns. He adopted the ancient Croatian red-and-white checkerboard shield, which had also been the emblem of the Ustasha regime. His response to the shock felt by Serbs and other non-Croats who remembered the genocide practiced by that regime was to say that if they did not like the new shield they could leave Croatia. Tudjman's legislature ignored the demands of the non-Croats to define Croatia as "a state of free peoples," defining it instead as "the national state of the Croatian nation."[61] Insensitive measures such as these led the more excitable members of the Serbian minority in Croatia to conclude that Tudjman was preparing the same kind of genocide against Serbs that the Ustasha regime had practiced.[62] The Belgrade media, controlled by Milošević, encouraged and abetted this overreaction, greatly inflaming the situation.

It was one thing for Slovenia to declare its sovereignty, since it has no coherent ethnic minorities and has a well-defined border with its neighbors. It was another thing for Croatia to do the same without taking special precautions to mollify its Serbian minority. The Serbs of Croatia are not a compact group, although a few local government units contain a majority of Serbs. Nevertheless, with the encouragement of Milošević and Vuk Drašković in Belgrade, not to mention some even more extreme fanatics like Vojislav Šešelj, who styled himself a Chetnik, arrayed himself in bandoleers, and talked about killing Croats, the leaders of the Serbian minority that lived in the poor mountainous regions of Croatia now began systematically to prepare for secession. By the end of July 1990 they created the Serbian National Council as their representative body, and in August they undertook a clandestine referendum allegedly showing that almost 100 percent of the Serbs in southwestern Croatia favored autonomy. Less biased observers noted that the area the Serbs sought to control, which they called Krajina, was only about two-thirds Serbian, the rest being Croats and other nationalities, and that an autonomous Krajina would contain only about one-quarter of the Serbs living in Croatia. Nevertheless, on October 1, 1990, the Serbian National Council declared the Krajina autonomous, and in February 1991 it formally announced its secession from Croatia as the Independent Republic of Krajina and expressed its desire to unite with Serbia.

Had this process of Serbian dissociation from Croatia been as peaceful as the previous paragraph makes it sound, Yugoslavia might have survived in some form. But it was far from peaceful. From the time of the 1990 election, when Franjo Tudjman began to assert a new Croatian nationalism, violence between Croats and Serbs in Croatia escalated. In August 1990, when Croatian police in the town of Benkovac tried to disarm some Serbian reservists, armed Serbs barricaded roads and patrolled the streets. From that point on, irregular Serb paramilitary forces began to arm themselves, to disrupt communications by downing trees across roads, and to destroy Croatia's tourist industry with slashed tires, brawls, and worse. The number of incidents multiplied, as did the outlandishness of the rumors and the virulence of the hostility. Tudjman called the Serbian actions "an armed uprising," while in Belgrade Vuk Drašković called for a "declaration of war" to prevent further Croatian genocide against the Serbs. In November 1990 Milošević's government began imposing a tariff on goods imported from Croatia and Slovenia, to which the Croats responded by instituting a confiscatory tax on all properties held in Croatia by Serbs from Serbia, which included a large number of summer homes on the Adriatic Coast.

Meanwhile, the Slovenes continued to put pressure on federal authorities either to reach a reasonable agreement or to resign themselves to losing Slovenia. On December 23, 1990, a large majority of Slovene voters approved a referendum in which they vowed to declare their independence in six months if a satisfactory arrangement could not be reached. In February 1991 the Slovenian assembly began passing enabling laws that would permit them to become independent, the government made plans to print Slovenian money and to open missions abroad, and border guards entered training. In March 1991 the assembly advised Slovenian youths that they could choose to serve in Slovenian territorial defense units or police instead of answering their conscription calls to the Yugoslav National Army, and in May it announced that Slovenia would secede from Yugoslavia on June 26, just six months after the referendum of December. The Croats announced they would follow suit.

In the end, Milošević proved willing to let Slovenia go, but not Croatia. In June 1990, while discussing the new constitution he wanted to install, he said that Serbia "links its present administrative borders exclusively to a Yugoslavia constituted as a federation. . . . If one does not want a federal state, the question of Serbian borders is an open political question."[63] By this formulation Milošević presented the Croats with an impossible choice: either they had to accept a federation dominated by Milošević or face a Serbian attempt to add one-third of Croatian territory, and possibly regions of Bosnia and Herzegovina as well, to a Greater Serbia. If he could control the Yugoslav army (Jugoslovenska narodna armija—JNA), either through the federal presidency or indirectly through Serbian generals, Milošević would have an overwhelming force at his disposal to put that policy into effect. With no really good options but unwilling to knuckle under to Milošević's threats, Croatia began, like Slovenia before it, to prepare for what increasingly seemed inevitable—secession.

The unknown quantity in this volatile situation was the JNA. The army was the only remaining Yugoslav institution that seemed to be functioning adequately on a federal basis at the end of 1990, but since about 70 percent of its officers were Serbs or Montenegrins and since its leadership consisted of old partisan warriors who refused to acknowledge that Communism was dying in Eastern Europe, many feared that it would either throw its weight behind Milošević or that it would seize power in a coup of its own.[64] A bizarre document leaked early in 1991 suggested that many army officers believed that socialism was the greatest accomplishment of the twentieth century, that the CIA had worked with Gorbachev to destroy the Warsaw Pact, that the LCY was the most progressive force still in Yugoslavia, and that the Slovenian and Croatian leaders were essentially traitors.[65]

The final humiliation of the federal government came in May 1991, when, by the normal rotation agreement, Borisav Jović was to step down as chairman of the presidency and the Croatian member was to succeed him. That Croatian member was Stipe Mesić, a critic of Serbian policy in Kosovë. Once in office, he promised, he intended to visit Kosovë to report on the conditions of oppression there. The Serbs used their four votes (Serbia, Vojvodina, Kosovë, and Montenegro) to deadlock the eight-member presidency so that Mesić could not achieve the majority needed to take office. In protest the Croatian and Slovenian delegates to the federal assembly walked out. With only one month to go before the promised Slovenian declaration of independence, Yugoslavia found itself with a rump federal legislature and no executive authority.

Hope for a rebirth of a new Yugoslavia now rested with the republics. It seemed a good sign, therefore, that in March 1991 the presidents of the six republics began face-to-face weekly meetings at a number of Tito's old personal retreats in an effort to stop what everyone conceded was a freight train running out of control. At these meetings the presidents of Macedonia, Kiro Gligorov, and of Bosnia-Herzegovina, Alija Izetbegović, acted as mediators between the two basic positions that had divided Serbs and Croats from the time of Bishop Strossmayer and Prince Michael. The first position supported by Croatia and Slovenia, was that Yugoslavia should be a voluntary association of sovereign republics. The second, supported by Serbia and Montenegro, was that Yugoslavia be a united state in which the federation exercised control over banks, foreign affairs, security, and similar matters. The conferees at first thought they could conduct a federation-wide referendum to resolve this question, but this proved impossible. Gligorov and Izetbegović proposed what they called an "asymmetric federation," a murky idea that was nevertheless the only potentially viable proposal made in the months leading up to civil war. But neither Serbia, which insisted on maintaining the old Yugoslavia and held that the Croats were mistreating Serbs (they never mentioned Kosovë), nor Croatia, which complained the Serbs were in armed rebellion with Milošević's encouragement and rejected any plan for meaningful autonomy for its Serbs, would even discuss the proposal.

As June 26 approached, violence in the Serbian parts of Croatia continued to increase. Late in February and early in March an effort by Serbs to disarm Croats in their newly proclaimed Republic of Krajina led for the first time to the intervention of the Yugoslav army.[66] In April, Serbian terrorists attacked Croatian settlements in the unique ecological area around Plitvice Lakes, and in April the army mobilized and took up positions throughout the Serbian parts of Croatia. By May sporadic but bloody fighting was taking place in a number of Croatian towns, but it was difficult to say just which side started shooting first and what role the army was playing.

By this time public opinion in both Serbia and Croatia had been completely inflamed by vigorous campaigns of disinformation and propaganda. Each side ran hours of television stories showing mass graves from World War II being dug up and describing the bestial atrocities committed, always by the other side of course, in gruesome detail.[67] One observer commented that Yugoslavia seemed to be turning into a country of necrophiliacs.

On June 25, 1991, one day before planned, the Slovenes declared themselves independent and the Croats quickly followed suit. When previously trained Slovene guards moved to take over border posts, the Yugoslav National Army decided to intervene. Miscalculating completely the nature of their opponent, the army apparently believed it could send a few armored columns to the Slovenian border posts and simply occupy them. But the crafty Slovenes expertly blockaded the highways, cutting off the columns, while at the same time surrounding and seizing many caches of arms stored around the country. The Yugoslav military doctrine in case of foreign invasion had been to retreat to the hills and to fight a guerrilla war along the lines of the partisan effort. Toward this end, the army had stored large amounts of arms in isolated places throughout the country. When the Slovenes seized many of these caches in the first three or four days of the army's operations, they suddenly went from being a weakly armed militia to being a force reasonably well equipped with antitank and armor-piercing weapons. With its columns stalled along the Slovenian highways and the Slovenes able to destroy a significant amount of their armor, the army now thought better of its intervention. Within three weeks it had retreated back to Croatia. From that time on Slovenia continued an accelerating process of turning itself into an independent country. Early in 1992 it achieved formal diplomatic recognition from the European Community.

Croatia, however, was another story. There the situation in 1991 went from bad to worse to appalling. The armed confrontations of the first half of 1991 now turned into active efforts by an aroused and well-organized variety of Serbian paramilitary forces, including volunteers from within

Serbia itself, to seize as much of Croatia as it could, while the disorganized and poorly armed Croats, aided by mercenaries from abroad, tried to resist.[68] At first the Yugoslav National Army seemed to be acting to keep the two sides apart, but with the collapse of the federal government it soon became apparent that the army had entered the war on the side of the Serbs. With no clear front, atrocities and virulent propaganda on both sides, incompatible aims, and murky lines of authority, the Yugoslav civil war became bloody and mean-spirited. Bitter hatred born of friends killing lifelong friends, of mutilations, of wanton destruction, of complete economic ruin for hundreds of thousands of refugees so contaminated all the parties that it is hard to imagine Serbs and Croats living peacefully together for at least a generation.

The European Community reacted with shock at the outbreak of civil war almost in its midst but found it very difficult to find an effective response. The Conference on Security and Cooperation in Europe proved to be useless in the face of this level of conflict, as did the West European Union. The European Community attempted to bring the warring sides together in a series of meetings in The Hague, but when truce after truce was immediately broken, it had to admit defeat, although desultory negotiations continued. Finally, a United Nations negotiating team, headed by former United States Secretary of State Cyrus Vance, was able to achieve a break in the fighting, and in the spring of 1992 blue-helmeted United Nations troops, operating under a mandate from the Security Council, took up positions in Croatia. By the time of the arrival of the United Nations force, Serbs had been able to seize about one-third of Croatia's territory, which, under the truce arrangements, they continued to occupy.

At about the time the UN forces arrived in Croatia, a new arena of conflict heated up. Bosnia and Herzegovina (called simply Bosnia below) was the most ethnically mixed of the Yugoslav republics. The largest group, about 43 percent of the population, consisted of Muslims, or Bosnians as they are also known. These descendants of people who either converted or immigrated centuries earlier during the Ottoman era speak Serbo-Croatian but, because of their religion and culture, they consider themselves a separate people. Serbs constituted about 32 percent of the population of Bosnia and Herzegovina, Croats about 17 percent. None of these three groups lived in ethnically compact regions that could be encompassed by any rational border. President Izetbegović likened Bosnia to the skin of a leopard, with each spot a different group.

Serbian and Croatian nationalists both have claimed that Bosnia should be theirs, but in 1992 it was the Serbs who provoked the Bosnian war. Influenced by Serbian nationalistic enthusiasms of the late 1980s, Bosnian Serbs, under the unbalanced leadership of Radovan Karadžić and with the encouragement of Slobodan Milošević, began a propaganda campaign against Izetbegović, whom they falsely accused of being a Muslim fundamentalist. By raising the issue in this way they brought back primitive memories of the Ottoman period, which Serbian tradition characterizes as one of bloody oppression of Serbs. Serbian activists started establishing local units of government, creating militia to "protect" themselves, and proclaiming their desire to become part of Milošević's Serbia.

As the war progressed in Croatia, the situation in Bosnia became more and more tense. The issue that set the mix on fire was diplomatic recognition in the spring of 1992. The European Community had not immediately recognized either Slovenia or Croatia when they declared their independence in 1991. The United States in particular did not believe it would be fruitful to do so while Serbian aggression was going on and a civil war was in progress. But Germany insisted, perhaps because of historical ties to Slovenia and Croatia, and in December 1991 the European Community agreed to recognize those former Yugoslav states that met certain requirements, including the protection of human rights. This was more or less a subterfuge, since Germany said it would recognize Slovenia and Croatia on January 15, 1992, regardless. The commission examining the documentation found that only Slovenia and Macedonia met the requirements for recognition, but because of the German demarche, on January 15, 1992, the European Community formally recognized Slovenia and Croatia. Since this action substituted a partial solution for the all-Yugoslav solution the negotiators at The Hague had advocated, it almost certainly contributed to a worsening of the situation.[69]

In the case of Bosnia, the European Community suggested that a referendum on the question of independence would be appropriate. When the overwhelming majority of those voting in the election of March 1, 1992, approved, the Western powers recognized Bosnia's independence. But this move galvanized the already agitated Serbs, who had boycotted the election. Within days armed Serbian detachments were seizing territory in Bosnia and Serbian troops began a seige of Sarajevo, Bosnia's capital. By the summer Bosnia had degenerated into a chaotic and brutal three-sided civil war. Franjo Tudjman's government sided with the Bosnians, but at the same time managed to carve out some of Herzegovina for itself, and of course Milošević supported the Serbian rebels. Milošević ordered the Yugoslav National Army to withdraw from Bosnia, but when it did so it left its enormous supply of arms in the hands of Serbian irregulars, so that whereas the Serbian military forces in Bosnia were mainly local free-booters out of the control of any centralized command, they were very well armed. These Serbian forces quickly occupied two-thirds of Bosnia and terrorized the Muslim Bosnians into the greatest flight of human refugees Europe had seen since World War II. The Serbs conducted a policy of "ethnic cleansing," by which they meant killing or causing to flee all the non-Serb population of the areas they held. By utilizing the most primitive and brutal methods imaginable, including the purposeful mass rape of Muslim women with the dual goal of making them unacceptable to their men and forcing them to bear Serbian children, the Serbs turned themselves into the pariahs of Europe. Western leaders began calling the Serbian leaders war criminals and making plans to convene a war crimes tribunal to deal with the terrible atrocities committed on all sides. Peace negotiations conducted in Geneva by United Nations and European Community negotiators produced plausible plans, but by 1993 the old multiethnic Bosnia, which Nobel Prize–winning Yugoslav novelist Ivo Andrić had described with such power in his novel *Bridge on the Drina*, was gone, perhaps forever.[70]

One other republic of the former Yugoslavia (the country that calls itself "Yugoslavia" today consists of Serbia and Montenegro, but it is no longer internationally recognized) remained in limbo during this period: Macedonia. Originally Macedonia was a geographical term, but early in the twentieth century, when the Ottomans were pushed out of the Balkan peninsula, Macedonia was divided among Greece, which received a little over half of the area; Bulgaria, which received about 15 percent; and Serbia, later Yugoslavia, which received the rest. The Macedonians speak their own Slavic language, are Orthodox Christians, and have their own national consciousness, although 20 to 40 percent of the population, depending on who does the counting, are Muslim Albanians. In 1945 the Communists created the Republic of Macedonia (it had been part of Serbia in the interwar years), and in 1991 this entity sought international recognition. Macedonia fulfilled the European Community's requirements, and by the end of 1992 it had Eastern Europe's only multiethnic cabinet (five Albanians, one Turk, the rest Macedonians). But recognition was prevented by the Greeks, who alleged that the term "Macedonia" was exclusively a Greek term and hid aggressive aspirations of the Macedonians to the northern part of Greece. It was not until early in 1993 that Macedonia was finally admitted to the United Nations under the name "The Former Republic of Macedonia." Macedonia's future, however, remained gravely in doubt.

And finally there was Kosovë, the initial focal point. Amazingly, leaders of the Albanians in Kosovë still continued to maintain at the end of 1991 that their hope was to enter a renewed confederation of sovereign and equal republics. But as that prospect grew less and less feasible, in the spring of 1992 the Kosovars declared their independence. The only country to recognize them was Albania. The Albanians in Kosovë have been remarkably restrained in the face of extreme provocations by the Serbs, perhaps because they are poorly armed and know that the Serbs will not hesitate to massacre them. But with unemployment in the 40 percent range, with education at a standstill, and with no governmental functions reserved for them, it remained in doubt how long they could maintain their moderate stance. Together with their conationals in Albania and other parts of Yugoslavia, the Albanians constituted a population of about five and one-half million, more than the Croats and almost three times as numerous as the Slovenians. How long could it be before they attempted to assert that position in the Balkans to which ethnic politics seemed to entitle them?

8

Nationalism, Responsibility, and the People-as-One: Reflections on the Possibilities for Peace in the Former Yugoslavia

The success West Europeans have enjoyed since World War II in creating supranational structures that produced both political stability and economic development gave them, until recently at least, a sense that they had entered a new stage of history, one that left bestiality behind. The depression, the violence of war, the holocaust—these were the unclean emanations of the past, the result of national, racial, and ideological claims that had since been tamed. Postwar Europeans were well pleased that they had found a prosperous way to put these passions behind them and to live together, if not without tension, then at least without killing. The inhumanity of the wars of Yugoslav succession therefore came as a shock to everyone who believed that such grotesque cruelties were a thing of the past. The disasters in southeastern Europe have rekindled respect for the institutions of Western Europe that have maintained the civility of public life and lent a renewed urgency to the issues posed by nationalism.

The most pressing problem of nationalist excess is how (and if) Serbs, Croats, and Bosnians, not to mention Kosovars and Macedonians, can find a way to live peacefully with one another after the bitter passions engendered by the inhumanity of their conflicts. The East Central European countries, along with Romania and Bulgaria, seem to be proceeding on their varied pathways toward eventual integration in the postwar structures of international cooperation, but the former Yugoslav lands have

From *Studies in East European Thought,* 46 (1994), pp. 91–103. Reprinted by permission of Kluwer Academic Publishers.

gone in the opposite direction, especially in the case of Serbia, which finds itself formally characterized by the United Nations as an aggressor and its leaders labeled by Western officials as war criminals. The purpose of this chapter is not to discuss the Yugoslav conflict directly, nor to formulate a policy agenda, but rather to suggest the general terms that will have to characterize a lasting settlement in the Yugoslav lands, and, by extension, anywhere that nationalist controversies exist. Unfortunately, the conclusion will be that those most mobilized by the extreme nationalist rhetoric that characterizes the wars of Yugoslav succession will be the least likely to accept these terms.

Having unleashed the demons, can the Serbs and Croats enter into the common European home again? There is at least one relatively recent example of a nation that committed gruesome atrocities and yet returned to a position of honor and strength in Europe, and that is of course Germany. The Germans cannot take all of the credit for this happy result, since the main reason they could turn away from their Nazi past was that the allies utterly destroyed their political infrastructure, occupied their lands, forced new political forms on them, and brought them into the cold war calculus. But Germany reentered Europe on new terms not only because of this coercion. Germans undertook their own serious and successful efforts to accept responsibility for their problematic history. This painful renegotiation of the past was absolutely essential to the creation of a democratic Germany and a stable Europe. The acceptance of responsibility that characterized postwar Germany consisted of three elements, what one might call the three Rs of responsibility: reconciliation, remembrance, and regret.

In Germany's case reconciliation meant primarily reaching an accommodation with France, which it had invaded three times within seventy years. Konrad Adenauer's greatest achievement was the Franco-German reconciliation that assured peace in Western Europe. He championed the Coal and Steel Community in 1950, was a strong supporter of the Treaty of Rome in 1957 that established the European Community, and signed the Franco-German Friendship Treaty of 1963. The shock of Germany's devastating defeat in World War II, the enormity of the Nazis' crimes and the realization that the *Stunde null* offered a chance for a new beginning created the conditions in which Adenauer could follow a policy that so contrasted with German's aggressions of the recent past. The creation of the European Community on the basis of a politics of accommodation established the principle of reconciliation in a concrete political structure that all participants accepted. Each member of the EC participates fully and voluntarily in its activities and politically accepts the consequences of the community's decisions. Within this supranational structure it is possible to be a national, or even a regional, patriot without feeling at the same time the necessity of subduing one's neighbor by force. Reconciliation for the Germans after World War II, therefore, meant not only making a conscious decision to seek accommodation with a former enemy, but also entering willingly into self-enforcing multinational political structures that internationalized the reconciliation and made it semipermanent.

It goes without saying that reconciliation of this sort is at present completely foreign to the situation in the former Yugoslavia. There is no likelihood that some beneficent foreign power will conquer Serbia and Croatia and force them to become democratic, although it is true that considerable pressure can be brought to bear from abroad. There are few signs that the tiny internal groupings who advocate reconciliation have any hope of achieving power. Indeed, every instance of conflict in the Yugoslav crisis is blamed entirely on the other side, and hundreds of thousands of people have become convinced that they can never be reconciled to neighbors who slaughtered members of their family.

A second step the Germans took was to enter into a pluralist discourse of remembrance, in which it was considered not only legitimate but essential that bitter and painful memories of the past be brought to the surface and confronted. One of the persistent characteristics of totalitarian states is the tampering with memory, and even in democratic states it is sometimes difficult to face up to embarrassing realities, as in the case of the Austrians' refusal to recall the level of their enthusiasm for Hitler in World War II. But starting in the late 1950s, West Germans have engaged in constant public discussion of the disasters and missteps of the past, and of the level of guilt they should bear for them. Historical questions that in other countries were left to high school textbooks and academic specialists became the matter of spirited and long-lasting public debate: the nature of Bismarck's impact on the disastrous outcome; the level of German responsibility for World War I; the level of personal guilt involved in living a normal life while knowing others were being purposefully sent to their deaths; the absence of a democratic past. These and many other issues have filled German media for years, to the point that they have become an ordinary part of Germans' self-image, even a tiring one.

Remembrance stabilized German public life by keeping the record of the past on the surface, where it could be dealt with, instead of hidden under the surface, unattended, unhealed, and unappeased. This is what happened in East Germany, which blamed Hitler's excesses on bourgeois capitalism and refused to countenance the suggestion that Germans living under socialism might have had any responsibility for the Nazi past. When the two Germanies came together in 1990 and the lid was removed, some East Germans, unfamiliar with the forty years of dialogue that had shaped their Western counterparts, found it difficult to understand that their antiforeign, anti-Semitic, and antidemocratic ideas were no longer acceptable to most West Germans.

In Yugoslavia the situation was similar to that of East Germany. The communist regime refused to permit open discussion of the Ustasha, Chetnik, and Partisan atrocities except in terms of bad old bourgeois society versus good new socialist society. As a result, although the wounds of the war were covered over, they were never allowed to heal. The entire policy of reconciliation rests on the moral and ethical foundation of remembrance. When the discourse of the past is manipulated in such a way as to prevent a more-or-less honest confrontation with the skeletons it contains, reconciliation is not possible. As German president Richard von Weizsäcker put it in 1985, "We must understand that there can be no reconciliation without remembrance."[1]

Finally, the Germans went beyond simple remembrance and actually expressed regret for their actions in the past. The most obvious case of this is explicit measures taken to compensate Jews who survived the war, to establish and maintain good relations with Israel, to make gestures of repentance, as Willy Brandt did when he visited the memorial to the Warsaw ghetto in 1970, and to build new synagogues for the few Jews remaining in Germany. Anti-Semitic racism is punishable by law in Germany today, and the first step taken by the new East German legislature when it met in April 1990 was to make good the forty-year hiatus and to express its sorrow and regret at the crimes of Germans during World War II.

At this point, of course, the situation in Yugoslavia has not matured to anywhere near the point that expressions of regret are conceivable. But there is a post-1989 example of regret that is relevant to a strategy of stability. It is the two treaties Germany and Poland signed in November 1990 and in June 1991, the first guaranteeing the border along the Oder/Neisse line and the second a treaty of "good neighborliness and friendly cooperation." By the first treaty Germany assured Poland of the finality of the post–World War II border adjustments, and by the second the two countries entered into a set of remarkable agreements for the systematic protection of minority rights, the development of the economies along their mutual frontier, and the provision of German advice in social services such as health insurance. The agreements, and the speeches and letters that accompanied them, are notable for the repeated expressions of regret about "die leidvollen Kapitel der Vergangenheit," as the Treaty on Good Neighborliness and Friendship begins.[2] "Vor unseren Augen stehen die Leiden des polnischen Volkes in der Zeit der deutschen Besetzung," Hans-Dietrich Genscher said in his speech at the signing of the first treaty, to which Jan Krzysztof Bielecki responded at the signing of the second one: "der letzte Weltkrieg, entfesselt durch die nationalsozialistische Aggression gegen Polen, brachte dem polnischen, aber auch dem deutschen Volk ein Unmass von Leid und Elend."[3] The memories of the German brutalities are clear here, but less well remembered was the ferocious, if understandable, way in which Poles, with the help of the Red Army, expelled Germans in 1945 from East Prussia and what is now western Poland. On their side the Germans killed perhaps 3 million Poles and 3 million Polish Jews, while during the last months of the war perhaps as many as 1.7 million Germans died during the expulsion.[4]

The Polish treaties are consistent with the general thrust of post–World War II German foreign policy, and the signatories to the treaties explicitly recognized them as standing in the footsteps of the Franco-

German treaty of 1963. The Germans have gone on to sign similar treaties with other East European states, but for the Poles the treaties are the cornerstone of an original and constructive policy that directly confronts their geographical position between Germany and Russia (or Belarus and Ukraine). Instead of bemoaning their geographical bad luck, they have gone out and concluded similar agreements with their other neighbors, having relatively minor difficulties only with Lithuania.

In undertaking this policy of good neighborliness, the Poles have put behind them one of the underlying causes of instability in Eastern Europe throughout the twentieth century. This factor is the complete inability of nationalists to accept responsibility for their own nation's past. Even in stable, well-disciplined countries, leaders rarely admit that their country has erred, and nationalists in particular seem to think they have a natural right never to say they are sorry. They see such admissions as shameful, as in themselves harmful to the national spirit. Past actions may indeed be shameful, but expressions of regret for them are quite the opposite— honorable in that they constitute a simple recognition of fact rather than an obfuscation and an avoidance of responsibility. As Adam Michnik puts it, "If—being German—I feel proud because of Goethe, Heine, and Thomas Mann, even though it wasn't I who wrote their books, I also have to feel shame because of Hitler, Himmler, and Goebbels, even though I never had any sympathy for that ensemble."[5]

Nationalism, as Michnik points out, is a device for avoiding responsibility. By identifying "the other," which may be an ethnic minority, neighbors, or even just political opponents, as an enemy bent on subverting the nation, nationalists can shift blame for every social ill from themselves. An excellent example of this style of political fingerpointing has been the various excuses and explanations given over time by Vladimir Mečiar of Slovakia, who contends that all criticisms of him are Czech plots and that whatever may be wrong in Slovakia is the fault of the Hungarians, the Czechs, or even the Germans—everyone, that is, except the Slovaks and him. Another is the refusal of Russian nationalists to discuss amending the Russo-Hungarian friendship treaty to include an expression of the two people's "mutual desire to overcome the legacy of totalitarianism, especially that of the invasion of Hungary in 1956." One nationalist deputy found it unacceptable for Russia to be "constantly bowing and scraping to the rest of the world."[6]

Why is it so difficult for nationalists to accept the three Rs of responsibility? There may well be deep-seated psychological motivations at work that lie outside the ability of political analysts to penetrate, but among the accessible ideological ingredients the most significant factor driving the rejection of mechanisms that could ameliorate strife is the belief that the nation is and should be ethnically, religiously, linguistically, and culturally homogeneous. This idea is as old as the ancient idea that three types of government exist: autocracy, aristocracy, and democracy. In the eighteenth century, the view was widely held that each of the three possible ruling entities, the monarch, the nobility, and the people, was a single unit with a single interest. Rousseau's notion of the general will was based on this premise. When the people asserts the general will it does so as a homogeneous whole, not a plurality of factions and individuals pursuing partial interests. The general will differed from individual opinions precisely because it was the single view on any given issue that truly reflected the virtuous will of the generality. Thinkers as diverse as Edmund Burke, John Adams, and the Abbé Sieyès agreed. "Parliament is a *deliberative* assembly of *one* nation with *one* interest, that of the . . . general good, resulting from the general reason of the whole," said Burke. For Sieyès, legislators were "not the representatives of portions of society, their electors for example, but of the entire nation." American president John Adams maintained until his death the idea that the people were the virtuous single order of a mixed government.[7]

The American constitution of 1789 was the first major political document that undermined this monistic interpretation of the people's will. Before the revolution of 1776 American radicals believed that the "tyranny" they suffered at the hands of state governors appointed by the king would be overcome when legislators elected by the people made laws in the people's interests. But as soon as the revolution gave state legislatures significant power, it became apparent that legislatures too could be tyrannical, or at least could pass easy-money legislation, repudiate debts, and refuse to pay the confederation its levies. Unlike the French revolutionaries, however, the men who saw themselves as the natural leaders of the American revolution learned an important lesson from this failure of the people to achieve harmony and virtue through revolution.

James Madison, in the most famous of the Federalist Papers, noted that "as long as the reason of man continues fallible, and he is at liberty to exercise it, different opinions will be formed. . . . The latent causes of faction are thus sown in the nature of man."[8] Madison pointed out that there were two ways to deal with the fundamental datum that human beings are by nature contentious: either repress the differences of opinion when they arise, or create a republic in which the powers accorded to the state were "so divided and balanced among several bodies of magistracy as that no one could transcend their legal limits without being effectually checked and restrained by the others."[9] In the American system, the people remained seized of their sovereignty, only dispensing "such portions of power as were conceived as necessary for the public welfare . . . to such bodies, on such terms, and under such limitations, as they think proper."[10] This was the essential invention of the American revolution: to abandon the ideal of the general will, the single representation of the popular sovereignty, and to replace it with the idea of limited government in which sovereignty was apportioned among various public entities.

On the continent, however, the idea of a single people with a single will was not abandoned. French revolutionaries adopted it from the beginning. The Chapelier Law of 1791, for example, stated in its preface the following: "Sovereignty being one and indivisible, and belonging to the entire nation, no administration of a *department,* no district administration, no municipality, commune or section of a commune, nor any section of the people has the right to execute any act of sovereignty."[11] In the next century the idea expanded in two seemingly opposite directions. The first direction was laid out by Marx, for whom the proletariat was the materialist version of Rousseau's virtuous people. By seizing the means of production, the proletariat would eliminate the category of class and establish an unalienated and truly human society based on the understanding that the proletariat was a single entity with a single interest. Leninism posited that the vanguard party of the proletariat was the entity that embodied this understanding, and eventually Stalin became the single individual who embodied it. This reductio ad absurdum of the notion of the virtuous and homogeneous people—one virtuous individual representing all of humanity—was not necessarily a logical outcome of Marxism, but it was an actual one.

The second direction in which the idea of the people-as-one developed was in the Central European style of nationalism. The view that a specific social conception represented the character of the Volk began in Germany in the eighteenth century, became explicit in the nineteenth century, and by the beginning of the twentieth century had become one of the basic tenets of Central European nationalism. Nationalists in every ethnic group came to claim that only if they had their own state could they preserve the character of the community they imagined they represented. In the nineteenth century this idea appeared to be democratic, since its practitioners argued that the great Central European empires—the Russian, the German, the Austrian, and the Ottoman, none of which were based on democratic principles—were denying them their right to govern themselves through their own free choices. The nationalists constructed their advocacy on the basis of popular sovereignty and self-determination, and thus appeared to be democratic. Once these nationalists achieved power after World War I, however, the monistic and nonpluralistic character of their nationalism became clear. In every East European country the dominant national group used its new power to confront enemies and to benefit its own members. Claiming that only members of the majority culture had the right to govern, the nationalists insisted further that only they fully understood the correct characteristics of the national culture. The failure of East European democracy under the nationalist dispensation was clear by the late 1930s, but its full implications were hidden first by the Nazi incursion and then by Soviet domination. These foreign intrusions permitted the East European nationalists to evade responsibility for their errors—the disasters clearly were, in fact, the fault of outsiders. Unlike the West Europeans, the East Europeans did not have an opportunity to assess and understand the destructive potential of exclusionary nationalism at the end of World War II. They had no *Stunde null.*

Despite the almost complete failure of Marxism to address the problem of nationalism, communism and nationalism were similar in their contention that a single "correct" vision of social organization existed. They had taken different pathways from the eighteenth century, but both of them had chosen the first of James Madison's two choices when confronted with human contentiousness: repression in the name of unity. Both the Communists and the nationalists seek purity, the Communists in their purges, the radical nationalists in their insistence on ethnic homogeneity. It is no accident that so many of the most virulent nationalists in today's Bulgaria, Slovakia, Romania, Serbia, and Croatia are former Communists. These men (but few women) continue to believe, despite an entire human history to the contrary, in the ancient ideal of a homogeneous and virtuous people, on whose behalf, of course, they presume to speak.

While nationalism and communism were going their special ways, the pluralism characteristic of the American constitution on the one hand and the principles of equality and fairness introduced by the French Revolution on the other hand were having their impact as well. North America, England, France, and, after World War II, even Germany were creating democratic political systems characterized by tolerance and openness and by market-style economic systems that permitted ease of entry. During both halves of the twentieth century this pluralist style of politics by accommodation and economics by relative openness proved able to survive extremely powerful social and economic strains. The principles of openness, democracy, pluralism, and market became the founding dogmas of the European Community, so that, when the revolutions of 1989 occurred, pluralism was recognized throughout Eastern Europe as the only viable sociopolitical model. It is just the openness of pluralism that both the Communists and the nationalists cannot abide. The ideal of the homogeneous people is their device to fend off the radical indeterminacy of pluralism, the assertion of the democratic states that it is process that is important, not ends. Pluralism evades control, that is its strength. But Communists and nationalists insist on turning the public space into their private sphere, refusing to grant to others the rights and privileges they demand for themselves.[12] This is why pluralism and nationalism can never be fully compatible.

The problem for the nationalists then is clear. Their vision of the purified state with its monotonously correct history, its canon of acceptable viewpoints, its stultified public rituals, and its exclusionary politics is irreconcilable with pluralism. Therefore every time the more extreme East European nationalists assert themselves in a way they believe will bring them dignity as the masters of their own space they alienate themselves from the international system they claim they wish to be a part of. And since the quality of their ideology is such that it precludes accepting responsibility for their past, not to mention expressing regret for it or seeking reconciliation with those they define as their enemies, their consistent tactic of blaming others will only estrange them further from their goal.

They face a vicious cycle of resentment causing rejection causing greater resentment, and so forth. And none of this will have anything to do with the real problems of economic restructuring and political organization that they face.

Homogenizing nationalism contains a second self-defeating tendency as well, the self-destruction of culture. The creative power of pluralist culture is a product of its diversity and its openness. Historically, diversity has been one of the strengths of East European culture as well—the colorful variety of peoples, cultures, and ideas that have cross-fertilized each other in the region for centuries. But by purposefully excluding all those who are different from some arbitrarily set national norm and by leveling all cultural creations to a single standard set by political leaders who feel threatened by any originality that they cannot control, East European nationalists undermine the very cultures they seek to glorify.

Ethnic cleansing destroys an external threat to the people-as-one by removing all those who are alleged not to fit into the adopted national category. But the nationalists also insist on cleansing their own societies internally in the sphere of culture. They seek to impose their particular understandings of art, fiction, and poetry, but in particular they stake claim to the writing of history. The principle tenet of pluralist historiography is that the past constitutes an infinitude of data out of which historians construct narratives. Every narrative is open to contestation on a variety of grounds, such as selection, ordering, logic, or even context. In a pluralist society there may be privileged styles of history, but they are constantly enriched and adjusted as the discourse proceeds, producing a vibrant and stimulating conception of the self as placed in the dynamic process of time. The nationalists reject openness of entry into the historical discourse. They maintain that there is a single, self-evident, static, and glorious past that is so unproblematic that all members of the nation should willingly and enthusiastically accept it. They seek to hide the fact that the narrative they privilege is authored, because that admission would open it to contestation, which is where the threat to their own power, or rather to their own unproblematic sense of self and to their denial of process lies. This not only prevents the "rough bustling in of a new truth," as Thomas Hobbes put it, but deadens the minds of both those who are denied entry into the discourse and those who are offered no alternatives to it. Extended to all spheres of culture, the result is an intellectual wasteland. Michael Howard has summed up the impact of the cultural homogenization characteristic of the people-as-one style of nationalism as follows: it "is a process of self-starvation, almost of self-castration. No culture is complete and adequate in itself. Deprived of constant cross-fertilization it loses all creativity."[13]

Not all Serbs and Croats are unaware of the dangers of the-people-as-one syndrome. The weekly *Vreme*, for example, still published regularly in Belgrade, has regularly criticized this view. For example, in the issue of March 1, 1993, Miloš Bobić wrote that "if politics has no other vision than a nationally, culturally, and socially single-sided and homogeneous community, that will be an excellent sign and an important measure of its backwardness."[14] But as long as the nationalists now in charge in the former Yugoslavia reject the three Rs of reconciliation and insist on the people-as-one style of nationalism, the Yugoslav peoples cannot and will not become participating elements of Europe, since the principles on which they operate are just as unacceptable to the Western democracies as the communist principles were, and for many of the same reasons. In their unwillingness to accept responsibility for their own pasts, to express regret for the shameful events of those pasts, and to seek reconciliation with their neighbors they are operating in exactly the same antipluralist way as their communist predecessors, and destroying the creative diversity of their own people in the process. Perhaps this is all one can expect in a time of war, in which every sinew is strained toward the struggle. But the structural inadequacies of the extreme nationalist position have penetrated deeply into Yugoslav societies. No matter what peace proposal eventually is patched together by the international community, it will be a long time before those societies will be able to accept responsibility for their past. Without that acceptance, however, there will be no lasting peace.

III

1989: PROLOGUE, LESSONS, PROSPECTS

The East European revolutions of 1989 captured the imagination and attention of the world like nothing else since the end of World War II. After forty years of being considered slavish satellites of the Soviet Union—the general public did not differentiate clearly among communist states that in actuality were quite different—suddenly, and seemingly without warning, the East Europeans rose up and threw off their oppressive regimes almost without bloodshed. Such a dramatic upheaval required explanation, and many rushed in to fill the breach. Political partisans in the United States credited the foreign policy of Presidents Reagan and Bush for pushing the communist regimes towards collapse, whereas Soviet scholars noted that nothing could have happened unless Mikhail Gorbachev had tried to reform socialism. East European specialists tended to find explanations that gave the initiative to the peoples of the region, their favorite theory being that the emergence of a civil society undermined illegitimate communist regimes.[1] Inspired primarily by the Polish experience with Solidarity and by the rhetoric used by Polish intellectuals, this explanation posited that the utter lack of legitimacy of the communist regimes in Eastern Europe, especially after 1968, left the door open for creating legitimate autonomous societies. Antipoliticians in Czechoslovakia, such as Václav Havel, ignored the party and the state, living "in truth" and acting "as if" they were free. The Solidarity movement mobilized ten million Poles, challenging the Leninist notion that only the Communist party had the right to speak for the working class.

But the notion of civil society only takes us so far in explaining 1989. It works well in Poland, where during the 1980s thousands of publications, clubs, and initiatives of all kinds created a powerful sense of society standing in contrast to the party and to the state—us versus them. It might work to a certain extent in Hungary, where a process of bourgeoisification enabled a growing number of people to create alternative forms of property. But elsewhere the revolutions of 1989 exploded on a people whose rulers had almost completely denied them any autonomous public space.

Economic failure was a significant factor in the revolutions, of course. One can assume that if Soviet socialism had produced prosperity similar to that in much of the world after World War II the revolutions would not have occurred. But people can live with a creaky economic system, even if they do not like it. Soviets had been doing so since the 1930s. In 1989 the people of Leipzig, Prague, Timişoara, and Sofia did not get out on the streets to shout "Volkswagen, Refrigerator, and Deutschmark." The words they used were the traditional abstractions of modern politics: freedom, democracy, and nation. Even East Germans, desperate to reap some of the economic benefits they had long seen on West German television, shouted "We are one people," urging from the beginning that their socialist state disappear into West Germany.

In other words, ideas had an autonomous power in the revolutions of 1989. East Europeans did not know exactly what democracy was, although the word was commonplace. They sensed that it meant more control over their lives and the direction of their countries than they had under Soviet tutelage. Neither were they sure just what market economies entailed, but they knew they had to be better than the economies of shortage. When offered the opportunity—the opening of the Hungarian border in the summer of 1989, for example, or the disturbances in Timişoara in December of that year—they rallied around the abstractions. In this way, the revolutions of 1989 confirm the lessons of the nineteenth-century experience in southeastern Europe. Political ideas have an autonomous strength that is not necessarily rooted in social relations or economic development.

Because ideas are mobilizing in their own right, policy makers need to pursue what I call soft-nosed analysis as well as the more ordinary kinds of strategic, military, and economic analysis that is favored by "realists." Those who attended to these forms of expression in the 1980s had a much better sense of what was happening in Eastern Europe in 1989 than those who did not. There are other lessons of 1989, but the most important reminder that those unexpected revolutions provided is that we cannot predict the future. The revolutions of 1989 show us again that events have their own logic. They progress by means of unpredictable human reactions in moments of stress, usually on the basis of scant or faulty information.

Nevertheless, one does try to read the tea leaves. The last chapter in Part III is based on the final chapter of my book on the collapse of Communism in Eastern Europe.[2] It does not predict the future in any specific way, but it does attempt to present a positive picture of the great opportunities that have opened up to the 140 million people who live in the region. Media coverage of Eastern Europe, like that in other parts of the world, necessarily concentrates on problems. Academics also make their living by analyzing difficulties. The horrible wars in Yugoslavia have focused attention on the worst possible outcome of collapse. In my view, however, these inclinations tend to create a false range of possibilities. The future of the surviving Yugoslav states is indeed precarious, but when criticizing other parts of Eastern Europe we often tend to forget that our own societies are far from perfect, that democracy is a contentious discipline, that crime characterizes all industrialized societies, and that patriotism, not to mention nationalism, is a constant of modern politics. East European societies are not going to develop into textbook examples of harmonious societies with a chicken in every pot. But they are on the pathway to creating their own varied versions of pluralist societies. This is an enormous step forward from the experiences they have suffered through most of this century.

9

Modes of Opposition Leading to Revolution in Eastern Europe

With the exception of a handful of books on Poland, work by a few Western social scientists on factories in Hungary, and the studies of two notable anthropologists who worked in Romania, essentially no social history of the post–World War II period comparable to the work that has been done for twenty years or more in the West exists concerning Eastern Europe before 1989. The most obvious reason for this is that the communist regimes forbade such work, since the findings of any real social science were likely to undermine the claims of the vanguard party. The entire sociology department of Charles University in Prague was disbanded after 1968, and in Bulgaria the field of anthropology is a post–1989 product. The primacy of the cold war paradigm also hindered the development of investigations in the West that were not overtly political or economic. Even Western interest in the democratic opposition in Eastern Europe tended to lead to theoretical constructs, such as the widespread use of the concept of civil society, rather than to concrete research into the sociological ingredients of this opposition.

I begin with this disclaimer because I am about to make an argument that, with the exception of Poland, the revolutions of 1989 in Eastern Europe were not social revolutions in the way we have thought of them in the past. Whether this view is a construct of the data, or rather the lack of

From George Reid Andrews and Herrick Chapman, eds., *The Social Construction of Democracy, 1870–1990* (New York: New York University Press, 1995), pp. 241–263. Reprinted by permission.

data, or whether it has a more substantial basis remains to be seen. We are only at the beginning of our investigations of these events, and it will be some time before we have the fine-grained analyses on which more substantial conclusions can be based.

In Poland a self-activating workers' movement that created democratic forms of social interaction over a period of at least twenty years was the force behind the creation of Tadeusz Mazowiecki's government in August 1989, but none of the other countries of Eastern Europe experienced even a modest mobilization of either the working class or the peasantry prior to 1989. Neither did the new technocratic class provide a social basis for their revolutions, as some thought possible twenty years ago. In Hungary the growth of alternative forms of ownership and the reforms of the early 1980s that opened Hungary's internal market and its foreign trade furthered a process of embourgeoisement, but the beneficiaries of this policy played almost no direct role in Hungary's negotiated revolution. The social force of an aroused public did play a fundamental role in 1989, as demonstrators by the millions convinced communist regimes that their time had come; but street demonstrations, whatever their short-term effects on public memory, are poor substitutes for the thick organization of pluralist societies, very little of which existed in any East European country by 1989.

The lack of obvious social determinants has caused some analysts to question whether the events of 1989 can be called democratic revolutions at all, especially because they lacked a level of violence normally associated with the concept of revolution. Even the Romanian events were small potatoes compared to the bloody traditions of the great revolutions. And in contrast to earlier social revolutions, the revolutions of 1989 were not progressive because they restored or sought to copy social and economic norms that had previously existed in Eastern Europe or that had proven successful elsewhere rather than opening new avenues for human development, as presumably the French Revolution did and as the Bolshevik Revolution claimed to be doing. Neither were they democratic in the sense that they created truly interactive forms of political discourse. The political mobilization of East European populations in the early 1990s proceeded not primarily by means of the self-activization of individuals forming primary groups but through appeals to the citizenry to join this or that political party formed and led by elites. For all these reasons I refer to the 1989 revolutions with a small "r" and with adjectival prefixes, such as "negotiated revolution."

But to deny that the events of 1989 were revolutionary because they were not sufficiently democratic or were not progressive is both to apply an ideal rather than a realistic standard to them and to miss their fundamental importance. None of the great revolutions actually produced an ideal democracy, a contested concept in any event; and the very notion of progressive was itself a product of the dialectical modes of thinking characteristic of the system that was overthrown in 1989. The term "progressive" is a product of nineteenth-century positivistic optimism and of its teleological relative, the dialectical process. Both ideas today have a distinctly anachronistic tone. The new notion in Eastern Europe is pluralism, which is not progressive, and not even a system, but rather a process whose outcome is unknown and whose structures vary, albeit within a particular type of worldwide economic system. Pluralism is not new, of course, since it emerged from the same eighteenth-century milieu from which Marxism emerged. But if the events of 1989 can be understood as the recognition that the centrally planned system failed, then it seems appropriate at the very least to term those events revolutionary in the negative sense that they interred any realistic hope that the teleological experiment in the use of human reason to transform society in its entirety might succeed. (The hope itself had died twenty years earlier.)

From a more positive point of view, the changes introduced in 1989 were startling. They hold significant hope for the development of the countries of Eastern Europe into functioning pluralistic societies. Not only were the former authorities overthrown, except perhaps in Romania, but the ideological justifications advanced by the vanguard party were rejected in their entirety; centralized planning was renounced, at least in principle; and private property was restored, once again at first mainly in principle. This latter change is now in the process of creating a basis for the emergence of another "new class" in Eastern Europe that eventually can be expected to fill the gap left by the decline and defeat of Djilas's "new class" of party and state agents that dominated the socialist societies of Eastern Europe since 1945. It is difficult to imagine a more sudden and more complete creation of the conditions for a social transformation than the events of 1989, especially if we understand that social change is the consequence of revolution just as much as it is the cause.

The revolutions of 1989 suggest in a newly powerful way that democratic forms are as much a product of the ethical and moral demands of the French Revolution, the calculus of freedom and the demand for equity, as they are of social determinants, although there clearly is a close relationship between pluralist economic systems and pluralist political forms. Of course, the question of how ideas turn into actions remains important, and it is people with ideas who make history, not the ideas themselves. Neither should it be inferred that the revolutions took place entirely in the ethical realm or that there were no underlying structural elements. In fact, it is highly unlikely that the revolutions would have occurred at all had not the centrally planned economies failed or had Mikhail Gorbachev not begun his reform process in the Soviet Union. The legitimacy of modern governments rests on their ability to deliver economic success, and East European governments were no exception. The extent of the economic failure of the centrally planned economies surpassed even the most pessimistic evaluations, and the responsible regimes paid the price of their failure. But if we concentrate on this factor alone or on the Gorbachev factor, we miss the most important part of the process: the utter moral rot that hollowed out the East European regimes and turned them into empty husks ready to be blown away by the first strong wind.

The initial Soviet incursion into Eastern Europe was no empty husk— it was the Red Army, which swept across the region in 1944 and 1945, and then, in varying degree, remained for the next forty-five years. The entire history of Eastern Europe from 1945 to 1989, in fact, can be considered one spasmodic imposition of Stalinism followed by forty years of adjusting, accommodating, opposing, reinterpreting, and rejecting. Naturally, this imposition did not occur on a blank slate. Each East European country had its particular historical background and characteristic political culture. Post–1989 events have suggested that despite the strenuous efforts of the Stalinists, these historical roots still exist and still play their role. But during the first few years of the Stalinist imposition, East European societies underwent a forceful transformation of enormous brutality that temporarily blotted out that past.

The Communists who imposed Stalinism did not believe that they were creating a monster. Jacob Berman, interviewed in the early 1980s, believed that the Communists saved Poland from being crushed between a revanchist capitalism, by which he meant Germany supported by the United States, and an occupying army from the Soviet Union. Even at that late date Berman was still "convinced that the sum of our actions, skillfully and carefully carried out, will finally produce results and create a new Polish consciousness; because all the advantages flowing from our new path will be borne out, must be borne out."[1] Berman's lingering enthusiasm illustrates something that tends to be forgotten today. In the immediate postwar period many people, not only Communists catapulted to power by the Red Army, welcomed the chance to transform Eastern Europe. Charles Gati points out that approximately 50 percent of the Hungarian electorate in 1945 wanted radical change, and in Czechoslovakia all major parties favored nationalization of large industry, which actually took place before the final communist takeover in 1948.[2] As G. M. Tamás puts it: "It is true that the Communist party dictatorship was brought to the small East European countries by the victorious troops of Stalin, but we should admit that we were ready for it."[3]

But since Stalinism was imposed by force, because it was perceived as being Russian, and because it did not work economically, it was only natural that opposition arose. In the 1960s the term *dissident* became the popular descriptive term for oppositionists in both the Soviet Union and Eastern Europe, but it was never a particularly good choice. For one thing, it hid the diversity of the opposition. Charter 77, for example, was made up of former communist officials like Zdeněk Mlynář, revolutionary socialists like Petr Uhl, conservative Catholics like Václav Benda, and completely apolitical intellectuals like Václav Havel. The term *dissident* also implied that the opposition was static, a dissident in the Soviet Union in the 1960s being essentially equivalent to a dissident in Czechoslovakia in the 1980s. As the very term "Solidarity" suggests, the myth of a homogeneous opposition temporarily obscured the normal sociological facts of diversity and of process over time. In other words, opposition had a history.

That history is conceived here as the convergence of two originally antithetical tendencies that eventually came together in 1989. The first tendency began with the violent opposition put up by suicidal military and guerrilla movements that continued to resist communist occupation in some places for several years following World War II. The second tendency began with the dissimulation practiced in the face of overwhelming force, to which Czesław Miłosz has given the name "ketman."[4] The first might be termed the heroic strand of opposition, the second the survival strand.[5]

The violent military confrontations of opponents to the communist regimes in the early postwar period have yet to find their historian, but their futility was heart-wrenching and complete. Facing a mobilized and energetic Red Army, or, in the case of the Chetniks, a mobilized and energetic Yugoslav army, traditional guerilla movements were totally outgunned and crushed with complete finality. A significant number of persons were involved in these actions, but most people in Eastern Europe who were unhappy with the new regimes and who were not killed or did not emigrate adopted a survival strategy of dissimulation and public accommodation justified with a whole variety of private reasonings. Czesław Miłosz describes many forms of this "ketman," as he calls it, such as the aesthetic person who conforms to all the canons of socialist realism in public life but maintains reproductions of "real" art on the walls of his or her flat, or the national dissimulator who hides his or her own nationalism under an exaggerated display of affection for the Soviet Union.

Almost all persons under communist rule practiced dissimulation of this sort with varying levels of intensity throughout the entire socialist era, some quite cynically, and the majority of the population did not get much beyond this level even at the end. But dissimulation was the characteristic form of dissent only in periods of the most severe repression, which, not coincidentally, were the periods in which regimes were run by individuals who so strongly believed in their cause that they insisted on genuine conversion rather than the mere observation of forms.

The Hungarian Revolution of 1956 was the polar opposite of accommodation, and it constitutes the next step in the heroic tradition of opposition.[6] It was a less violent confrontation than the postwar guerrilla wars because it took place in only one country and lasted only ten days. Following Stalin's death, other countries had achieved some working space within the socialist commonwealth without violence. The Polish October (1956) was ecstatic but generally peaceful, although serious repressions took place in Poznań, and the right of Yugoslavia to tread its separate path to socialism had been recognized the previous year by Khrushchev. But in Hungary the unprepared events of October got out of hand. Whereas by 1956 the Yugoslavs had been thinking about how to construct a non-Stalinist socialism for five or six years, and in Poland vigorous discussions with the party, among the intellectuals, and at the workplace took place throughout

1956, Hungarians entered their revolution socially and intellectually un-prepared. Suddenly finding hundreds of thousands of people in the streets, Imre Nagy moved precipitately, declaring Hungarian neutrality and with-drawing from the Warsaw Pact. When the Red Army re-entered Budapest shooting, the Hungarians shot back. The Hungarian Revolution of 1956 was an unconsidered but heroic outburst of rage and defiance that ended, as romantic tragedy does, in death but not in ultimate defeat.

Stalin's death permitted the beginning of a new phase of the survival mode of opposition also: the Marxist critique. Agreeing that Stalinism was a distorted form of Marxism, both governments and oppositionists began a search for ways to create a better socialism. On the side of the govern-ments, the main pressure came from economic reformers. Even the colle-gial leadership that came to power in the Soviet Union immediately following Stalin's death agreed that a "new course" was needed in the economy, and by the 1960s economic reformers were finding ways to introduce marketizing concepts while still using Marxist terminology. The publication of a famous article by E. G. Liberman in *Pravda* in 1962 began a debate in the socialist countries of how best to reform their economies. In Yugoslavia Branko Horvat suggested that marginal prices were theo-retically the best device for allocating resources, although, he claimed, they were not practical. In Poland, Oskar Lange proposed a "normal price" that sounded a good deal like Adam Smith's "natural price," while Włod-zimierz Brus argued that indirect measures would be more effective than direct control for stimulating the economy. In Czechoslovakia Ota Šik struggled to get a hearing for his "humane economic democracy," and in Hungary actual reform got underway after three years of detailed planning with the introduction of the New Economic Mechanism of 1968. Even East Germany and Bulgaria got into the act with superficial reform mea-sures.

While none of these economic discussions were undertaken by opposi-tionists, they all posed the question of reform in ways that were antithetical to centralized planning and to direct party control of the economy. But all were couched in terms of Marxian economics. By the middle of the 1960s only a few persons had read any of the Austrian or neoconservative econo-mists (Václav Klaus, later Czechoslovak prime minister, came across Hayek while studying in North America in 1962, for example), and cer-tainly no one was publicly advocating any sort of market economy.

Political oppositionists also presented their cases in Marxist terms. The most famous of these was Milovan Djilas, whose *The New Class,* published in 1956, remains in print today. Djilas had been a major player in Yugoslav Communism since the late 1930s and had risen to be second in command of the new revolutionary state. But Djilas remained morally an adolescent, which is to say he never stopped asking sophomoric questions and there-fore never lost his moral edge. After leading an underground communist movement to power, he, unlike any other leader in Eastern Europe—or elsewhere, for that matter—refused to stop his critique of the abuse of power. His view that a new class of party officials had replaced the bourgeoisie as the dominant class in socialist societies, including Yugoslavia, remains a basic contribution, and his prediction of its end was positively prescient. "When this new class leaves the historical scene, and this must happen," he said in 1956, "there will be less sorrow over its passing than there was for any class before it."[7]

During the 1960s the most notorious critique of Polish socialism was, if anything, even more steeped in Marxism. It came from the pen of two young activists, Jacek Kuroń and Karol Modzelewski, today pillars of the post-1989 establishment. Although they are now embarrassed about their "Open Letter to the Party," which presented a Trotskyite interpretation of what had happened in Poland since World War II, the authors' style was characteristic of opposition in the revisionist era. The two authors agreed that Poland needed to develop economically and that a vigorous program of growth had gotten under way, but, like Djilas, they observed that the deadening hand of bureaucracy had stifled the country. Djilas did not offer any solutions to this problem, although he eventually went on to reject Marxism completely, but Kuroń and Modzelewski argued that only a direct workers' democracy would create the conditions for development in Poland. Their suggestions got them three years in prison.

The most sophisticated Marxist oppositionists in the 1960s were those surrounding *Praxis,* the Yugoslav journal that attracted socialist writers from around the world. The *Praxis* group consisted of a variety of intellectuals unified by their interest in the implications of the writings of the young Marx and their concern with problems of alienation. They did not believe, as even the relatively liberal League of Communists of Yugoslavia claimed, that socialism had put an end to alienation. Indeed, they found that it was precisely the existing communist parties that "cripple human beings, arrest their development, and impose on them patterns of simple, easily predictable, dull, stereotyped behavior."[8] They advocated free transformative activity and commitment that draws out genuine needs, not the false ones they observed around them. In this way the *Praxis* group began to penetrate to the main theme of later oppositionists, the ethical vacuity of "real existing socialism," the difference between its claims and its actuality. But they did not abandon socialism. Rather they sought to adjust the socialist actuality through critical inquiry.

The heroic tradition of opposition and the survival tradition, as represented by the economists and political theorists, came together momentarily in Prague in 1968. The Prague Spring was much better prepared than the Hungarian Revolution of 1956, in the sense that both the oppositionists and the party reformers had been advocating change in public forums for more than a year. But the main impetus for reform came not from civil society—indeed, no such entity existed in Czechoslovakia—nor from the working people, but from within the party, which meant that the Prague Spring remained a reform movement in the Marxist mold. The main vehicle the party proposed for improving political communication between the people and the regime, for example, was the National Front, in which differing views of public issues could be raised and forwarded to the party. But the abandonment of censorship that went with the airing of reform possibilities brought out not only oppositionists from the Left but also for the first time activists who suggested going beyond socialism. When Václav Havel suggested that perhaps it would be better having two political parties rather than merely permitting differing opinions to exist within the National Front, everyone was shocked, especially the Soviets. The economic reforms of the Prague Spring also remained in the tradition of tinkering with centralized planning, assuming that the dawn of the computer age would make a just and efficient plan possible through sophisticated technological innovations.

By the manner in which they suppressed the Prague Spring, the Soviets showed that they had learned something from 1956. Rather than marching in the Red Army, they called upon their surrogates, the Warsaw Pact forces. When the Czechs and Slovaks did not shoot, the invaders did not shoot back. The Czechs and Slovaks resisted in ways calculated to annoy and to hinder the invading forces, and the Husák/B'ilak regime imposed a much longer-lasting regime of normalization than János Kádár had in Hungary, but August 1968 represented a significant de-escalation of violence in the heroic tradition of confrontation.

It almost goes without saying that 1968 destroyed any chance for socialism with a human face to be taken seriously in Eastern Europe, since the invasion proved that the Soviet Union would not tolerate anything except its own rigid forms. The March Days in Warsaw and the student demonstrations in Belgrade, both of which occurred in 1968, reinforced that conclusion in Poland and Yugoslavia. With the exception perhaps of the Budapest School in Hungary and of East German oppositionists like Robert Havemann and Rudolf Bahro, both of whom continued to find Marxist discourse useful, and with the temporary exception of Romania, where Ceaușescu's nonparticipation in the invasion of Czechoslovakia produced a surge of party membership, the events of 1968 ended the viability of Marxist discourse in Eastern Europe.

Less recognized is the fact that Soviet decisions in 1968 constituted an economic watershed as well as a political and a psychological one. Politically the Prague Spring is remembered for the Brezhnev Doctrine, and psychologically it is the moment when belief in the genuineness of socialism became impossible. But economically, the decision not to permit socialism to evolve in a democratic direction also ended the possibility that the centrally planned economies would be reformed along the lines suggested in the 1960s by revisionist Marxist economists. Instead of rejecting the exhausted extensive strategy of development in favor of an intensive strategy, which presumed a competitive entry into the world market, Brezhnev scuttled the modest Liberman reforms and forced his satellite states in Eastern Europe to hunker down once again within the sheltering arms of Comecon (Council of Mutual Economic Assistance, the Soviet-sponsored international trade organization for socialist economies). Every East European country, except Poland, which had not introduced significant reforms in the 1960s anyway, recentralized its planning and control mechanisms in the early 1970s, even Hungary and Yugoslavia. The East Europeans took these steps backward at a time when the environment of world trade was changing dramatically. During the 1970s the newly industrializing countries of the Pacific Rim began to come on line; the oil crises forced industrialized states to become more efficient; service industries began to replace manufacturing as the characteristic economic activity in the older industrialized states; and the information revolution began to transform the ways business was conducted. It may not have been possible to reform the centrally planned economies adequately in any event, but the failure to try sentenced the economies of Eastern Europe to permanent backwardness. The combined loss of ideological confidence and economic competence utterly destroyed the claims of the East European regimes to legitimacy.

Before 1968 many people had already recognized that their regimes were totally false, but it was still possible to hope that things could be improved. After 1968 almost everyone understood that public life was a lie. Polish workers learned, both in 1956 and in 1970–1971, that the regime would not keep its promises of reform; economists learned that proposals that threatened major interests would be scuttled; ordinary citizens learned that the cost of suggestions for innovation or change was dismissal or disciplinary action. Millions of people sensed their own humiliation and even mentioned it to each other in private. But Soviet force made their situation seem hopeless. What to do in such a situation? Many decided to opt out, giving the state its minimal due and focusing instead on gardening, sex, or alcoholism. Some, like Milan Kundera, gave up and emigrated, arguing that it was a waste of time for intellectuals to send blurry carbon copies of their poetry to one another in the face of such overwhelming force. But these admissions of defeat were a dead end that left public life in the hands of false regimes. The new question after 1968 for those who did not give up was not how to adapt to the system or how to change it according to its own principles, but how to live an authentic life in spite of it. As Jacek Kuroń put it later, "What is to be done when nothing can be done?"[9]

Leszek Kołakowski provided one of the earliest and most compelling answers to this question in an article entitled "Hope and Hopelessness" published in the Paris journal *Kultura* in 1971.[10] The situation is hopeless, Kołakowski argued, because every effort at democratization in the Leninist state appropriates some aspect of the total control the regime enjoys and will not relinquish. But precisely because the leaders have no intention of relinquishing their power, they will be forced to cover the conflicts of interest that will inevitably occur among them with a false ideological screen. This will continually undermine their claim to meaning and therefore their claim to eternal power. But true hope does not lie in the working out of this historical process, which is in itself a false claim of the regimes, but rather with the power of individuals to believe that hope is possible. Hope lies in living an ethical life, not in forming an opposition party, which would only create the same desire to impose "correct" solutions on society that was the failing of the communist regimes. As Adam Michnik put it later, "By using force to storm the existing Bastilles we shall unwittingly build new ones."[11]

Others in East Central Europe brought forward similar strategies in the hopeless situation. In 1967 Ludvík Vaculík had already enjoined his fellow Czechoslovaks to live "as if" they were free, and a decade later a group of Czechoslovak intellectuals formed Charter 77 to be a public, open grouping dedicated to the international norms of human rights. Charter 77 eschewed not only politics but any organizational structure at all. "Charter 77 is not an organization," the founding document stated. "It has no rules, permanent bodies, or formal membership. It embraces everyone who agrees with its ideas, participates in its work, and supports it."[12]

Václav Havel presented the most engaging and penetrating theory of the new style of antipolitics in his essay, "The Power of the Powerless." For Havel real life resided in the realm of the ethical, not in the realm of the political. "Under the orderly surface of the life of lies," he wrote, "there slumbers the hidden sphere of life in its real aims. . . . The singular, explosive, incalculable political power of living within the truth resides in the fact that living openly within the truth has an ally, invisible to be sure, but omnipresent: this hidden sphere."[13] This was the power of the powerless: to "live in truth." Only in this way could one experience the certainty that things make sense, and only in this way could one begin the hopeless project of creating a decent life.

The antipolitical project constituted an entirely new phase of opposition, and a devastating one. No longer accommodating and no longer using Marxist discourse, the antipoliticians simply told people to ignore the regime and to live an honest life. Communist governments knew how to compromise dissemblers and how to silence oppositionists who spoke their own language, but now they found themselves contesting a space they could not even enter. One Polish author, Konstanty Gebert, put it this way: "A small, portable barricade between me and silence, submission, humiliation, shame. Impregnable for tanks, uncircumventable. As long as I man it, there is, around me, a small area of freedom."[14]

If antipolitics was a more thoroughly grounded and ethically engaging evolution of the survival strategy of opposition, the next stage in the history of East European opposition came from a genuine social movement that adopted an antipolitical ethic. Solidarity transformed the ideal of living in truth, a strategy born of isolation and hopelessness, into a broad movement aiming to create an independent society in which all, or many, citizens could achieve a sense of freedom. By the 1970s every East European country, although some to greater degrees than others, possessed a population that was significantly alienated from its regime. But Solidarity was the only organization until 1989 that was able to tap that discontent in a politically forceful way. One reason was that the workers of Poland were the only ones in their region to devise their own mechanisms for self-activization. It seems clear from the work of Roman Laba that the idea of an independent trade union, along with the tactics of the occupation strike and the interfactory strike committee, was first invented by the coastal dock workers of Szczecin in 1971, and that these innovations, reinvented in 1980 by the workers of the Lenin Shipyard under Lech Wałęsa's leadership, were the creative basis of Solidarity.[15]

Nevertheless, Solidarity was in intent an antipolitical movement. Its goal was not to create a political party that would seize power and impose its views. That was the failure of the past. Solidarity simply sought autonomy to pursue goals of interest to itself—the freeing of the workers from the heavy hand of the party. Even in the strikes of 1970 and 1971 the force behind the strikes was not, as one striker put it, "the compulsion, the use of force so much, but the moral element, the element of honor."[16] The second paragraph of the Solidarity Program of 1981 reads in part: "What we had in mind were not only bread, butter, and sausage but also justice, democracy, truth, legality, human dignity, freedom of convictions, and the repair of the republic. . . . Thus the economic protest had also to be simultaneously a social protest, and the social protest had to be simultaneously a moral protest."[17] Solidarity's position was also the position of the intelligentsia. Jan Józef Lipski, one of the organizers of the Worker's Defense League (KOR), which was a group of intellectuals who came to the defense of strikers in 1976 and formed the intellectual core of the Solidarity movement, stated in his study of that organization that its mission was "to appeal above all to ethical values and to general moral standards rather than political attitudes," and after the Bydgoszcz crisis within Solidarity in 1981 Andrzej Gwiazda said that in his view Solidarity was primarily a "moral revolution."[18]

From the beginning the Solidarity movement was self-limiting, maintaining that it was simply a labor union and not a political opposition and remaining as true as it could to its antipolitical roots. Wałęsa and the others feared the intervention of the Soviet Union, and they hesitated to sacrifice labor union gains by forcing a political confrontation. But Solidarity, despite its ethic, could not remain an antipolitical movement. Politics is about power, and when a movement encompasses more than half the active workforce of a society and has the ability to call these workers out on strike, it has no choice but to enter the political arena.

The state recognized this better than Solidarity did. When it decided to act, it did so brutally and with determination. Many were sent to prison and others were badly beaten, lost their jobs, and experienced harrassment; but in comparison with 1945, 1956, and 1968, the imposition of a state of war, as martial law was called in Poland, represented another de-escalation of violence on the part of the Soviet Union, an amelioration of their response to heroic opposition. This time neither the Soviets nor their

Warsaw Pact partners invaded, and there was no foreign occupation. Instead, a local surrogate who was far from being a Stalinist subdued Solidarity. At the time martial law in Poland seemed yet another example of how impossible change was in Eastern Europe and how certain repression was in the face of genuine aspirations. But the balance had tipped in a decisive way. After World War II the problem facing East European societies was how to adjust to the Stalinist state; after 1981 in Poland the question became how the state was going to adjust to society. Instead of dissimulating, reforming, or opting out, oppositionists had found a positive democratic agenda of their own that would reshape the state in a new form altogether.

This is not the way it looked at the time. The depression among Polish oppositionists was as great in 1983 as it was among Czechs and Slovaks in 1970, but there was a difference. In Poland millions of people realized that opposition to the vanguard party and its state was possible for two reasons that were peculiar to the Polish experience. The first was the existence of a Polish Pope. In the late 1970s the activities of KOR, which included an impressive amount of underground publishing, mobilized many students and intellectuals and reached tens of thousands of workers, but it left most of society untouched. The elevation of Karol Wojtyła to Pope in 1978, and his visits to Poland in 1979 and 1983, galvanized millions of Poles and proved to them in a visceral way that another form of loyalty was possible. The second was underground Solidarity's success in keeping alive the flame of the movement that had attracted ten million members during its short existence. The breadth of underground publishing, radio broadcasts, videotape recording, and educational efforts during the years of martial law was amazing, so that by the late 1980s Solidarity was, in the minds of Poles, synonymous with democracy, unionism, pluralism—in short, of everything that the regime was not. The difficulties were great, the conflicts within the opposition epic, the discouragements profound, but the existence of a large public with the memory of an independent church and a free union provided a unique resource for the ultimate transformation of Poland. General Jaruzelski eventually recognized this. In 1986 he began a series of moves that led to the roundtable talks, the election of June 1989, and the installation of a Solidarity government.

The coming of Solidarity to power in September 1989 proved to be one of the most significant ingredients in the rush to revolution that stunned the world in the last three months of that year. During that period the declining violence of Soviet reaction to defiance in Eastern Europe reached its ultimate conclusion—the Soviet Union did not intervene at all. This was not a simple matter of leaving the troops in the barracks. Given the dynamics of Mikhail Gorbachev's policies, he no longer had the choice to intervene.

Gorbachev's new thinking had both a domestic and a foreign thrust. Coming to power at a moment when the Soviets realized they could not continue to compete technologically with the West in armaments, and understanding even more clearly that the Soviet Union could not sustain its great power status by simply being a Third World state with missiles, Gorbachev undertook to restructure the Soviet economy. In order to push the painful changes called for by *perestroika,* he understood that he needed to mobilize both the intellectuals and the population at large. *Glasnost* was the device he proposed to engage the intellectuals; and *demokratsiya,* which meant free but still limited elections, was the device he hoped would engage the people. Gorbachev seems to have believed that appreciative intellectuals and grateful people would rally to his support, thereby out-flanking the party stalwarts who stood in the way of change. In foreign affairs, Gorbachev decided to make a virtue out of the Soviet Union's inability to match the West technologically by signing the INF treaty (it abolished intermediate range nuclear missiles) and otherwise reducing arms, and to undermine the influence of the United States in Western Europe by pursuing the slogan "our common European home." Whereas Brezhnev believed in offering the West the vinegar of military strength, Gorbachev and Shevardnadze offered the honey of a secure Euro-Asian continent.

The dual thrust of Gorbachev's interrelated campaign constitutes the most daring and ambitious effort to transform the European geopolitical stage peacefully in the twentieth century. If the Soviet Union could become an economically viable country with moderately democratic forms, it might find itself accepted into Europe, thus enhancing its security by lessening American engagement. And if it could be accepted into Europe, it could find the credits and the technology that its economic transformation required.

Poland was best prepared to enter the space that Gorbachev opened up for Eastern Europe by 1988. Tested and well-known opposition leaders undergirded by a real social base produced a dramatic result. Only one other country in Eastern Europe was similarly prepared for change, and that was Hungary. There economic reforms begun in the 1960s and rein-forced by important innovations in the early 1980s led to a process of embourgeoisement that invigorated the economy and encouraged re-formers within the party. The emergence of a new stratum of private and semiprivate economic actors constituted a potential social basis for the creation of a political movement. But the small antipolitical opposition in Hungary did not base its claim to be heard on support from this new stratum. Whereas in Poland the organizational experience that made an independent society possible occurred in the workplace and involved the initiative of working people, in Hungary the organizational experience that produced a new oppositional leadership grew out of public demonstrations.

Starting in 1985 with small demonstrations against the Gabčikovo-Nagymaros dam project, the Hungarian democratic opposition was able by 1988 to draw thirty thousand people onto the streets of Budapest to demonstrate against the dam, another thirty thousand to protest

Ceauşescu's village reconstruction plan, and ten thousand for the May 15 anniversary of the Hungarian Revolution of 1848. The meetings' organizers, who were mainly Budapest intellectuals and student leaders, provided the nucleus of democratic leadership that emerged in that year.

The episodic generation of street demonstrations did not have the organizational thickness that interfactory strike committees gave to Solidarity, but they nevertheless proved to be a vital form of social mobilization. The demonstrations gave the organizers experience, a temporary constituency, and public visibility. They tapped the widespread alienation of those parts of the urban population who knew the regime was false but had never known what to do about it. But street demonstrations are not broadly based social movements. In Hungary they mobilized a very large proportion of the urban young and the more educated middle classes, but they were very thinly populated with workers and peasants. In fact "people power," as it has been called since Corazon Aquino's rise to power in the Philippines in 1986, is a fickle form of social mobilization whose democratic content depends greatly on the elites who call it forth. Whereas in Hungary, Czechoslovakia, and East Germany the leadership came from highly ethical antipolitical backgrounds and was able to focus the crowds on democratic change, in Serbia a narrow and self-interested leader was able to draw hundreds of thousands of people onto the streets in support of a racist ideology and in support of a vicious war. The key element in the revolutions of 1989, therefore, was not so much the mechanisms of street demonstrations that provided the impetus for change but the fact that they were fomented by a leadership committed to a democratic outcome. Of course the Hungarian opposition used nationalist arguments—their rallies were skillful evocations of Hungarian historical moments—but they did not evoke racial hatred or make irredentist claims, as Slobodan Milošević did in Serbia.

At the same time a Hungarian opposition leadership was discovering its voice on the streets of Budapest, a reform wing was achieving power in the Hungarian party. In Poland the most reform-minded group within the party were the three main generals who ran the country. It was they who forced the Polish party in January 1989 to accede to roundtable discussions. A reform wing had always existed in the Hungarian party, and when Gorbachev came to power it began to elbow the aging János Kádár aside, which it accomplished in 1988. Gorbachevian in their plans for Hungary, leaders like the economist Rezső Nyers undertook measures to push Hungary back into the world economy, such as a banking reform and an income tax, while political reformers like Imre Pozsgay, hoping to mobilize broader social support, entertained democratizing reforms.

The dramatic moment in which the street met the reforming party was the rally held in June 1989 on the occasion of the reburial of the remains of Imre Nagy. The climax of a year of change in the party and increasing pressure from rallies, this emotional occasion symbolized the restoration of Hungarian dignity. Everyone believed that the Hungarian Revolution of

1956 had not been a retrograde counterrevolutionary outburst, as the party had maintained for thirty years, but a nationwide effort to take Hungary back from the Russians and the Communists. With that historical memory now restored, the two parties—the oppositional leadership gathered together in a number of protopolitical parties on the one side and the reform Communists on the other—undertook their own roundtable discussions that led eventually to the creation of a new Hungarian democracy.

In the other countries of Eastern Europe, nothing similar to the mobilizations that took place in Poland and Hungary occurred. As of 1985 Romania and Bulgaria had no opposition at all, while in East Germany opposition consisted of only small groups of church-supported peace advocates. The only major opposition grouping in these four countries was Charter 77 in Czechoslovakia, and even it was pitifully small. In the other three countries the first glimmerings of a substantial political opposition occurred only in the late 1980s. In Bulgaria Ecoglasnost, an environmental group growing from protests in Ruse in 1987, enlisted members of the Bulgarian intelligentsia, and in Sofia a democratic discussion group entitled the Club for the Discussion of Perestroika and Glasnost emerged in 1988. In Czechoslovakia oppositionists specifically decided to become more political in 1988, while in East Germany the democratic opposition coalesced into a political organization only in September 1989. Romania did not even have such a group, although individuals made brave gestures and in 1989 a group of six senior party members dared to write Ceauşescu demanding changes.

All of these oppositional movements endorsed the antipolitical view that the party had destroyed normal life. Under "real existing socialism" it was impossible to live as a person in the twentieth century had a right to live, that is, as an autonomous individual making his or her own choices about religion, politics, art, sexual preference, or ethics. But because of repression, none of the oppositional movements in these four countries penetrated very far into society. They were all small, and—worse—they did not know how to translate their growing understanding that society at large despised their regimes into effective political action. No East European country outside of Poland had a self-activating workers' movement. Occasionally work stoppages occurred in each country, even quite violent ones such as the demonstrations in Braşov in 1987, but regimes had always been able to prevent the communication of whatever lessons these strikes offered to those who had not participated in them. Except in Poland and Hungary, therefore, very few non-Communists in Eastern Europe had experienced any autonomous participation in public life. Because of the lack of a workers' movement, the Polish experience offered inspiration more than a usable organizational example, although the roundtable proved to be a useful device everywhere.

East German collapse began when Hungary opened its borders in May 1989. During the August vacation season, thousands of East Germans crossed the border into Austria en route to their final destination, West Germany. In the early 1980s some scholars detected a distinct East German national feeling, a sense the regime assiduously nourished. But the GDR had always labored under the burden of being "the first workers' and peasants' state on German soil" rather than being simply Germany, as the Federal Republic of Germany styled itself. In other parts of Eastern Europe democracy was considered a desirable goal, but the concept was more or less empty, since most of society had very little direct contact with the West. In East Germany, however, constant contact between East and West made the notion of democracy real and specific: it meant life as lived in West Germany. The mass mobilization of hundreds of thousands of emigrants in 1989 was not the self-activated mobilization of the citizenry into a civil society so much as it reflected a yearning for a better life constructed from the images of West Germany. This is one of the reasons why the East German opposition, many of whom regretted the thirst for capitalism, were swept aside so easily by the organized parties of the West in the elections of 1990, even though it was they who had provided the impetus for the rallies that toppled the regime.

Elsewhere in the region the roots of alienation lay to the East, in Soviet domination and in the sense that one did not have control over one's own life. East Germans felt the same alienation, but their attention focused on the West rather than the East. Most East Germans did not want to follow their democratic opposition and to build their own pluralist society, thereby creating the conditions for reentering Europe—they wanted to enter the West directly. When the GDR joined West Germany it was left with no indigenously developed democratic tradition. The influx of West German political parties, economic administrators, and professors preempted the public space in eastern Germany, leaving little room for self-activated movements there. The East German revolution was a social revolution in the sense that broad masses of the population were involved, and it was democratic in the narrow sense that democratic forms now exist in a formerly totalitarian country. But mobilization did not occur on behalf of an indigenous democracy, and the new forms were imposed from the West, albeit on a willing population, without preparation, so that it will take time to fill them with real democratic content. Perhaps the form will create its content, but the resentments unification has created are immense and account in significant measure for the antisocial behavior that characterized public life in the five east German *Länder* in the years immediately following unification.

The democratic turn in Bulgaria was not a broad popular movement either, since it was initiated by party reformers who pushed Todor Zhivkov out in November 1989. In Bulgaria, the mobilization took place after the change, which makes it interesting that developments there give promise that an indigenous and stable democratic system will take root. Todor Zhivkov resigned the day after the Berlin Wall fell, but the transfer of power to the democratic opposition came only with the election of Zhelyu

Zhelev to a five-year term as president in January 1992. Historically, Bulgaria has never had the same sort of antagonistic relationship with Russia as have the other peoples of Eastern Europe. The Russian army liberated them in the nineteenth century, and even in 1945 the Red Army did not stay long enough in Bulgaria to create the antagonisms it did elsewhere. Many Bulgarians speak Russian, and all educated Bulgarians can read it. In addition, from the late 1970s, one of the three Bulgarian television channels was a Russian channel. Bulgarians could follow Gorbachev's progress toward reform more directly than could any other non-Soviets. By 1987 Russian newspapers regularly sold out, an unprecedented event in Eastern Europe, and Bulgarians had become obsessed with Gorbachev, whose program cast a very poor light on the phony reforms attempted by their own leaders.

Still, no truly popular movement emerged in Bulgaria until reformers in the party itself began the process by ousting Zhivkov. Once again the main experiential learning came in the street, the organization of which provided the United Democratic Forces, the coalition of the new democratic parties, with its first public education. The process of creating new parties in Bulgaria was not as artificial as it was in the former GDR, but after the first few months the process of mobilizing a democratic opposition proceeded mostly through the mechanisms of party and union organization, that is, not through grassroots self-activization but rather through the propagation of formally inclusive structures by elites. Even this innovation was so novel in Bulgaria, however, that more than 80 percent of the eligible voters turned out for the fall 1991 elections to the national assembly, a significantly greater proportion than in other East European countries.

The difference in Czechoslovakia's velvet revolution lay in the quality and availability of its leadership, not in the emergence of a civil society there. The Jakeš regime proved able to contain street demonstrations late in 1988 and early in 1989 and was able to argue that Czechoslovakia was in better economic condition than Poland. But after the Berlin Wall came down the pressure in Czechoslovakia escalated. When the government suppressed a student demonstration on November 19, allegedly killing a student, the crowds that gathered on the streets of Prague shouted "This is it" and "Now is the time." The opposition leadership available from Charter 77 emerged from the cellars and doorways to create Civic Forum, and the government collapsed. No civil society existed in Czechoslovakia, although the Catholic Church did provide a node of attraction for many, especially Slovaks, but the existence of a recognizable antipolitical leadership permitted a rapid transition to democratic forms to take place.

The leaders of Civic Forum saw themselves as guiding a movement of national regeneration, not a political party. They had worked together for years despite fundamental political differences, and they believed that the spirit of change that suffused the velvet revolution should carry over to the transition period. The leaders of Solidarity had much the same feeling.

The leaders of the Union of Democratic Forces (UDF) in Bulgaria, however, as well as those of the democratic opposition (DEMOS) in Slovenia, specifically created their organizations as coalitions of protoparties that agreed to come together for the purpose of contesting elections with a united front. Therefore, whereas Civic Forum and Solidarity enjoyed genuine popularity in the beginning, they both disintegrated and thereby undermined their self-actuating mythology. Nationalism and regionalism, which are not inherently democratic, emerged to threaten the ethical spirit of cooperation characteristic of the antipolitical opposition. In Bularia the UDF also split, but this did not undermine the fundamental goal of the main coalition, which achieved a plurality in the election of 1991 and took power. A similar contrast exists in Hungary between the Free Democrats, the leaders of which were the main oppositionists in the 1980s, and the Young Democrats, who consider themselves an electoral party.

Finally, Romania. The conditions surrounding the revolution there remain murky, with plot theories abounding, but the initial outburst in Timişoara, at least, seems to have been an authentically spontaneous moment. When authorities attempted to remove a Hungarian reform minister from his parish, an ethnically mixed group of parishioners and townspeople surrounded his house and prevented it. This led to rioting in Timişoara, an intervention by the army that led to a number of deaths, and the outbreak of spontaneous demonstrations in other parts of Romania. The most important of these was one convened by Nicolae Ceauşescu himself in Bucharest, during which the crowd turned against the dictator. In a series of violent and still confusing events a group of leaders emerged, formed a National Liberation Front, and took over the revolution.

The Romanian revolution remains, however, a revolution *manqué*. The brief outburst of violence that brought people into the streets for a few days quickly ended. New authorities presented themselves and established their position with very little or no preparation of their public. They had not been an antipolitical opposition, they did not emerge from a workers' movement, and they had not even organized substantial street demonstrations. Indeed, most of them were lifelong party members in good standing at the time of the revolution. This meant that not only were they unprepared by experience for the mechanisms of democratic opposition, but citizens too were unprepared by any but the briefest experience with self-activization. Romania's leadership consists entirely of refurbished Ceauşescu Communists who found it useful in the beginning to bring the equivalent of brown shirts to Bucharest to beat up opponents. The Democratic Convention is trying its best to encourage the growth of pluralist politics, but the prerevolutionary lack of any substantial opposition has made its task extremely difficult.

The history of opposition to communist regimes in Eastern Europe had two tendencies: a declining violence of intervention by the hegemon, and progression of opposition from simple dissimulation to a Marxist critique, thence to antipolitics, and finally to a reassertion of politics. One of the strengths of Communism was that for approximately one hundred years it occupied the high moral ground of opposing oppression. The loss of this high ground in Eastern Europe, especially after 1968, when a large proportion of the citizens came to recognize that the regimes were totally false and supported only by force, created a reservoir of discontent waiting to be tapped. The most thoroughgoing process of reasserting politics took place in Poland, where the creation of a civil society over a period of fifteen years by Solidarity created a social basis for Solidarity's electoral victory in 1989. Czechoslovakia did not develop such an independent society, but the antipolitical Charter 77 movement identified leaders with the moral stature to step in when a spark brought the people onto the streets. In Hungary, where a reformist party elaborated its own means of destruction, the creation of alternative forms of ownership prepared the way for Hungary's post–1989 economic success but did not create a social basis for Hungary's negotiated revolution. East Germany's case was unique, since its mobilization was based on the promise of unification. Neither Bulgaria nor Romania experienced much pre-1989 social mobilization.

Behind the collapses of the East European regimes lay their moral hollowness. No regime in the world can make good on all its promises. There is a cant and a bluster about modern politics that every thinking person recognizes. But in pluralist societies the level of distrust and resistance to this falsity remains on the surface, a matter for debate and conversation but not a deep humiliation, because whatever the realities might be, there is always a feeling that change is possible. In Eastern Europe distrust and resistance penetrated deeper because domination by the Soviet Union suppressed the sense of possibility. The events of 1968 confirmed that economic and political change was impossible and that public life would remain monochromatic. The result was a malaise that went beyond politics into the personality itself. "Even if people never speak of it," Václav Havel said in his open letter to Gustav Husák in 1975, "they have a very acute appreciation of the price they have paid for outward peace and quiet: the permanent humiliation of their human dignity."[19] Restoration of dignity is what the social movement Solidarity sought, what the antipoliticians of Charter 77 sought, and eventually what the street demonstrators in Leipzig and Prague sought too.

In most of the revolutions of 1989 the main social element was people power, crowds on the street. The demonstrations were contagious, first gathering momentum in Hungary, then in Leipzig and throughout East Germany, then in Sofia and Prague, and finally in Romania. But street demonstrations, whatever useful organizational lessons they teach their sponsors and whatever lingering memories of participation they may leave in the minds of their participants, are no substitute for the longer-lasting and more varied experiences of pluralism. They do not create habits of dialogue and compromise that are the lifeblood of democracy, however it is defined; they do not formulate programs or policies useful for transition;

and they do not create structures of interaction. The real social basis of the revolutions of 1989, therefore, did not come before the events but is currently in the process of creation, as each society attempts, within the boundaries of its own historical experience, the qualities of its leadership, and the intensity of its ethnic problems, to create a democratic society.

10

Lessons of the East European Revolutions of 1989

At the beginning of 1989, most specialists recognized the political and economic dangers facing the communist regimes of Eastern Europe. Foreign debt, loss of legitimacy, weakening of support from the Soviet Union, and the pathologies of central planning were only the most obvious and well-known deficiencies of the region. However, these weaknesses did not seem to be significantly undermining the ability of most East European regimes to maintain control over their societies. Even in Poland, where roundtable discussions led to the stunning elections of June 1989, negotiations had been stalled for four months and legalization of Solidarity faced serious opposition among party leaders. The other countries of Eastern Europe seemed no closer to real reform than they had been in 1970 or 1980. In the German Democratic Republic, Erich Honecker was trying to avoid *perestroika* by ignoring it. A smooth transition of power from Gustav Husák to Miloš Jakeš in Czechoslovakia had produced no change in the strict social controls that had been in force since 1968. Romania's dictator Nicolae Ceauşescu, despite having ruined the country's already weak economy, had little trouble crushing the few brave but isolated dissidents. And in Bulgaria, Todor Zhivkov continued to propagate purposefully ineffective reform proposals.

One year later, Eastern Europe was unrecognizable. Not only was Honecker replaced, but the Berlin Wall was down and what had been called East Germany was on a headlong path toward becoming eastern

From *Problems of Communism*, LX (Sept–Oct 1991), pp. 17–22.

Germany. Hitherto illegal Solidarity had formed a government in Poland and had begun to apply shock therapy to the country's moribund economy. Václav Havel, almost straight from prison, was president of Czechoslovakia, and Czechs were greeting historical videos of their former leaders with a devastating response: laughter. Ceauşescu was dead, and Zhivkov was gone. If one believes that a widespread change in government personnel, coupled with total rejection of the philosophy of the previous system, dynamic efforts to utterly transform an economic system, and the creation of a new social basis for rule constitute a revolution—whatever the level of violence—then 1989 was a year of revolution, or at least a year in which the necessary beginnings of a revolutionary transformation took place.

Now, only two years later, our memories of the revolutions of 1989 have become dominated by conventional wisdoms about the fate of Communism, the failures of centralized planning, and the virtues of Western policy, while the efforts of the East Europeans to right themselves, so to speak, increasingly are greeted with yawns. Before the thrilling moments of 1989 lose all their freshness, therefore, it seems appropriate to attempt a sketch of what lessons those dramatic and unanticipated events might hold for students of Eastern Europe.

There is little doubt what the greatest lesson of 1989 is: Communism failed. This failure was not a parochial event limited in its significance to Eastern Europe, to the resolution of the cold war, or to Western policy initiatives, but rather it was a moment of global importance in the family of most important events of the last few hundred years. These long-term phenomena do not have a satisfactory general name, even though we all know how fundamental they are. We can call them the industrial revolution, modernization, the great tranformation, the single transition, the emergence of capitalism, or the energy revolution, but whatever name they go by, the unprecedented economic and social changes they have brought about in just a few generations have forced every human society to find new ways of organizing itself. In my view, three basic genres of solutions to the fundamental challenges of the past few hundred years, all first broached in the eighteenth century, have been tried in the twentieth century: the antirationalist genre, the hyper-rationalist genre, and the pluralist genre.

By the first of these, I mean those movements of rage and rejection from the first half of the twentieth century that craved the power of the great transformation—the technology, the military strength, and the standard of living—but rejected the economic calculus of market capitalism and the political calculus of parliamentary democracy. Instead they espoused what Thomas Mann called "a highly technical romanticism," adopting Friedrich Schelling's view that the universe contains "a primal, non-rational force that can be grasped only by the intuitive power of men of imaginative genius."[1] Nazism and fascism repudiated the eighteenth-century bases of middle-class culture for what they believed were the superior principles of mass culture, rejecting reason for power, individuality for *sacro egoismo,* virtue for vainglory, transparency for obscurantism, constitutions for the *Führerprinzip,* humanitarianism for racial fanaticism, objectivity for prejudice, and, in the end, the guillotine for the gas chamber.

The hyper-rational genre, on the other hand, moved in the opposite direction by routinizing the application of reason into a rigid political formula. Stalinism is the reductio ad absurdum of Descartes's assertion that we humans can "render ourselves the masters and possessors of nature," a dream that found a confident echo as late as 1961 in the statement of the Hungarian author who wrote that socialism was on the verge of "the *final* maneuvers . . . for the *ultimate* conquest of the material world."[2] In the twentieth century, the agent for accomplishing this end was, first, the Leninist vanguard party sustained by its allegedly scientific (i.e., rational) understanding of human history, then, the vanguard of the vanguard, and, finally, the great leader, who imposed himself as the ultimate source of human rationality that was to transform the world.

The third genre is pluralism, which, in contrast to the other two genres, is not so much a system as it is an indeterminate set of political devices for structuring process. Because pluralist institutions are based on the prosaic observation that human beings are fallible and liable to contention, they are designed to prevent any "primal non-rational force" or "vanguard scientific party" from directing the affairs of society for very long. This does not mean they will not err, but it does mean that they will change—not immediately, not easily, and often with a great deal of pain and political struggle, not to mention cant and humbug. Pluralism's balanced and multilayered political configurations and processes, variety of ownership forms, diversity of associational possibilities, and openness of public discourse have proven flexible enough to match the protean surge of economic and social development that has characterized the past two hundred years.

Without going into any detail, it seems to me that the experience of the twentieth century has taught us something about political organization that we did not know when the century began; namely that both the antirationalist and the hyper-rationalist genres are incapable of successfully solving the problems posed by rapid social and economic change. The year 1945 revealed the bankruptcy of the antirationalist genre, and 1989 demonstrated the bankruptcy of the hyper-rationalist genre. The message of the twentieth century is not, as some observers would have us believe, that pluralism is the final answer to the challenges of modernity and that history is over. Indeed, the paradox of Francis Fukuyama's notorious recent claim is that the "end of history" has occurred because of the victory of the only genre within which history can occur. Both the antirational and hyper-rational systems sought final solutions and found stasis instead. The ease with which pluralism incorporated the information revolution of the past fifteen years, compared to the difficulties socialist systems had with computerization, is a recent instance of pluralism's ability to respond to the unexpected.

But this does not mean that pluralism has adequately solved the modern problematic. When we observe the misery in which not just most people in the Third World, but a large number of people in the First World, live, we understand that many issues remain on the agenda, not the least of which is the problem of finding a plausible framework for opposition to injustice in societies that are suffused with self-satisfaction. The great message of the twentieth century is not the positive accomplishments of pluralism, although there are many, but the negative message of the other two genres: we have not learned what works as surely as we have learned what does not work. Pluralism has its problems, but the other two genres are dead ends. History is not over, just the twentieth century.

The most important lesson of 1989—the reason that year can be added to the short list of dates that students will learn as the landmarks of the modern era (the others are 1789, 1848, and 1945)—is that the second of the twentieth century's two great experiments failed. "We have made one important contribution," Soviet reformer Yuriy Afanas'yev said, "We have taught the world what not to do."[3]

Unfortunately, however, that failure does not present the same kind of unique opportunity for positive reconstruction that the failure of the antirationalist genre in 1945 did. In 1945, Europe was devastated not only physically, but psychically as well. The optimism of the nineteenth century was not only long gone, but the entire civilization that had spawned the disasters of two great wars seemed spent. This was a calamity, but a calamity with a positive side. Moments like 1945 are rarely seen in history—a wiping of the slate, if not clean, then close to it. Of course, the wiping was done with blood—not something we would choose—but it was precisely the grotesque and bloody futility of the great thirty years' war from 1914 to 1945 that convinced men like Alcide de Gaspari, Konrad Adenauer, Henri Spaak, Robert Schuman, and Jean Monnet—in a way that conferences, speeches, articles, and diplomacy never could have—that the old obsessions could not form the basis of a stable Europe. They built their new community not on *sacro egoismo,* but on voluntary association and the politics of accommodation.

Surprisingly, given all the ink that has been spilled about the failure of the early dreams of creating a European political union, in a little more than thirty years this new community has become not just a strong economic unit, but also a vertical structure for containing the passions that burst the traditional European system of empires apart earlier in the century. Today, if you live in Florence, for example, you can be a booster of your neighborhood and city, a Tuscan patriot, a citizen of Italy, and an advocate for Europe, all at the same time, or singly on the appropriate occasions. One may fear that the increasingly inward-looking preoccupations of the European Community will eventually turn Europeans into multinational nationalists, but the absurdity today of Germans shooting

Frenchmen or Italians bombing Spaniards, both commonplaces of our fathers' time, is obvious.

One of the greatest costs of Stalinism in Eastern Europe was that it excluded the East Europeans from the unique caesura that made new solutions possible in the West. Eastern Europe had no *Stunde null.* In 1989, many East Europeans emerged from their own devastating era of grotesque obsessions with no sense of despair over the collapse of civilization, but rather harboring both enthusiastic expectations and a host of ideas from the past that had been suppressed for forty years. François Furet has said that the most striking thing about 1989 was the absence of new ideas.[4] East Europeans are exuberant at their release from lies, but some of them appear anxious to create their own deceptions; other East Europeans are convinced that their particular people has been unjustly treated for forty years, but stand ready to do the same to others; East European elites are frustrated by a long generation of humiliating compromises, but for that very reason find it difficult to practice the politics of accommodation. Some authors have suggested that these data show that the East Europeans have reverted to the mentality of the 1920s and 1930s, to that moment at which they distanced themselves from Europe sixty years ago. It would be more accurate to say that, having missed the unique window of opportunity that the bitter tonic of 1945 offered to others, they have not yet had the chance to learn firsthand the futility of some of the old ideas. This does not mean they will find it impossible to create the structures that will contain their passions, because, unlike in 1918, the existence of the European Union will exert a constant pressure on them to democratize and to marketize. But, feeling that their predicament is not their fault but rather something imposed on them from outside, being socialized to the ethic of a paternalistic state, and retaining a sense that some of the bad old ideas are not really all that bad, they will find it more difficult to take advantage of their particular caesura.

A third thought on the revolutions of 1989 came to me when I saw those first pictures of Soviet tanks being loaded on trains in Hungary for their journey east. For the past forty years, Western governments have quite naturally focused on the military and economic strengths of the Soviet Union and Eastern Europe. Enormous bureaucracies are devoted to understanding and countering every military threat, especially at the technological level, to evaluating relative strengths in the leadership elites, and to analyzing the details of trade, finance, and investment. In the world of power relationships that civil servants and politicians inhabit, only data of that sort carried the conviction of being realistic. The hard-nosed analyst was preoccupied with studying the implications of the "nth" party congress; charting CMEA statistics to estimate the none-too-good prospects of the next five-year plan; assessing the meaning, or even the existence, of the Sonnenfeldt Doctrine; or analyzing the disposition of Warsaw Pact forces.

The academic community was preoccupied with similar concerns.[5]

Studies in conflict resolution, security issues, economic analysis, policy options, and various kinds of modeling focused attention on those areas of public life that are quantifiable, that are consistent with social science theorizing, or that have policy implications. Fearing, with good reason, that they might be considered soft or unscientific, academics too gravitated toward "realistic" assessments of East European affairs.

The events of 1989 clearly show how limited a view this was, how, if you like, unrealistic. If anything is clear about the sudden swoon of the hollow East European regimes in November and December 1989 it is that those collapses were the result of moral rot at least as much as of economic or political failure. After the Soviet invasion of Czechoslovakia convinced East European intellectuals that it would be impossible to create socialism with a human face, they turned from debating how to reform the system to something much more devastating—total rejection of the regimes' thorough-going falsity. It was not economic deprivation that brought the people onto the streets in Eastern Europe in November and December 1989. They had suffered economic hardship for a long time, and in countries like Czechoslovakia and Bulgaria, times were not even that hard. It was their humiliation, their disgust with the falsity of their regimes, their desire for freedom. That is why when the fall took place it was the uncompromised advocates of living in truth—cultural leaders such as musicians, historians, philosophers, sociologists, and playwrights—who came to power. All the studies of strategic balances proved inappropriate and useless. The Soviet troops simply got on their trains and went home.

The events of 1989 have not only shown that strategic studies do not adequately take into account such intangibles as ethical values, religion, and national sentiment, but they have greatly altered the kind of analysis we need in the future. At least when we faced an adversary with massive nuclear forces who was competing with us in many parts of the world using an ideology that claimed ultimate victory, there were excellent justifications for concentrating on the strategic balance. After 1989, however, the situation changed. Without question, we must continue to study our policy options, to analyze the economic strengths and weaknesses of our competitors, and to monitor the status of military forces in the world. I do not propose giving up such vitally important work. But as confirmed by the surprising outcome of the Iraq war, which unleashed the unexpected outpouring of Kurdish fears, we need to spend more time on the intangibles.

For example, it was quite clear in 1975 what we meant by our support for human rights. We meant that oppressive regimes, particularly communist ones, should permit more freedom of speech, more free travel, and so forth. We purposefully avoided the obvious fact that human rights also means minority rights, since minority issues occur typically within already established states rather than among them and imply that established borders might have to change. Today minority rights, which in the Wilsonian era went under the name "self-determination of peoples," are a central issue of East European politics that threatens the stability of the region, and even the existence of two of the states. How are we to deal with the apparent incompatibility of our advocacy of self-determination (minority rights) and stable borders? At this point we do not know. But strategic studies alone will not provide a fully adequate answer, because the issues involved are cultural, religious, ethical, and emotional, as well as strategic.

Michael Howard has put this point well in his recent book, *The Lessons of History*. The real lessons of history, he says, are not so much about pride, folly, and stupidity, as about "people, often of masterful intelligence, trained usually in law or economics or perhaps political science, who have led their governments into disastrous miscalculations because they have no awareness whatever of the historical background, the cultural universe of the foreign societies with which they have to deal. It is an awareness for which no amount of strategic or economic analysis, no techniques of crisis management or conflict resolution . . . can provide a substitute."[6] Professor Howard wrote those words in 1981, but they constitute an elegant way of saying that 1989 made a good case for soft-nosed analysis.

My fourth suggestion is closely connected with this third point. The events of 1989–1991 showed how important leadership is.[7] For a historian like myself, there is little question that we all operate within a historically determined and relatively limited range of creative possibilities. But 1989 has shown once again, if it needed showing (and it apparently does), how important and unpredictable is the ability of individual leaders to stretch that range. Whatever the final assessment will be of Mikhail Gorbachev, whether he is the Alexander II of our day, beginning a reformer and ending a conservative, or the Kemal Atatürk who completely changed his nation's direction, there seems little doubt that his decision to let Eastern Europe go was original, unexpected (probably even by him), and difficult. If there was one thing we thought we knew for certain about the Soviet relationship with Eastern Europe, it was that whatever else might happen, the Soviet Union would never relinquish its special relationship with the region. To have done so was not a socioeconomic imperative or a structural necessity, although arguments in that vein are being made. The loss of Eastern Europe was the outcome of a policy conceived and introduced by a particular individual, representing a significant strain of Soviet thought, who saw, perhaps briefly, a possibility to revivify socialism while at the same time creating a constructive place in Europe for the Soviet Union that it had never had in the past. If we compare Gorbachev's rhetoric about autonomy of choice and his actions about arms reduction and withdrawal from Afghanistan with what we reasonably might have expected from his Brezhnevian rival from 1985, Viktor Grishin, we can grasp the power and originality of Gorbachev's leadership.

And Gorbachev was not the only original leader of 1989. It was not written that a German chancellor should have moved as single-mindedly as Helmut Kohl did toward unification, nor that he should have done so in such a relatively restrained and un-nationalistic way.

For the next few years, I think, leadership will be a key factor in determining whether the individual countries of Eastern Europe will be able to make rapid transitions in the aftermath of 1989. One of the striking differences between East Central Europe and Southeast Europe lies precisely in this sphere. Moderate men with great prestige now lead Poland and Czechoslovakia, and even in Hungary, József Antall at least understands parliamentary democracy. Unlike many of the politically inexperienced members of their societies, both among the public and among elites, these men recognize the fragility of their current position, know that it takes time to create the institutions of interest representation, and understand that democracy is a politics of accommodation. This is true even of Lech Wałęsa. Despite the fears many Poles express about the possibilities of a Piłsudskian resolution in Poland, one of the basic characteristics of Wałęsa's early career was his ability to seek out solutions rather than confrontations. During the Solidarity period, he probably spent as much time advising the workers not to strike as in any other single activity.

In Southeast Europe, by contrast, we have at least one and probably more inward-looking and radically selfish leaders in Yugoslavia, a self-appointed and none-too-legitimate government in Romania, and a scramble that has not yet produced any clear leadership in Bulgaria, although Zhelyu Zhelev's honesty and common sense have begun to have an impact. This contrast can only have a differential impact on the future development of these two regions. Unfortunately, we can only dream of the benefits for Yugoslavia if Serbia and Croatia had leaders of the stature of a Wałęsa or a Havel. Structural analysis is useful and important, particularly when it is turned to past events. But 1989 has reminded us that leaders can make original decisions and that they can shape forces. We hardly notice, however, because these decisions quickly enter the structure of our presuppositions, changing them radically but almost imperceptibly as we go along. The dramatic reversals in our perceptions of Soviet possibilities based on our assessment of Gorbachev—in 1987, still skeptical; by the Congress of People's Deputies in 1989, enthusiastic; by the bloody intervention in Lithuania in early 1991, gloomy; in mid-1991, after an apparent agreement with Yeltsin and the republics, more optimistic; and so forth—illustrate the point.

Although leadership was important, I do not want to give the impression that it was leadership alone that brought 1989 about, or that Gorbachev simply called the tune and the East Europeans danced. Centralized planning failed, regimes lost their moral underpinnings, and Soviet policy changed, but unless internal developments in Poland and Hungary had created a strong independent society in the first case and forces for reform both inside and outside the government in the second, Gorbachev's initiatives might have had far less effect. When we admire Poland and Hungary's primary role in getting the avalanche of 1989 started, we tend to forget that Honecker, Jakeš, Ceauşescu, and Zhivkov rejected *perestroika*. Had Jaruzelski turned out to be a Honecker, and Kádár a Husák, or, put another way, had the internal developments in Poland and Hungary been less pluralistic in the 1980s, then 1989 might not have been 1989 at all.

This point is linked with a much larger theme, the last one I want to raise. Many people understood the weaknesses of centrally planned systems very well. But the actual drama of 1989 was foreseen by no one. The final lesson of 1989 is to remind us of something that in an intellectual sense we already know: the near-term future is unpredictable. And yet laymen and specialists alike harbor a touching hope that we will find just that knowledgeable person who can tell us what the future holds. Anyone who has given a public talk about Eastern Europe or the Soviet Union recently can attest that the first question posed after the talk is certain to be "What is going to happen next?" One of the things that sustains the hope that someone will know the answer, I think, is that historians find it possible to trace causal strings though past events. We feel that the same kind of linear logic should permit us to extrapolate events into the future. But linearity only works backward. Forward, we live in a nonlinear world where surprises lurk. The historian's ability to trace causal strings is an illusion, a sleight of hand granted us by the fact that we already know, in a certain sense at least, what happened.

The future, by contrast, is subject to what chaos theory calls the butterfly effect, which is the modern version of that old tale of how the empire was lost for want of a nail. Its point is simply that no matter how large the amount of data we accumulate about complex systems, there always exist uncertainties that radically transform outcomes.[8] Václav Havel has a more personal way of putting the point: "We never know when some inconspicuous spark of knowledge, struck within range of the few brain cells, as it were, specially adapted for the organism's self-awareness, may suddenly light up the road for the whole of society, without society ever realizing, perhaps, how it came to see the road."[9] The year 1989 has turned the post–World War II era from current events into history, so that we now can talk about postwar Eastern Europe with a confidence that we did not have in 1985, let alone 1975 or 1960. We know what happened. But we must resist the temptation of turning our newfound confidence that we understand 1989 into a newfound memory that we understood it was coming, because that will only continue to sustain our already overdeveloped hunger to predict the unpredictable.

The basic lesson of 1989, then, is that the twentieth century is over, with both antirationalism and hyper-rationalism having proven to be political, economic, and moral dead ends. This has not provided humanity with any magic solutions for the future, but it has lessened the likelihood that we will repeat the grossest of errors. Unfortunately, however, the East Europeans will probably not profit as rapidly from their deliverance from hyper-rationalism in 1989 as Western Europe did from its deliverance from antirationalism in 1945, although the goal of entering Europe does provide them with powerful positive incentives. Another strength that East Europeans bring to their efforts to find a pathway back to Europe is that their revolutions of 1989 were moral events as well as political and economic ones. Insufficiently measured in strategic assessments during the cold-war period, moral and cultural factors will have to be taken into account to a greater extent in the postcommunist era. The quality of leadership in individual countries also will be an important ingredient in the differential development that appears to be the destiny of East Central Europe and Southeast Europe. Finally, 1989 offers a trenchant reminder that human affairs remain nonlinear. However persuasively we are able to trace the causes of events that have already happened, the only prediction we can make with complete confidence is that surprises await us.

11

Is It Possible to Be Optimistic
about Eastern Europe?

First of all, it is not possible to be optimistic about the former Yugoslavia. Careful observers of the situation in the summer of 1993 believed that stability in Bosnia would not be achieved soon, even if a partition plan could be agreed upon, and that Kosovë and possibly Macedonia remained gravely at risk. The feckless behavior of Europe and the United States had amply demonstrated to Serbia and to its increasingly criminal leadership that no substantial obstacles existed to creating a modern version of the Balkan federation under Serbian control that Prince Michael Obrenović had dreamed of in the nineteenth century. Slobodan Milošević envisions an Orthodox consortium stretching from Cyprus to Belgrade, and since Greece, his main ally, is a member of NATO and the European Union, there appeared every possibility that he, or even more vicious successors, would achieve that goal. The cost will have been enormous. Serbia and the regions it has ruined will not be economically or socially viable for a long time, nor will Croatia or Bosnia and Herzegovina. But Milošević's hand has not trembled.

Neither can one generate much optimism about Albania. When American negotiators first came to Tirana to discuss restoration of diplomatic relations in 1990, the Albanians informed them that Albania's true gross domestic product was about $500 million annually, or approximately the amount IBM spends monthly on research. Since that time, production has dropped perhaps 60 percent. The best Albania was hoping

From *Social Research,* 60:4 (Winter, 1993), pp. 685–704. Reprinted by permission.

for in 1993 was to lower its reliance on foreign charity for its supply of basic necessities to 50 percent.

These cases are clear. But for the rest of the former Soviet bloc in Eastern Europe (Poland, Hungary, the Czech Republic, Slovakia, Romania, and Bulgaria) and for Slovenia the picture is more mixed. This is the first time that these countries have been in a position to determine their own fate. After the European empires collapsed during World War I, East Europeans had only a very short time to try on their new democratic clothing before Hitler's Germany and then Stalin's Soviet Union overwhelmed them. Today, however, Germany is a democracy that treads relatively lightly in Eastern Europe, at least compared to imperial and Nazi Germany, and the Soviet Union has disintegrated into its constituent parts, each with is own weaknesses and problems. For the first time and perhaps only temporarily, and East Europeans are in a position to create the conditions for their own future.

It is easy to be pessimistic about their progress. Politics, for example, has proven much more vicious than anyone in the pre-1989 days thought possible. The ordinary squabbling characteristic of all open political systems is intensified in Eastern Europe today by the fact that almost everyone in those societies adapted themselves to the communist regimes. Only a few people were brutal torturers or totally corrupt, and they were matched by a few heroic antipoliticians on the other side. The overwhelming majority of people found ways to live under the oppressive regimes as people always do, thereby becoming complicit in the totalitarian project. Today they unite in what Jiřina Šiklová has called the solidarity of the culpable.[1] There have been some scandalous cases of accusation, such as the charges against Jan Kavan, and some absurd ones, in which Lech Wałęsa and Václav Havel found themselves accused of alleged contamination. But much more damaging are the accusations of collaboration and of supposed leftist tendencies that are made almost on a day to day basis. Often it is the people who sat on their hands during the communist era who make these accusations most vigorously, accusing precisely those persons who courageously spoke.[2] These accusations and the defenses offered by those accused are all the more bitter because however self-righteous they sound, all parties are aware deep in their hearts of their own compromises. Politics can be a nasty enterprise, but this element makes East European politics particularly wounding.

In the economic sphere the situation seems hardly better. The Council for Mutual Economic Assistance (CMEA) did not work particularly well, but at least it worked. When the Soviet market collapsed, East Germany entered the Deutschmark region, and the CMEA disintegrated, the weaknesses of the East European economies were exacerbated, and the drop in production accelerated. Unemployment hovers around the 12 percent level or higher throughout the region and much higher in particular pockets. Privatization of the great dinosaurs of socialist heavy industry is more or less stalled (except in the Czech Republic and in the former East

Germany) as each country debates, changes, and fails to implement its privatization plan. Social problems hidden under the old regime have burst to the surface. Health care is now understood to be substandard. Street crime has greatly increased. The usual suspects in a downturn—the aged, the retired, orphans, the small farmer—have been hurt, and their relative position seems to be deteriorating. Pollution has been revealed to be not only atrocious, but also too expensive to fix.

Then there is ethno-politics. The Yugoslav situation has brought this problem acutely to the public's attention, but it is an issue in almost every East European state. The problem of the Hungarian minorities in Transylvania, Ukraine, Slovakia, and Vojvodina is perhaps the most potentially disruptive of these situations; however, the Turkish minority in Bulgaria may yet cause problems, the former Sudeten Germans in Bavaria are raising claims on the Czechs, anti-Semitism has raised its head in Hungary, and everywhere the Roma (gypsies) are treated like the despised minority most East Europeans consider them to be.

This brief litany could be expanded and made perhaps more vivid. Almost any discussion with an East European intellectual will provide several good anecdotes showing how bad things are in his or her country, why there is so little hope for the future, and who is to blame (the speaker's political opponents usually come first in responsibility, with Germany and the United States next, closely trailed by the traditional ethnic enemy). A good deal of this is real. There is absolutely no question that the problems facing Eastern Europe are difficult, disruptive, and discouraging. But at least some of our understanding of these problems is a matter of perception. Pluralist democracy, even in the West, turns out to be considerably more messy close up than at a distance.

For most of the former Soviet bloc, democracy was an empty concept, the positive side of the negative icon of Yalta. If the West had abandoned Eastern Europe to division at Yalta (a faulty historical statement), then at least it seemed that the West could offer a positive vision of democracy. But democracy to most East Europeans was only a generalized ideal, not a real experience. It represented an aspiration, a hope for deliverance rather than any true grasp of how democracy works in practice. Just as East European emigrants early in the twentieth century believed that the streets of the West were paved with gold, during the cold war some east Europeans believed that democracy was characterized by the harmonious pursuit of common goals. This image was abetted by the success the antipoliticians had working together despite their political differences. When that enemy collapsed, it was a bitter disappointment to some of the Charter 77 activists and to many in Solidarity that they could no longer maintain their unity in the newly open circumstances.

The public too has been disappointed. They find that their new politicians are petty, venal, ambitious, bombastic, and machiavellian. What they do not realize is that in the West politicians are also petty, venal, ambitious, bombastic, and machiavellian, and they always have been. We have forgotten the turmoil and chaos that attended the creation of Western democracies. Gordon S. Wood, for example, noted the comment of William Maclay in August 1789 after entering the first Senate of the United States. "I came here," Maclay recorded in his diary, "expecting every man to act the part of a God. That the most delicate Honor, the most exalted Wisdom, the refined Generosity was to govern every Act and be seen in every deed." Instead he found only too often "rough and rude manners Glaring folly, and the basest selfishness apparent in almost every public Transaction." "Everything seemed to be coming apart [after the revolution]," says Wood. "Murder, suicide, theft, and mobbing became increasingly common responses to the burdens that liberty and expectation of gain were placing on people. . . . Fistfighting even broke out repeatedly in the Congress and the state legislatures."[3]

The difference between Eastern Europe and the developed democracies is that over a long period of time the Western democracies established a level of civility that does not yet exist in the East. Václav Havel has called for an increase in civility in public life without great success, but I do not refer here to the ordinary decency in public intercourse that he rightly seeks to enhance. Rather I mean that in the West the rules of parliamentary behavior, of governmental change, and of respect for the law are deeply ingrained in the public psyche. George Bush, no matter how bitterly he resented his loss to Bill Clinton, nevertheless shook the new president's hand, showed him around the White House, and retired to Houston. He did not, as one legislator did this year in the Serbian parliament, smack his adversary in the nose, nor did he, as did a Bulgarian politician, start a hunger strike to get the new president to resign. The inconceivability of such acts bespeaks a long experience with the intense emotion of political infighting and represents what I mean by civility in Western public life. We tend to forget that our democracies were not built in calm debate but rather in revolutions, civil wars, bitter political impasses, fierce personal confrontations, and periods of devastating disillusionment. When we see a similar process going on in Eastern Europe we should not be surprised. Human beings are a contentious lot.

There is a tendency to criticize the economic actualities through rose colored glasses as well. One of the most powerful, albeit discredited, explanatory ideas about capitalism is Max Weber's notion that there is a connection between the Protestant ethic and the capitalist spirit. This view is congenial to apologists for capitalism. The entrepreneur prospers because he works hard, saves his money, is a good steward, and is frugal—an edifying picture and not a false one. But the other side of the coin is true also. Pirates, slavetraders, and speculators who have been willing to subjugate the weak, work people to death, and cheat the public have also built the capitalist system. It is not remarkable that such people exist—they always have and always will. What is remarkable is that a workable mixed system of resource allocation that has created enormous wealth and has been at least as fair if not fairer than any preceding system has evolved anyway. Many in Eastern Europe have gotten a bad impression of the market system because of the remarkable swindles that were pulled off in the first few years of reform. In Poland, two enterprising men took advantage of the decrepit Polish banking system with a massive check kiting scheme that netted them something like $300 million in only a few months. Former members of the *nomenklatura* have arranged sweetheart deals for themselves that frustrate those not in a position to make such deals. Rival local mafias threaten fledgling entrepreneurs as soon as they start to make a profit. These things are not good, but are they unexpected? Not by anyone seasoned by observing such aspects of American capitalism as the operation of the Teamsters' Union, the practices of junk bond promoters, or the eagerness with which allegedly upstanding bankers swindled the savings and loan industry out of a half-trillion dollars.

So a certain amount of our discouragement with Eastern Europe is a matter of perception. In addition, some of the most positive happenings are little reported, such as the rash of genuinely cooperative ventures that have gotten under way in the past two or three years. Despite doubts in the Czech Republic, the four East Central European states put the so-called Visegrad Free Trade Agreement into effect on March 1, 1993. During the first phase of the agreement, which lasts until 1997, the object is to lower tariffs on "noncontroversial" items, which means 30 to 60 percent of the items in trade, depending on the state. During the second phase, border checks are to be phased out, and by the year 2001 the signatories have agreed to reach fully free trade and to have conformed their trade laws to those of the European Community. The Visegrad group is only one of several international initiatives that are modifying the East European tradition of looking primarily to the West or to the East. The Central European Initiative, for example, is attempting to bring together the old nations of the Habsburg realm (Slovenia, Croatia, Austria, the Czech Republic, Slovakia, Hungary, Poland, and others) into an organization devoted to better relations. The Black Sea Economic Cooperation Organization, which eleven Black Sea countries brought into being in 1992, is now launched and has started to organize a Black Sea Trade Development Bank. Local cooperative efforts are trying to bring subregions into closer cooperation as well, such as the Carpathian regional initiative and the efforts of Brandenburg and Gorzów, neighboring German and Polish districts, to create a Eurozone.

The reason that West Europeans are no longer threatening each other with war as they have done for centuries is that they found a way after World War II to construct an institutional structure within which they could interact. By pooling aspects of their sovereignty, they created a quasi-federal system: the European Union.[4] One of the characteristics of a federal system is that its constituent entities constantly struggle for position and power. These struggles are currently the primary concern of the West Europeans. For example, when the French and the Germans have differences, they do not consider war as they might have over the past several hundred years. They hasten to take their claims to one or another of the dozens of negotiating nodes that constitute the European Union or, alternatively, to GATT, to G-7, to CSCE, to WEU, or to some other appropriate entity. This enormously complex and confusing grid of international negotiating arenas did not come into being by some natural process of evolution, and its viability was not inevitable. The international institutional network that contains conflict among the West European states to a tolerable level of nonphysical violence was built by politicians and public figures more or less on purpose. This is why the cooperative initiatives under way in Eastern Europe are so important. They suggest that many East European leaders have realized that the institutional arrangements in which they act have to change. One can not know at this point what the outcome will be, but the fact that East Europeans are undertaking such projects is not unhopeful.

None of these ventures is a substitute for the main East European goal, which is to enter the European Union. All the East European countries have signed association agreements with the EU, and many Western leaders have said they support the entry of these countries, especially those in East Central Europe, into the community. The question, of course, is when. The East Europeans have been badgering the West to set a date of 1996 to begin serious negotiations that would get them into the community by 2000, but the community has demurred, citing the queue of other countries that have already applied, the necessity to regularize relations with EFTA, recession, and their own difficulties with monetary union. The difference between now and 1918 and 1945, however, is that everyone at least gives lip service to the necessity of reaching an agreement with Eastern Europe. This does not mean it will happen by the target date of 2000, but it does mean that the agenda is clear: find a way to maintain and enhance European unity or face a deteriorating situation the possible outcome of which the crisis in Yugoslavia makes frighteningly clear.

Even in the economic sphere the news is not entirely bad. Poland especially seems to be moving in the right direction. In the first three months of 1993, for example, Polish industrial production increased 5.4 percent and productivity went up about 10 percent. Poland's trade deficit was increasing and real wages continued to drop slowly, but gross domestic product turned upward in 1992 for the first time since the massive drop of 1990 and 1991. More encouraging than these figures was the constructive attitude that many of the most successful businessmen in Poland have adopted. Some places seem stuck in the old ethic of unproductive and self-defeating parochialism. Complaints and delays by the old-fashioned local leadership in Łódź, for example, finally scared off Sarah Lee, which was considering modernizing a textile plant in that dreary city of obsolete textile mills. But in Wrocław, another working-class city, a young and aggressive mayor has been able to invigorate the region to the extent that Wrocław can now boast of Poland's second international airport. In the confectionery industry, after Pepsico bought Wedel, the famous sweets maker, its successful and cash-rich Polish competitor decided to sell out to Suchard, the Swiss giant, in order to stay competitive. The shipyard in Szczecin has a substantial list of backorders, and Fiat has finalized its huge investment in FSM. As one business analyst put it, the best Polish managers are now starting "to think strategically."[5] On a smaller scale, old Polish hands driving through the Polish countryside are surprised to see spruced up shops appearing in formerly forlorn villages. In the same countryside, local governments, while inexperienced and often floundering, also are slowly taking responsibility for their own affairs. Zakopane, for instance, is now completing its long-awaited natural gas pipeline, which should greatly lessen the pollution in that resort area.

These positive signs are not readily visible to those who follow only Warsaw politics, which have been perhaps the most chaotic in Eastern Europe. But even here the situation is not as bad as the recent fall of the Suchocka government makes it appear. Suchocka's regime had some real successes, which in the end Lech Wałęsa supported. It passed the so-called "small constitution" reform, a mass privatization bill, and a new electoral law, all of which Wałęsa signed. It dealt firmly but fairly with a serious rash of strikes, and it struggled valiantly to keep the Polish budget in line. Wałęsa helped in the latter case by vetoing a bill to increase pensions that the legislature passed against the government's wishes.

Perhaps the most significant change in Polish public life, however, has been the policy of reconciliation the government has pursued toward its neighbors and toward Jews. Often overlooked has been Poland's rapprochement with Germany. By means of three agreements, one guaranteeing the Oder-Neisse border, the second a treaty of friendship, and the third an agreement concerning refugees and asylum seekers, the Poles and the Germans have achieved an extraordinarily close relationship. Explicitly recalling the Élysée agreement between Adenauer and DeGaulle in 1963, both the Germans and the Poles have expressed regret for terrible events of the past and promised to do better. Such an admission is the first and most basic step toward reconciliation. "There can be no reconciliation without remembrance," German President Richard von Weizsäcker correctly stated in 1985.[6] Starting from that base, the two neighbors have guaranteed each other's minority rights and initiated fruitful steps on their borders that promise better economic development and better relations in the future. In March 1993 Prime Minister Suchocka, while visiting the former German lands that now constitute western Poland, praised the German work ethic, suggested that German success should evoke admiration, not hostility, and said that ethnic diversity was one of the region's major assets. These statements about a former bitter enemy suggest the distance toward pluralist stability that Poland has traveled in a short time.

Poland has replicated its policy of rapproachement with Germany with all its neighbors, including Belarus, Ukraine, and even Russia. Russian recognition of Soviet culpability in the Katyn massacre has removed an enormous symbolic barrier to better Russo-Polish relations. Now that

Russian investigative reporters themselves are revealing more and more of the details about Katyn, the Poles seem almost no longer to care about it. This is a perfect example of the power of remembrance and reconciliation working to pacify a formerly bitter relationship.[7]

Despite its bad reputation with American and European Jews, Poland is also doing a good job of combating anti-Semitism. Although there are very few Jews left in Poland today and while polls show that many Poles retain some anti-Semitic views, the nation's leaders have explicitly, publicly, and repeatedly rejected anti-Semitism in contrast to the attitudes of the prewar period and some periods during the postwar era. Despite a nasty argument about a Carmelite nunnery that for a while existed at Auschwitz, at the fiftieth anniversary of the Warsaw Ghetto uprising of 1943 Cardinal Józef Glemp said a mass for Jews and Christians as believers in the God of Abraham, Isaac, and Jacob, and offered words of contrition for "all the crimes against the Jewish people, the crimes of the holocaust, all forms of anti-Semitism and intolerance, all hatred and violence."[8] These words reflect the explicit hostility that the Polish establishment increasingly shows toward anti-Semitism and the serious efforts now underway to investigate and clarify the historical relationship between Poles and Jews.

The issue of anti-Semitism and exclusiveness has raised its head in Hungary, where a fraction of the ruling Hungarian Democratic Forum under the leadership of Sándor Csurka has staked out a conservative and nationalist program it calls the Hungarian Path. Budapest contains the largest concentration of Jews (perhaps 80,000) left in Eastern Europe. But despite Csurka's anti-Semitic statements, the level of practical discrimination—in housing, jobs, and education—is very low. The leading party of the government coalition, the Hungarian Democratic Forum, waffled for some while over Csurka, but expelled him and his closest allies in the early summer of 1993, perhaps thinking ahead to the elections scheduled for 1994.[9] Many elements of Hungarian society outside the MDF have condemned his ideas. The Jewish community also has proven responsive to Hungarian sensibilities. When the head rabbi of Budapest made offensive statements about Hungarian culture, the Jewish organization of Hungary abolished his post. The rooting out of prejudice is a constant process; Csurka is not going to go away. But in comparison to the pre–World War II period, when creeping anti-Semitic legislation gradually ghettoized Hungarian Jews, the current situation is rather healthy.

The most explosive ethnic problem in Hungary is not Jews (or Roma, who are badly treated) but Hungarians living across the borders in the Vojvodina, Romania, Ukraine, and Slovakia. Much of the heat in Hungarian foreign relations is expended on the condition of Hungarians in Transylvania, where the reactionary and chauvinist mayor of Cluj is doing his best to Romanize Transylvania at the expense of its Hungarian minority. The situation in Serbia, where Hungarian army recruits are systematically abused, for example, is critical, and the protocommunist government of Slovakia has been unable to make reasonable concessions to its

Hungarian minority. But even in this sphere the picture is not altogether gloomy. As part of the agreement that brought it membership in the Council of Europe, Slovakia now permits birth registration of non-Slovak names and is pledged to improve minority relations. The Hungarian parliament adopted a model law on minorities and ratified a treaty of friendship with Ukraine that grants wide-ranging reciprocal cultural autonomy for each country's ethnic minority. Despite opposition from Csurka's group, which objected to the renunciation of border changes, the Ukrainian treaty sailed through the Hungarian parliament in the spring of 1993 with a substantial majority. Now a joint commission is working on creating the textbooks that will be used in the Hungarian schools in the Transcarpathian oblast of Ukraine, introducing Ukrainian classes in two Hungarian high schools, and setting up special trading zones between the two countries.

Industrial production has not yet turned up in Hungary, although it is expected to do so in 1993. Neither have the Hungarians privatized very many of their large concerns. On the other hand, many of those same firms have been restructured, Hungary has received close to $5 billion in foreign investment, and small privatization has turned Budapest into a booming European city.

The most successful privatization took place in Czechoslovakia. It is still too early to tell whether the voucher scheme will prove an economic success, since a new bankruptcy law came into effect in the summer of 1993 and it remains to be seen what impact this law will have on the large number of technically insolvent Czech firms. However, from the psychological point of view the voucher plan was a great success. For Poles, privatization is a distant process, the concern of the state. The still-to-be-implemented mass privatization plan in Poland, although it contains a voucher component, is seen as a scheme put forward by politicians for arcane reasons. In the Czech Republic, however, almost every active citizen registered his or her vouchers, and today almost every Czech knows how his or her vouchers are invested. Active trading in shares has commenced on the Prague stock exchange. The goal of Prime Minister Václav Klaus in pushing the voucher plan was to create a value for businesses of unknown worth, to promote efficiency through the profit motive, and to create a capital market—all of which seems to be happening. A key additional goal was to change the way Czechs think. By involving people directly in the process of change, Klaus sought to teach them the concepts of private ownership, profit, and risk taking in a direct and palpable way. This huge project of social engineering, which cuts to the core of the attitudinal structures that are appropriate for market democracies, so far seems to be having the desired effect. Czechs see privatization as something that affects them, not as an exercise conducted by faraway politicians.

The psychological boost provided by the voucher plan in the former Czechoslovakia has been balanced negatively by the split of Slovakia from the Czech Republic, an event that has cast a pall over both peoples. The divorce may have been velvet, but it has left everyone with a vague sadness. In the Czech Republic this sadness is tempered by economic good news. The unemployment rate is only 3 percent, although the operation of the new bankruptcy law may cause that figure to rise; foreign reserves have risen rapidly to about $1 billion, and the government estimates a positive growth rate in 1993. The picture in Slovakia is much less positive, although the plummet of Vladimir Mečiar's popularity in mid-1993 indicates that his tried-and-true methods of always blaming someone else may not be working as well as they formerly did. Slovak production will probably fall slightly this year, its foreign reserves are running low, and it is having trouble attracting foreign investment. Mečiar has not been particularly forthcoming to the sizeable Hungarian minority in Slovakia, but relations with Hungary are proceeding in a formal and not entirely hostile manner. Both sides, for example, have agreed to submit the Gabčikovo-Nagymaros dam controversy to the International Court of Justice.

The two states of Southeastern Europe, Romania and Bulgaria, have not moved as rapidly toward marketization. In Romania, political democracy has not matured as rapidly as one might wish despite the certification by international observers that the most recent national elections in 1992 were fair. Earlier in 1992, local elections for mayors throughout the country showed a refreshing pluralism. A hard-core and nasty nationalist was elected in Cluj with support of the army, but an equally hard-core, if considerably less nasty, reformer was elected in Timişoara. Galaţi may have elected a Communist, but Suceava brought in an environmentalist. In Bucharest the victor was a member of the Democratic Convention, the main opposition coalition.

Romania's privatization plan is to divide the ownership of about 6,000 firms between two agencies, 30 percent to the Private Ownership Fund and 70 percent to the State Ownership Fund. Citizens have received "pre-voucher packages" that they will eventually be able to invest in the Private Ownership Fund. At an unstated future time shares in the Private Ownership Fund can be exchanged for shares in 1600 small enterprises through worker buyout schemes. This plan is a far cry from Klaus's voucher plan. By maximizing the state's participation, the Romanians will be perpetuating many of the inefficiencies of the past. Small privatization has not gone very far in Romania either, although the Romanian government has restored over 9 million hectares of land to some 4 million persons as part of a massive restitution plan. One sector of private enterprise has been very strong in Romania: print media. Hundreds of privately owned and printed magazines, journals, and newspapers have survived over the past three years; some of them, like *România Mare,* are scurrilous racist rags, but not a small number of them, like the newspaper *Cotideanul,* are very sophisticated. Even the old *Scinteia* has been reborn as an independent newspaper (*Adevarul*) that criticizes the government as often as not.

The Bulgarian economy has been hit hard by two massive jolts: the Iraq war and the blockade of rump Yugoslovia. With or without those jolts, however, the Bulgarians have been moving slowly on large privatization. According to official statistics, by mid-1993 only about 15 percent of the Bulgarian gross domestic product was being produced by the private sector (compared to 50 percent in Poland and 40 percent in Hungary). Visitors question whether this figure is entirely accurate, since the streets of Bulgaria's main cities have blossomed with apparently flourishing small shops. Under the leadership of Prime Minister Lyuben Berov, an economist and a former Communist, the Bulgarians have not been able to keep their budget within the 5 percent deficit guidelines of the International Monetary Fund, and PlanEcon does not see growth in the gross domestic product until 1994. Unemployment is about 16 percent and foreign investment has been almost nil ($50 million).

In two ways, however, the Bulgarians are doing quite well. They managed to survive both a communist government and an inept one and followed these with a government of technicians. This government was made possible by the political skill of the predominantly Turkish party, which has proven, along with President Zhelyu Zhelev, to be the most constructive force in Bulgarian politics. Economic problems may still create ethnic conflicts between Bulgarians and Turks, but on balance those relations are better than could be expected. This is reflected in Bulgaria's very friendly relations with Turkey, especially between the Bulgarian and Turkish military. In another surprise, considering Bulgaria's historic interest in Macedonia, the Bulgarians have been very circumspect on the Macedonian question. Bulgaria was among the first to formally recognize the Republic of Macedonia, although it did not recognize the existence of a Macedonian people, and the government has taken strong measures against pan-Macedonian movements that have cropped up.

On balance, then, what is happening in Eastern Europe? The first step in thinking about the region is to drop the concept "transition." Since 1989 literally hundreds of conferences have been held to discuss aspects of "Transition in Eastern Europe," but the very term indicates a false perception of the processes under way there. The term "transition" has a teleological edge to it and implies that there will come a moment in the future when Eastern Europe will have arrived at some state of completion—the transition "to" something will be over. This is not only not true, but it also betrays a static understanding of what constitutes market-style democracy. Pluralism, as Jean Monnet once said about the European Community, is not a thing; it is a process. This is precisely the mistake that the communist regimes made. They assumed that it was possible "to build socialism," and that once they had done so their job would be over. But pluralism is not a system as such. It is a set of voluntarily entered into institutional arrangements that permit societies to govern themselves while at the same time remaining open to change. The European Community and the multitude of international organizations that surround and interpenetrate it constitute the best continental example of such a set of pluralist institutions.

In societies with totalitarian aspirations, real problems are not publicly discussed. The illusion is sustained that the regime is fully in control, that it understands what needs to be done, and that it is taking the proper measures. But since this is entirely false, the real dysfunctions that all living societies experience are not only not ameliorated, they are not even addressed. Thus, while the surface of public life appears smooth, the structure of the society becomes riddled with weaknesses. The hollow brittleness of the East European regimes that collapsed in 1989 amply demonstrated the devastating consequences of the long-term suppression of public confrontation with serious issues.

In a pluralist society, by contrast, all problems are open for discussion. Pluralist societies, therefore, are contentious and frustrating places. Public life often seems to be nothing more than a simultaneous tumult of controversies, most of which go on interminably; the weaknesses of a pluralist society are all too visible. But having been brought up to the surface, problems are also available for solution, or at least amelioration (since it would be fatuous to say that we ever fully "solve" questions of human relations and power). When, after interminable wrangling, posturing, and compromise, a solution is finally achieved, that particular element of social interaction drops unseen below the surface, where it becomes a structural strength of society; it is no longer discussed, but it creates stability. In other words, the strengths of the totalitarian system are obvious but superficial and its weaknesses are unseen but structural. In a pluralist society the situation is just the reverse.

The underlying problem in Eastern Europe since 1989 has been that *all* its many problems have suddenly emerged from below ground to become matters of public debate. Unlike in the West, which has had several generations of experience in how to cope with pluralism and has, therefore, evolved some basic norms of civility, even the most fundamental issues have been thrown open to discussion in Eastern Europe. East Europeans are writing new constitutions, redesigning their economies, coping with unemployment, reworking their public health, trying to understand new relationships between the central government and local governments, renovating education, and confronting many other issues that in major ways have long been regulated in the West. When one couples the sheer magnitude of the problems with the special shrillness in politics that comes from a compromised past, the wonder is not that the East Europeans are having difficulties, but that they are accomplishing anything at all.

Eastern Europe is not in transition. To one degree or another, every East European political system today is already pluralist. What we are seeing now is what we are going to get in the future—bitter political struggles, nasty elections, corruption, and fights over the media. This is what it means to have a normal political life. But what we need to remember is that these unseemly battles are over real issues, not contrived or phony ones as the rhetoric surrounding them makes them seem. As decisions are painfully reached on how to deal with specific problems, those decisions will drop beneath the surface of public consciousness and shape the structure of the new societies. This is already happening as decisions are made on abortion, education, local government, banking, catalytic converters, and hundreds of other matters. Some solutions will be areawide, abetted by the new initiatives in regional cooperation, and some will be national. But there is no reason why Romania has to be like Poland, any more than there is some reason why Ireland has to be like Sweden. Each of these countries in its own way has committed itself to the pluralist adventure and has embarked on it. If we compare this commitment and the progress made in what is, historically speaking, a very short time with the situation these societies faced in 1983, or 1953, or 1933, is it not possible to be at least a little bit optimistic about Eastern Europe?

Notes

Part I Introduction

1. John Lampe, "Imperial Borderlands or Capitalist Periphery? Redefining Balkan Backwardness, 1520–1914," in Daniel Chirot, ed., *The Origins of Backwardness in Eastern Europe* (Berkeley: University of California Press, 1989), pp. 177–209.

2. Diana Mishkova, "Modernization and Political Elites in the Balkans before the First World War," *East European Politics and Societies,* **9:1** (Winter, 1995), pp. 63–89.

3. Peter Sugar, "Railroad Construction and the Development of the Balkan Village in the Last Quarter of the Nineteenth Century," in Ralph Melville and Hans-Jürgen Schröder, eds., *Der Berliner Kongress von 1878* (Wiesbaden, Germany: Franz Steiner Verlag, 1982), pp. 485–98; Michael Palairet, "Farming in Serbia c.1830–1875: Impoverishment without the Help of Malthus," paper presented at the Woodrow Wilson Center, April 1987; Among Palairet's many debunking papers, see "Land, Labour, and Industrial Progress in Bulgaria and Serbia before 1914," *Journal of European Economic History,* 12 (1983), pp. 163–85.

4. In this way it is a reverse mirror of Marxism, which had very little national content.

1

1. Poland, Hungary, the Czech Republic, Slovakia, Romania, Bulgaria, Greece, Albania, Slovenia, Croatia, Bosnia and Herzegovina, Yugoslavia, and Macedonia.

2. Alan W. Palmer, *The Lands Between: A History of East Central Europe since the Congress of Vienna* (London: Weidenfeld & Nicolson, 1970).

3. For a recent explication of a similar argument see Dennis Hupchick, *Culture and History in Eastern Europe* (New York: St. Martin's Press, 1994). See also Jenö Szűcs, "The Three Historical Regions of Europe," *Acta Historica Academiae Scientiarum Hungaricae,* **29/2–4** (1983), pp. 131–84.

4. Peter Sugar, *Southeastern Europe under Ottoman Rule, 1354–1804* (Seattle: University of Washington Press, 1977), p. 3.

5. Hungarian, or Magyar, is a Finno-Ugric language. Although the only other European languages related to it are Finnish and Estonian, Hungarian is approximately as close to those languages as English is to Persian (both the latter are Indo-European languages).

6. Keith Feiling, *The Life of Neville Chamberlain* (London: Macmillan, 1946), p. 372.

2

1. See, e.g., Kemal Karpat, *Inquiry into the Social Foundations of Nationalism in the Ottoman State: From Social Estates to Classes, from Millets to Nations,* Center of International Studies Research Monograph No. 39, Woodrow Wilson School of Public and International Affairs (Princeton, 1973); and "Ottoman Relations with the Balkan Nations after 1683," *Balkanistica* **1** (1974), pp. 7–55.

2. Hans Kohn, *The Idea of Nationalism* (New York: Collier Books, 1967), and many other titles. Anthony D. Smith, *Theories of Nationalism* (New York: Harper and Row, 1971) gives the best typology of nationalism; see my review in *World Politics* **31** (1978), pp. 150–60.

3. Most structural models derive from the work of Karl Marx. Exceptions are Ernest Gellner, *Thought and Change* (Chicago: University of Chicago Press, 1963), and Karl Deutsch, *Nationalism and Social Communication,* 2nd ed. (Cambridge, Mass.: The M.I.T. Press, 1966).

4. "Reflections on the History of European State-Making," in Charles Tilly, ed., *The Formation of National States in Western Europe* (Princeton: Princeton University Press, 1975), p. 34. Besides the other articles in this collection, see Joseph R. Strayer, *On the Medieval Origins of the Modern State* (Princeton: Princeton University Press, 1970).

5. Robert Folz, *The Concept of Empire in Western Europe from the Fifth to the Fourteenth Century* (New York: Harper and Row, 1969), p. 145.

6. For the appearance of the new idea that the present did not have to copy the past, see Donald R. Kelley, *Foundations of Modern Historical Scholarship* (New York: Columbia University Press, 1970), and David O. McNeil, *Guillaume Budé and Humanism in the Reign of Francis I* (Geneva: Droz, 1975).

7. Theodore K. Rabb, *The Struggle for Stability in Early Modern Europe* (New York: Oxford University Press, 1975), p. 78.

8. See F. H. Hinsley, *Power and the Pursuit of Peace: Theory and Practice in the History of Relations between States* (Cambridge: Cambridge University Press, 1967), pp. 153–85.

9. See, e.g., Reinhard Bendix, *King or People: Power and the Mandate to Rule* (Berkeley: University of California Press, 1978), p. 7. The literature on this topic is enormous.

10. See Donald W. Hanson, *From Kingdom to Commonwealth: The Development of Civic Consciousness in English Political Thought* (Cambridge, Mass.: Harvard

University Press, 1970), and John G. A. Pocock, *The Ancient Constitution and the Feudal Law* (Cambridge: Cambridge University Press, 1957).

11. Two books that stress the importance of separating the idea of the nation from that of the ruler are Michael Walzer, ed., *Regicide and Revolution: Speeches at the Trial of Louis XVI* (Cambridge: Cambridge University Press, 1974), and, in a different context, Michael Cherniavsky, *Tsar and People: Studies in Russian Myths* (New York: Random House, 1969).

12. A superbly detailed account of how the hierarchical system worked in Europe is Jerome Blum, *The End of the Old Order in Rural Europe* (Princeton: Princeton University Press, 1978).

13. Peter Gay, *The Enlightenment, An Interpretation: The Freedom of Science* (New York: Norton, 1977), p. 399.

14. Louis went on, "To me alone belongs the legislative power. . . . The whole public order derives from me; I am its supreme guardian. My people exist only in their union with me; the rights and interests of the nation . . . are necessarily united with mine and rest only in my hands" (Kohn, *The Idea of Nationalism*, p. 220). For Louis XV, see Gay, *The Enlightenment*, p. 477.

15. One of the best studies of nation-formation in nineteenth-century Europe is Eugen Weber, *Peasants into Frenchmen: The Modernization of Rural France* (Stanford: Stanford University Press, 1976).

16. For further comments on this point, see my article, "Church and Class in Early Balkan Nationalism," *East European Quarterly* **13** (1979), pp. 259–70.

17. Halil Inalcik, "The Nature of Traditional Society: Turkey," in Robert E. Ward and Dankwart A. Rustow, eds., *Political Modernization in Japan and Turkey* (Princeton: Princeton University Press, 1964), p. 43. See also Peter F. Sugar, *Southeastern Europe under Ottoman Rule, 1354–1804* (Seattle: University of Washington Press, 1977), pp. 33, 272.

18. Michael Cook, ed., *A History of the Ottoman Empire to 1730* (Cambridge: Cambridge University Press, 1976), p. 7.

19. Inalicik, "The Nature of Traditional Society," p. 53. For the development of the *âyan* class, see Halil Inalcik, "Centralization and Decentralization in Ottoman Administration," in Thomas Naff and Roger Owen, eds., *Studies in Eighteenth Century Islamic History* (Carbondale: Southern Illinois University Press, 1977), pp. 27–52.

20. Peter Sugar stresses the importance of the practical political training local notables received (*Southeastern Europe under Ottoman Rule*, p. 221). Barbara Jelavich suggests that precisely this localization of politics for about fifty years around the turn of the nineteenth century created appropriate conditions for Balkan nation-formation; see "The Ottoman State and the Study of the Diplomatic History of South East Europe," paper presented at the International Conference on Turkish Studies, Madison, Wisconsin, May 26, 1979.

21. Fernand Braudel, *The Mediterranean and the Mediterranean World in the Age of Phillip II*, 2 vols. (New York: Harper Torchbook, 1975).

22. One of the clearest and most succinct descriptions of the meaning of the term "market" is found in Robert Heilbroner, *The Making of Economic Society*, 4th ed. (Englewood Cliffs, N.J.: Prentice-Hall, 1978), esp. pp. 14–77.

23. See Eric J. Hobsbawm, *Industry and Empire: An Economic History of Britain since 1750* (London: Weidenfeld and Nicolson, 1968), pp. 20–39.

24. This view, which derives from Marx, has been put forward most fully by

Immanuel Wallerstein, *The Modern World System* (New York: Academic Press, 1974).

25. Halil Inalcik, "The Ottoman Economic Mind and Aspects of the Ottoman Economy," in M. A. Cook, ed., *Studies in the Economic History of the Middle East* (London: Oxford University Press, 1970), pp. 207–18.

26. Halil Inalcik, "Capital Formation in the Ottoman Empire," *The Journal of Economic History* **29** (1969), pp. 97–140.

27. The importance of secure property rights to economic development cannot be overestimated. See, e.g., Douglass C. North and Robert Paul Thomas, *The Rise of the Western World* (Cambridge: Cambridge University Press, 1973).

28. Omer Lufti Barkan, "The Price Revolution of the Sixteenth Century: A Turning Point in the Economic History of the Near East," *International Journal of Middle East Studies* **6** (1975): 3–28.

29. Inalcik, "Capital Formation in the Ottoman Empire." See also Karl Max Kortepeter, *Ottoman Imperialism during the Reformation: Europe and the Caucasus* (New York: New York University Press, 1972), pp. 3–13, and Charles Issawi, "The Ottoman Empire in the European Economy, 1600–1914," in Kemal Karpat, ed., *The Ottoman State and Its Place in World History* (Leiden: Brill, 1974), pp. 107–17.

30. Thomas Naff, "Ottoman Diplomatic Relations with Europe in the Eighteenth Century: Patterns and Trends," in Thomas Naff and Roger Owen, *Studies in Eighteenth Century Islamic History* (Carbondale, Ill.: Southern Illinois University Press, 1977), pp. 91, 98–99.

31. Alfred C. Wood, *A History of the Levant Company* (New York: Barnes and Noble, 1964, orig. pub. 1935).

32. Paul Masson, *Histoire du Commerce Français dans le Levant au XVIIIe Siécle* (New York: Burt Franklin, 1967, orig. pub. Paris, 1896), pp. 431–32.

33. Issawi, "The Ottoman Empire in the European Economy," p. 114.

34. Robert Mantran, "Transportation du commerce dans l'Empire Ottoman au dix-huitième siècle," in Naff and Owen, *Studies in Islamic History*, pp. 217–35; Masson, *Histoire du Commerce Français*, p. 429; Issawi, "The Ottoman Empire in the European Economy," pp. 114–15.

35. Niyazi Berkes, *The Development of Secularism in Turkey* (Montreal: McGill University Press, 1964), pp. 23–85.

36. Immanuel Wallerstein, Hale Decdeli, and Resat Kasaba, "The Incorporation of the Ottoman Empire into the World Economy," paper delivered at the International Conference of Turkish Studies, Madison, Wisconsin, May 25–27, 1979, pp. 13–14. One great advantage of Wallerstein's approach is that it interprets historical change not as development, or modernization, or progress upward from backwardness, but rather as simply changes in the functions served by the systems involved. In this sense, although perhaps not in other senses, it is not normative: it does not define some places as "backward" and therefore inferior and others as "developed" and therefore superior.

37. Roderic H. Davison, *Reform in the Ottoman Empire, 1856–1876* (Princeton: Princeton University Press, 1963), p. 54.

38. Fred L. Israel, *Major Peace Treaties of Modern History, 1648–1967* (New York: Chelsea House, 1967), p. 948. I would like to thank Barbara Jelavich for bringing this point to my attention.

39. See the articles in the Winter, 1975, issue of the *East European Quarterly*. The authors could not find any impact of the Enlightenment on the Balkans.

40. Gale Stokes, "The Absence of Nationalism in Serbian Politics before 1840," *Canadian Review of Studies in Nationalism* 4 (1976), pp. 83–85.

41. Tom Nairn, *The Break-up of Britain; Crisis and Neo-Nationalism* (London: NLB, 1977), p. 340.

42. Guenther Roth and Claus Wittich, eds., *Economy and Society*, vol. 2 (New York: Bedminster Press, 1968), p. 928.

43. Kenneth Jowitt, "The Sociocultural Bases of National Dependency in Peasant Countries," in Kenneth Jowitt, ed., *Social Change in Romania, 1860–1940* (Berkeley: Institute of International Studies, University of California at Berkeley, 1978), p. 17. My argument has been heavily influenced by Jowitt.

44. For a discussion of the consequences of dissynchronization between value systems and environment, see Chalmers Johnson, *Revolutionary Change* (Boston: Little, Brown and Company, 1966).

3

1. Ernest Gellner, *Thought and Change* (Chicago: University of Chicago, 1965).

2. Barrington Moore, Jr., *Social Origins of Dictatorship and Democracy* (Boston: Beacon Press, 1966), p. xii. For a discussion of Moore's work, see Dennis Smith, *Barrington Moore, Jr.: A Critical Appraisal* (Armonk, N.Y.: M.E. Sharpe, Inc., 1983).

3. Iván T. Berend and György Ránki, *Economic Development in East Central Europe in the Nineteenth and Twentieth Centuries* (New York: Columbia University Press, 1974), p. 32; and Arnošt Klíma, "Agrarian Class Structure and Economic Development in Pre-Industrial Bohemia," *Past and Present* 35 (1979), p. 53. The work of Berend and Ránki provides a solid basis for the discussion of economic development in East Central Europe. See especially Berend and Ránki, *East Central Europe in the Nineteenth and Twentieth Centuries* (Budapest: Akademiai Kaido, 1977); Berend and Ránki, *The European Periphery and Industrialization, 1780–1914* (Cambridge: Cambridge University Press, 1982); and Berend and Ránki, "Underdevelopment in Europe in the Context of East-West Relations in the Nineteenth Century," *Studia historica* 158 (1980).

4. Joseph Rothschild, *East Central Europe between the Two World Wars* (Seattle: University of Washington Press, 1974), p. 134.

5. For a discussion of Czech democracy after World War I, see Gregory F. Campbell, "Empty Pedestal?" with comments by Gale Stokes, "Czech National Democracy: A First Approximation," and by Roman Szporluk, "War by Other Means," followed by Campbell's reply, "Politicized Ethnicity–A Reply," *Slavic Review* 44 (1985), pp. 1–29.

6. Arnošt Klíma, "Industrial Development in Bohemia, 1648–1781," *Past and Present* 11 (1957), p. 87.

7. Franklin Mendels, "Proto-Industrialization: The First Phase of the Industrialization Process," *Journal of Economic History* 32 (March, 1972), pp. 241–61; Eckart Schremmer, "Proto-Industrialization: A Step toward Industrialization?" *The Journal of European Economic History* 10 (1981), pp. 653–70; Herbert Matis, "Proto-Industrialization, Industrialization, and Economic Development in the

Habsburg Monarchy: A Commentary," *East Central Europe* 7 (1980), pp. 269–78; John Komlos, "Thoughts on the Transition from Proto-Industrialization to Modern Industrialization in Bohemia, 1795–1830," *East Central Europe* 7 (1980), pp. 198–206; and Richard L. Rudolph, "The Pattern of Austrian Growth from the Eighteenth to the Early Twentieth Century," *Austrian History Yearbook* 11 (1975), pp. 11–20. For the implications of Mendels's idea, see Charles Tilly and Richard Tilly, "Agenda for European Economic History," *Journal of Economic History,* 31 (1979), pp. 184–98.

    8. Arnošt Klíma, "Mercantilism in the Habsburg Monarchy—With Special Reference to the Bohemian Lands," *Historica* 11 (1965), pp. 95–119.

    9. Arnošt Klíma, "English Merchant Capital in Bohemia in the Eighteenth Century," *Economic History Review* 12 (1959), pp. 23–48.

    10. Richard L. Rudolph, "Social Structure and the Beginning of Austrian Economic Growth," *East Central Europe* 7 (1980), p. 217. See also Jan Zak, "The Role of Aristocratic Entrepreneurship in the Industrial Development of the Czech Lands, 1750–1850," in Miloslav Rechcigl, Jr., ed., *Czechoslovakia Past and Present,* Vol. II (The Hague and Paris: Mouton, 1968); and Arnošt Klíma, "The Role of Rural Domestic Industry in Bohemia in the Eighteenth Century," *Economic History Review* 27 (1974), pp. 48–56.

    11. For an excellent discussion of how the standard of living was dropping in mid-century due to populaton growth, see John Komlos, "Stature and Nutrition in the Habsburg Monarchy: The Standard of Living and Economic Development in the Eighteenth Century," *American Historical Review* 90 (1985), pp. 1149–61. Komlos suggests that by the 1750s the Habsburgs "perceived this decline in the standard of living and adopted countermeasures," p. 1157.

    12. Franz A. J. Szabo, "Kaunitz and the Reforms of the Co-Regency of Maria Theresa and Joseph II, 1765–1780," Ph.D. diss., University of Alberta, 1976, pp. 270–91. Maria Theresa decided free trade was to be "the fundamental rule and unyielding guiding principle," but Joseph II remained a mercantilist and protectionist who believed in self-sufficiency.

    13. Arnošt Klíma, "Agrarian Class Structure," and William E. Wright, *Serf, Seigneur, and Sovereign: Agrarian Reform in Eighteenth-Century Bohemia* (Minneapolis: University of Minnesota Press, 1966), pp. 50–52.

    14. Arnošt Klíma, "Industrial Development in Bohemia," p. 97.

    15. Helen P. Liebel, "Free Trade and Protectionism under Maria Theresa and Joseph II," *Canadian Journal of History* 14 (1979), p. 366.

    16. Wright, *Serf, Seigneur, and Sovereign,* p. 75.

    17. David F. Good, "Modern Economic Growth in the Habsburg Monarchy," *East Central Europe* 7 (1980), p. 252.

    18. Berend and Ránki, *Economic Development,* pp. 112, 114, and 116.

    19. Berend and Ránki, *Economic Development,* pp. 115–18. See also Arnošt Klíma, "The Beginning of the Machine-Building Industry in the Czech Lands in the First Half of the Nineteenth Century," *Journal of European Economic History* 4 (1975), pp. 49–78; Arnošt Klíma, "Industrial Growth and Entrepreneurship in the Early Stages of Industrialization in the Czech Lands," *The Journal of European Economic History* 6 (1977), pp. 549–74; and Jaroslav Purš, "The Industrial Revolution in the Czech Lands," *Historica* 2 (1960), pp. 183–272.

    20. Bruce M. Garver, *The Young Czech Party 1874–1901 and the Emergence of a Multi-Party System* (New York and New Haven: Yale University Press, 1978), p. 37.

21. Garver, *Young Czech Party,* p. 91.

22. Garver, *Young Czech Party,* p. 96.

23. Zigismund P. Pach, "The Transylvanian Route of Levantine Trade at the Turn of the Fifteenth and Sixteenth Centuries," *Studia historica* **138** (1980). See also Ingomar Bog, ed., *Der Aussenhandel Ostmitteleuropas, 1450–1650* (Vienna and Cologne: Böhlau Verlag, 1971).

24. Zigismund P. Pach, "The Role of East-Central Europe in International Trade (XVI–XVII Centuries)," *Etudes historiques,* vol. 4 (Budapest, 1970), pp. 217–264; Zigismund P. Pach, "The Shifting of International Trade Routes in the 15th and 16th Centuries," *Acta historica* **14** (1968), pp. 287–321; Laszlo Makkai, "Der Ungarische Viehhandel, 1550–1650," in Bog, *Aussenhandel Ostmitteleuropas,* pp. 483–506; and Krystyna Kuklinska, "Central European Towns and the Factors of Economic Growth in the Transition from Stagnation to Expansion between the Seventeenth and Eighteenth Centuries," *The Journal of European Economic History* **11** (1982), pp. 105–15.

25. Peter F. Sugar, *Southeastern Europe under Ottoman Rule, 1354–1804* (Seattle: University of Washington Press, 1977), p. 20; and Istvan N. Kiss, "Die demographische und wirtschaftliche Lage in Ungarn vom 16.–18. Jahrhundert," *Südost-Forschungen* **42** (1983), p. 211.

26. Kiss, "Die demographische und wirtschaftliche Lage," p. 219. See also I. Kallay, "Management of Big Estates in Hungary between 1711 and 1848," *Studia historica* **146** (1980).

27. Andrew C. Janos, *The Politics of Backwardness in Hungary, 1826–1945* (Princeton: Princeton University Press, 1982), p. 36.

28. John Komlos, *The Habsburg Monarchy as a Customs Union* (Princeton: Princeton University Press, 1983), p. 54.

29. Komlos, *Habsburg Monarchy as Customs Union,* p. 52.

30. Komlos, *Habsburg Monarchy as Customs Union,* pp. 25–51; John Komlos, "Economic Growth and Industrialization in Hungary, 1830–1913," *The Journal of European Economic History* **10** (1981), pp. 5–46; and John Komlos, "Austro-Hungarian Agricultural Development, 1827–1877," *Journal of European Economic History* **8** (1979), pp. 37–60. For a discussion of some of the issues involved see Richard L. Rudolph, "The New versus the Old in Austrian Economic History," *Austrian History Yearbook* **11** (1975), pp. 35–43; David F. Good, "Issues in the Study of Habsburg Economic Development," *East Central Europe* **6** (1979), pp. 47–62; and David F. Good, "Stagnation and Take-off in Austria, 1873–1913," *Economic History Review* **27** (1974), pp. 72–87; Richard L. Rudolph, *Banking and Industrialization in Austria-Hungary* (Cambridge: Cambridge University Press, 1976); and Thomas Huertas, *Economic Growth and Economic Policy in a Multi-National Setting, 1841–1865* (New York: Arno Press, 1977).

31. William O. McCagg, *Jewish Nobles and Geniuses in Modern Hungary* (Boulder: East European Quarterly Press, 1972), p. 31. See also Joseph Held, ed., *The Modernization of Agriculture: Rural Transformation in Hungary* (Boulder: East European Quarterly Press, 1980).

32. Scott M. Eddie, "The Changing Pattern of Landownership in Hungary, 1867–1914," *The Economic History Review* **20** (1967), p. 294.

33. Brian R. Mitchell, *European Historical Statistics* (New York: Columbia University Press, 1976), p. 355.

34. Janos, *Politics of Backwardness,* p. 151. See also Nachum Gross, "Die Stellung der Habsburgermonarchie in der Weltwirtschaft," in *Die Habsburger-*

monarchie, Vol. 1, *Die wirtschaftliche Entwicklung,* Alois Brusatti, ed. (Vienna: Verlag der österreichischen Akademie der Wissenschaften, 1973), pp. 1–28; and Peter Sugar, "Railroad Construction and the Development of the Balkan Village in the Last Quarter of the Nineteenth century," in Ralph Melville and Hans-Jürgen Schröder, eds., *Der Berliner Kongress von 1878* (Wiesbaden, Germany: Franz Steiner Verlag, 1982), pp. 485–498.

35. Janos, *Politics of Backwardness,* p. 65. See also Peter I. Hidas, *The Metamorphosis of a Social Class in Hungary during the Reign of Young Franz Josef* (Boulder: East European Quarterly Press, 1977). For a discussion of this period, see Thomas Spira, "Problems of Magyar National Development under Francis I (1772–1835)," *Südost-Forschungen* **30** (1970), pp. 51–73.

36. McCagg, *Jewish Nobles and Geniuses,* p. 27. See also his earlier articles, William O. McCagg, "Ennoblement in Dualistic Hungary," *East European Quarterly* **V** (1971), pp. 13–26; and William O. McCagg, "Hungary's 'Feudalized' Bourgeoisie," *Journal of Modern History* **44** (1972), pp. 65–78.

37. Hanák has pointed out that this produced a cognitive dissonance not only among the Jews, but among the Hungarian upper class as well, which wished to emphasize the Christian nature of the Hungarian state. See Péter Hanák, "Problems of Jewish Assimilation in Austria-Hungary in the Nineteenth and Twentieth Centuries," in Pat Thane, Geoffrey Crossick, and Roderick Floud, eds., *The Power of the Past: Essays for Eric Hobsbawm* (Cambridge: Cambridge University Press, 1984), pp. 235–50.

38. George Barany, "'Magyar Jew' or: 'Jewish Magyar'? (To the Question of Jewish Assimilation in Hungary)," *Canadian-American Slavic Studies* **8** (1974), pp. 1–44. For several good articles on Jews in Eastern Europe, including a reprint of Barany, see Bela Vago and George L. Mosse, eds., *Jews and non-Jews in Eastern Europe, 1918–1945* (New York: John Wiley & Sons, 1974).

39. Scott M. Eddie, "Agricultural Production and Output per Worker in Hungary, 1870–1913," *Journal of Economic History* **23** (1968), pp. 220–21; Antal Voros, "The Age of Preparation: Hungarian Agrarian Conditions between 1848–1914," in Held, *Modernization of Agriculture,* pp. 21–129; Iván T. Berend, and György Ránki, *Hungary: A Century of Economic Development* (New York: Barnes and Noble, 1974), p. 40–48; and Eddie, "Landownership in Hungary," pp. 293–310. The area covered by farms over about 15,000 acres (10,000 holds) increased from 1867 to 1914 from about 2.25 million hectares to almost 5.5 million (i.e., from 8.5 percent of the area of landed property to 19.4 percent). This distribution did not differ markedly from that in Germany or Romania. Eddie, "Landownership in Hungary," pp. 302–33.

40. Hungarian historians hold that 1848 constituted a bourgeois revolution because noblemen lost their privileges and henceforth had to pay taxes, while all citizens received the right to own land.

41. Austrian industrialists cooperated with Hungarian grain growers and millers to sell textiles in Hungary and wheat in Austria. Eddie calls this the "marriage of textiles and wheat." Scott M. Eddie, "The Terms and Patterns of Hungarian Foreign Trade, 1882–1913," *Journal of Economic History* **37** (1977), p. 351. See also Scott M. Eddie, "Farmer's Response to Price in Large-Estate Agriculture: Hungary and Germany, 1870–1913," *Economic History Review* **24** (1971), pp. 571–88; and Scott M. Eddie, "The Terms of Trade as a Tax on Agriculture: Hungary's Trade with Austria, 1883–1913," *Journal of Economic History* **32** (1972), pp. 298–315.

42. Daniel Chirot, *Social Change in a Peripheral Society* (New York: Academic Press, 1976), p. 147; and Eddy, "Land Ownership," p. 296.

43. Andrew C. Janos, "Modernization and Decay in Historical Perspective: The Case of Romania," in Kenneth Jowitt, ed., *Social Change in Romania 1860–1940* (Berkeley: Institute of International Studies, University of California, 1978), p. 82.

44. Henry Roberts, *Rumania: Political Problems of an Agrarian State* (New Haven: Yale University Press, 1951).

45. Chirot, *Social Change.*

46. David Mitrany, *The Land and the Peasant in Rumania* (London: Oxford University Press, 1930), pp. 7–21.

47. The Hungarian gentry had a similar sense of inferiority and need. Janos, *Politics of Backwardness,* pp. 44–50.

48. John R. Lampe and Marvin R. Jackson, *Balkan Economic History 1550–1950: From Imperial Borderlands to Developing Nations* (Bloomington, Ind.: Indiana University Press, 1982), pp. 84, 93.

49. Janos, "Modernization and Decay," p. 90.

50. R. W. Seton-Watson, *History of the Roumanians* (Cambridge: Cambridge University Press, 1934), p. 354. For a thorough discussion of Romanian industrialization see David Turnock, "The Industrial Development of Romania from the Unification of the Principalities to the Second World War," in Francis W. Carter, ed., *An Historical Geography of the Balkans* (London: Academic Press, 1977).

51. Carol Iancu, *Les juifs en Roumanie (1866–1919): De l'exclusion à l'émancipation* (Aix-en-Provence: Editions de l'Université de Provence, 1978), p. 143.

52. Nicholas Spulber, *The State and Economic Development in Eastern Europe* (New York: Random House, 1966), p. 144.

53. Simon Dubnov, *History of the Jews,* 4th rev. ed., Vol. 5 (New York: Yoseloff, 1973), p. 630.

54. Spulber, *State and Economic Development,* pp. 100–2.

55. Dubnov, *History of the Jews,* p. 633.

56. Moore, *Dictatorship and Democracy,* p. 420.

57. Eugen Weber, "Romania," in Hans Rogger and Eugen Weber, eds., *The European Right* (Berkeley: University of California Press, 1965).

58. Moore, *Dictatorship and Democracy,* p. 420.

59. Moore, *Dictatorship and Democracy,* p. 438.

60. Deena R. Sadat, "Rumeli Ayanlari: The Eighteenth Century," *Journal of Modern History* **44** (1972), pp. 346–63.

61. For an excellent discussion of Bulgarian history from the achievement of independence to World War I, see Richard J. Crampton, *Bulgaria 1878–1918: A History* (Boulder: East European Quarterly Press, 1983).

62. For an excellent discussion of the deleterious effect of railroad building on the Balkan peasantry, see Sugar, "Railroad Construction."

63. *Statistički godišnjak kraljevine Srbije, Knj. 12. 1907–08* (Belgrade, 1913), pp. 277–90.

64. *Situation financière et économique du Royaume de Serbie* (Belgrade, 1910), pp. 14–5.

65. On the fundamental nature of this process, see Ernest Gellner, *Nations and Nationalism* (Ithaca, N.Y.: Cornell University Press, 1983).

66. Charles Jelavich, "Serbian Textbooks: Toward Greater Serbia or Yugoslavia?" *Slavic Review* **42** (1984), p. 618.

67. Andrija Radenić has chronicled the lessening intensity of peasant disturbances in Serbia as urban parties took leadership of the peasantry over from the patriarchal leaders of the first half of the nineteenth century. A summary statement of his view is Andrija Radenić, "Karakteristične crte buntovnih pokreta," in his *Iz istorije Srbije i Vojvodine, 1834–1914* (Novi Sad and Belgrade: Matica srpska and Istorijski institut, 1973), pp. 359–66.

68. Michael Palairet, "Fiscal Pressure and Peasant Impoverishment in Serbia before World War I," *The Journal of Economic History* **39** (1979), pp. 719–740.

69. Crampton, *Bulgaria,* pp. 30–31.

70. Crampton, *Bulgaria,* pp. 158–60.

71. The 1879–1883 index of 100 became 154 by 1889–1892. Crampton, *Bulgaria,* pp. 149, 208.

72. Joseph Rothschild, *The Communist Party of Bulgaria: Origins and Development, 1883–1936* (New York: Columbia University Press, 1959).

73. John D. Bell, *Peasants in Power: Alexander Stamboliski and the Bulgarian Agrarian National Union, 1899–1923* (Princeton: Princeton University Press, 1977), p. 55.

74. Michael Palairet, "Land, Labour, and Industrial Progress in Bulgaria and Serbia before 1914," *The Journal of European Economic History* **12** (1983), p. 177; and Crampton, *Bulgaria,* p. 358.

75. Dimitrije Djordjević, "Foreign Influences on Nineteenth-Century Balkan Constitutions," in Kot K. Shangriladze and Erica W. Townsend, eds., *Papers for the Fifth Congress of Southeast European Studies* (Columbus, Ohio: Slavica, 1985), pp. 72–102.

76. Theda Skocpol, *States and Social Revolutions: a Comparative Analysis of France, Russia, and China* (Cambridge: Cambridge University Press, 1979). For an expansion of Skocpol's emphasis on the state into the sphere of ideas see William H. Sewell, Jr., "Ideologies and Social Revolutions: Reflections on the French Case," *Journal of Modern History* 57 (1985), pp. 57–85.

77. Eric Hobsbawm, *The Age of Revolution, 1789–1848* (London: Weidenfeld and Nicolson, Ltd., 1962) p. xv.

78. Kenneth Jowitt, "The Sociocultural Bases of National Dependency in Peasant Countries," in Kenneth Jowitt, ed., *Social Change in Romania, 1860–1940* (Berkeley: Institute of International Studies, University of California, 1978), pp. 1–30.

Part II Introduction

1. For further development of this point, see Gale Stokes, *Politics as Development: The Emergence of Political Parties in Nineteenth Century Serbia* (Durham, N.C.: Duke University Press, 1990).

4

1. David Booth, "Marxism and Development Sociology: Interpreting the Impasse," *World Development,* **13** (1985), p. 762.

2. The notion that ideas have their own autonomous impact seems to be making a comeback. See, for example, William H. Sewell, Jr., "Ideologies and Social Revolutions: Reflections on the French Case," *Journal of Modern History* **57** (1985), pp. 57–85.

3. For a fuller discussion of the implications of this point see Gale Stokes, "Dependency and Nation Formation in Southeast Europe," *International Journal of Turkish Studies* 1 (1980), pp. 54–67. The most thorough discussion of economic dependency in Eastern Europe is Iván T. Berend and György Ránki, *The European Periphery and Industrialization, 1780–1914* (Cambridge: Cambridge University Press, 1982). The best individual study is Andrew C. Janos, *The Politics of Backwardness in Hungary, 1825–1945* (Princeton: Princeton University Press, 1982). On the inapplicability of dependency theory to the economic history of Southeast Europe, see John R. Lampe, "Imperial Borderlands or Capitalist Periphery? Redefining Balkan Backwardness, 1520–1914," in Daniel Chirot, ed., *The Origins of Backwardness in Eastern Europe: Economics and Politics from the Middle Ages until the Early Twentieth Century* (Berkeley: University of California Press, 1989), pp. 177–209.

4. Dimitri Obolensky *The Byzantine Commonwealth: Eastern Europe 500–1453* (London 1971).

5. *Državopis Srbije,* **16** (1889), pp. XX–XXII.

6. Michael Palairet, "Farming in Serbia c. 1830–1875: Impoverishment without the Help of Malthus," presented at the Woodrow Wilson International Center for Scholars, March 1989, p. 22.

7. Sergije Dimitrjjević, *Socijalistički radnički pokret u Srbiji 1870–1918* (Belgrade 1982), pp. 16–7; Scott M. Eddie, "The Changing Pattern of Landownership in Hungary, 1867–1914," *The Economic History Review,* **20** (1967), p. 293–310; and Jozo Tomasevich, *Peasants, Politics, and Economic Change in Yugoslavia* (Stanford: Stanford University Press, 1955), pp. 204–6.

8. Andrei Simić, *The Peasant Urbanites: A Study of Rural-Urban Mobility in Serbia* (New York and London, 1973), p. 29.

9. Tomasevich, *Peasants, Politics, and Economic Change in Yugoslavia,* p. 165.

10. Gregory Clark, "Productivity Growth without Technical Change in European Agriculture before 1850," *Journal of Economic History,* **47** (1987), pp. 419–32, as quoted by Palairet, "Farming in Serbia," p. 22.

11. See Robert Brenner, "Causes and Consequences of Backwardness," in Chirot, *The Origins of Backwardness in Eastern Europe,* pp. 32–33.

12. Tomasevich, *Peasants, Politics, and Economic Change in Yugoslavia,* p. 46.

13. Palairet, "Farming in Serbia," p. 19.

14. Tomasevich, *Peasants, Politics, and Economic Change in Yugoslavia,* p. 206. Michael Petrovich, who writes that the "penetration of money and credit and capitalist principles" led to "the disappearance of the zadruga" and the creation of "a landless peasant proletariat," states a few pages later that between 1884 and 1905 the export of agricultural products doubled, exceeding imports by 10 to 15 percent per year (*A History of Modern Serbia,* Vol. 2 [New York: Harcourt, Brace, Jovanovich, 1976], pp. 526, 531). Petrovich is correct that exports increased, but not that this was part of a process of creating a landless proletariat. Had accumulation and proletarianization occurred, Serbia might have entered into some sort of developmental process. The difficult question is why these things did not happen.

15. John R. Lampe and Marvin R. Jackson, *Balkan Economic History, 1550–1950* (Bloomington: Indiana University Press, 1982), pp. 115, 184.

16. The debate over whether or not peasants are economically rational is a long and vivid one. Two excellent contrasting studies in the debate are Samuel L. Popkin, *The Rational Peasant: The Political Economy of Rural Society in Vietnam* (Berkeley: University of California Press, 1979), and James C. Scott, *The Moral*

Economy of the Peasant: Rebellion and Subsistence in Southeast Asia (New Haven: Yale University Press, 1976).

17. Palairet, "Farming in Serbia," *passim*. Palairet has published many articles on the economy of the nineteenth-century Balkans, most of which are relevant to Serbia. See particularly "Merchant Enterprise and the Development of the Plum-Based Trades in Serbia, 1847–1911," *Economic History Review*, 2nd ser., **30** (1977), pp. 582–601; "Serbia's Role on the International Markets for Silk and Wine 1860–1890," *Acta Historico-Oeconomica Iugoslaviae*, **4** (1977), pp. 161–86; "Land, Labour and Industrial Progress in Bulgaria and Serbia before 1914," *Journal of European Economic History*, **12** (1983), pp. 163–85; "The Decline of the Old Balkan Woollen Industries 1870–1914," *Vierteljahrschrift für Sozial- und Wirtschaftsgeschichte*, **70** (1983), pp. 330–62; "Desindustrialisation à la périphérie: études sur la région des Balkans au XIXe siècle," *Histoire economie et société*, **4** (1985), pp. 253–74. Not all of these were available to me in preparing this article.

18. Thomas H. Aston and C. H. E. Philpin, eds., *The Brenner Debate: Agrarian Class Structure and Economic Development in Pre-Industrial Europe* (Cambridge: Cambridge University Press, 1985), which contains Brenner's original article from 1976, a number of criticisms, and Brenner's powerful response. See also Brenner's article in the Chirot volume.

19. For Brenner's further argument to this effect, see Robert Brenner, "The Origins of Capitalist Development: A critique of neo-Smithian Marxism," *New Left Review*, **104** (July–Aug 1977), pp. 25–93.

20. For example Olga Srdanović-Barać, *Srpska agrarna revolucija i poljoprivreda od kočine krajine do kraja prve vlade Kneza Miloša* (The Serbian Agrarian Revolution and Agriculture from the Late Eighteenth Century to the end of the First Reign of Prince Miloš) (Belgrade, 1980). Srdanović-Barać is well aware of the backwardness of Serbian agriculture at this time, a subject she discusses skillfully and at length.

21. Miroslav Hroch, *Social Preconditions of National Revival in Europe: A Comparative Analysis of the Social Composition of Patriotic Groups among the Smaller European Nations,* trans: B. Fowkes (Cambridge: Cambridge University Press, 1985). See also my review, *American Historical Review*, **91** (1986), pp. 625–26.

22. Lampe, "Redefining Balkan Backwardness," pp. 177–209. In the seventeenth and eighteenth centuries the Balkans maintained an export surplus, whereas in the twentieth century Austrian and other Habsburg banks and entrepreneurs were singularly unaggressive in Serbia. Lampe, who stresses the relatively rapid growth in the Serbian economy during the two decades preceding World War I, calls the Serbian case one of delayed development or arrested modernization, rather than one of self-sustained growth.

23. Dimitrijević, *Socijalistički radnički pokret u Srbiji*, p. 21.

24. Michael Palairet, "Fiscal Pressure and Peasant Impoverishment in Serbia before World War I," *Journal of Economic History*, **39** (1979), pp. 719–40.

25. For an argument that Balkan railroad construction had a much smaller effect on peasant life than one would assume, see Peter Sugar, "Railroad Construction and the Development of the Balkan Village in the Last Quarter of the Nineteenth Century," in Ralph Melville and and Hans-Jürgen Schröder, eds., *Der Berliner Kongress von 1878* (Wiesbaden, Germany: Fraz Steiner Verlag 1982), pp. 485–98.

26. I have used here the arguments of Klaus Offe as presented in Martin

Carnoy, *The State and Political Theory* (Princeton: Princeton University Press, 1984), in his chapter "The German Debate."

27. Brenner suggested that even in France "the centralized state appears to have developed (at least in part) as a class-like phenomenon—that is, as an *independent* extractor of the surplus" (*The Brenner Debate,* p. 55). But, see the criticism by Guy Bois and Brenner's qualifications of this statement (*Ibid.,* pp. 111, 262–63).

5

1. Vasilije Krestić, *Hrvatsko-ugarska nagodba 1868. godine* (Beograd, 1969), p. 334.

2. Ivo Lederer, "Comments," *Austrian History Yearbook,* III, pt. 2 (1967), p. 196; Charles Jelavich, "Garašanins Načertanije und das grosserbische Programm," *Südost-Forschungen,* **27** (1968), pp. 146–147. For two good examples of this tendency see Dimitrije Djordjević, *Carinski rat Austro-ugarske i Srbije* (Beograd, 1962), p. 19; and Dimitrije Djordjević, "Projects for the Federation of South-East Europe in the 1860's and 1870's," *Balcanica,* I (1970), 138.

3. Two good articles on this subject are Jaroslav Šidak, "Prilog razvoju jugoslavenske ideje do g. 1914," *Naše teme,* **IX** (1965), pp. 1290–1317; and Charles Jelavich, "Serbian Nationalism and the Question of Union with Croatia in the Nineteenth Century," *Balkan Studies,* III (1962), pp. 29–42.

4. The following is based in large measure on Krestić, *Nagodba;* Grgur Jakšić and Vojislav J. Vučković, *Spoljna politika Srbije za vlade kneza Mihaila* (Beograd, 1963); Jaroslav Šidak, et. al., *Povijest Hrvatskog naroda, 1860–1914* (Zagreb, 1968); Vojislav J. Vučković, ed., *Politička akcija Srbije u južnoslavenskim pokrajinama Habsburške monarhije 1859–1874.* (Beograd, 1965); and Vaso Čubrilović, *Istorija političke misli u Srbiji XIX veka* (Beograd, 1958). For a bibliography on the sources of Garašanin's foreign policy ideas see Jelavich, "Garašanins Načertanije," p. 132.

5. For an excellent, review of these plans and bibliographical references see Djordjević, "Projects for Federation," pp. 119–145.

6. In 1875, 1,337,393 persons lived in Bosnia and Herzegovina. Of these persons, 35.9% were Muslim, 48.4% were Orthodox and presumably Serbs, and 15.5% were Catholic and presumably Croats (Sidak, et al., *Povijest hrvatskog naroda,* pp. 91–92).

7. Louis Kossuth, *Memories of My Exile* (New York, 1880), pp. 327–328. Cf. Krestić, *Nagodba,* p. 333, where Krestić leaves out the remark about the Croats, thereby strengthening the feeling that Michael's idea of "an independent Balkan state" was analogous to the Yugoslav idea. See also Jakšić and Vučković, *Spoljna politika,* p. 323, for a critique of Kossuth's account.

8. Vučković, *Politička akcija,* pp. 5 and 2; Krestić, *Nagodba,* p. 337.

9. Krestić, *Nagodba,* p. 340; Jakšić and Vučković, *Spoljna politika,* p. 44; Vučković, *Politička akcija,* document 18; and Andrija Radenić, "Dokumentacija tajnog nacionalnog oslobodilačkog komiteta u Beogradu 1860–1861," *Godišnjak grada Beograda,* 14 (1967), pp. 61–80.

10. For a striking visual impression of how seriously the separate administration of the military frontier divided the Croatian lands, see the excellent map in Šidak, et al., *Povijest hrvatskog naroda,* p. 81.

11. Vučković, *Politička akcija,* p. 224.

12. Krestić, *Nagodba,* pp. 352–353.

13. See Beust to Filipović, March 11, 1867, cited by David MacKenzie, *The Serbs and Russian Pan-Slavism* (Ithaca, N.Y.: Cornell University Press, 1967), p. 12.

14. Russian officers who visited Serbia in 1867 were unimpressed with the army's capabilities (MacKenzie, *Serbs and Pan-Slavism,* p. 12). Alimpije Vasiljević tells in his memoirs, which are located in the Archive of Serbia in Belgrade, that a certain Captain Ostojić, in order to demonstrate the position of his main body of troops to the Russian observers, put a small group of his men some distance from the position of his main body of troops and told them to start firing in the air at a certain time. When he heard the firing in the distance he announced to his troops that the Austrians had penetrated into Serbia and the time had come to defend the homeland. As soon as the peasant soldiers heard that the Austrians were coming they fled into the woods and disappeared (p. 37).

15. Vučković, *Politička akcija,* document 137. See also documents 134, 139, 140, 142, and 148.

16. Since no minutes of the private meeting between Andrassy and Michael have survived, the intentions of the participants have been a matter of debate. For the standard interpretation of Andrassy's policies and for references see Peter Sugar, *Industrialization of Bosnia and Herzegovina, 1878–1918* (Seattle: University of Washington Press, 1963), pp. 19–22; and Jakšić and Vučković, *Spoljna politika,* pp. 396–403. See also Slobodan Jovanović, *Druga vlada Miloša i Mihaila* (Beograd, 1923), pp. 222–225, and Vučković, *Politička akcija,* documents 183, 194, and 198. Krestić believes that Andrássy was "thoroughly insincere" at Ivanka (*Nagodba,* p. 367), but correspondence between Kallay and Beust, and between Kallay and Andrássy, for the next several years shows that the Hungarians seriously considered the possibility of letting Serbia have Bosnia, as Nikola Petrović has shown in "Austro-ugarska nagodba, gradovi i istočno pitanje," in Vaso Čubrilović, ed., *Oslobodjenje gradova u Srbiji od Turaka, 1862–1867* (Beograd, 1970), pp. 263–279. See also R. W. Seton-Watson, "Les rélations de l'Autriche-Hongrie et de la Serbie entre 1868 et 1874," *Le monde slave* (1926), I, 211–230 and II, 186–204; and Nikola Petrović, ed., *Svetozar Miletić i narodna stranka: Gradja, 1860–1885,* 2 vols. (Sremski Karlovci, 1968–1969), I, documents 228, 254, 256, and II, documents 330 and 337. MacKenzie, p. 13, is almost certainly wrong when he says Michael did not accept Andrássy's offer at Ivanka.

17. Later Benjamin Kállay put it this way: "A happy solution of the Bosnian question and the complete estrangement of Croatian from Serbian interests can guarantee our future" (Kallay to Andrássy, December 23, 1868 [new style], *Svetozar Miletić: Gradja,* I, document 254).

18. There is an enormous literature on Svetozar Miletić and his movement. See "Bibliografija radova o Miletiću," *Dokumenti o Svetozaru Miletiću,* Branislav J. Vraničević, ed., (Novi Sad, 1951), pp. 115–136. Two brief pre–World War II biographies are Kosta N. Milutinović, *Svetozar Miletić* (Zagreb, 1939), and Vasa Stajić, *Svetozar Miletić* (Beograd, n.d.). Nikola Petrović is the major post–World War II interpreter of Miletić. Among other things, he has published a popular biography, *Svetozar Miletić* (Beograd, 1958), a collection of articles, *Oko Miletića i posle njega* (Novi Sad, 1964), and a collection of documents, *Svetozar Miletić i narodna stranka, Gradja,* 2 vols. (Sremski Karlovci, 1968–1969). For Miletić's early hopes in the Hungarians, see Vasa Stajić, *Gradja za političku istoriju* (Novi Sad, 1951), p. 333, and Petrović, *Gradja,* I, p. 325.

19. *Zastava,* May 26/June 7, 1866.

20. On the Omladina see Jovan Skerlić, *Omladina i njena knijiževnost* (Beograd, 1966, originally published 1906); *Ujedinjena omladina srpska:* Zbornik radova (Novi Sad, 1968); and Gale Stokes, *Legitimacy through Liberalism: Vladimir Jovanović and the Transformation of Serbian Politics* (Seattle: University of Washington Press 1974).

21. Vera Ciliga, "Narodna stranka i južnoslavenske pitanje (1866–70)," *Istoriski zbornik,* **17** (1964), p. 89.

6

1. Some of the research for this article was done at the Illinois Summer Research Laboratory for 1978. I would like to thank both the Russian Center at the University of Illinois and Rice University for making my stay at the laboratory possible.

2. The extensive efforts on behalf of the Yugoslav movement by South Slavic emigrants in North and South America will not be discussed in this article. For their influence on American policy see Victor S. Mamatey, *The United States and East Central Europe, 1914–1918: A Study in Wilsonian Diplomacy and Propaganda* (Princeton: Princeton University Press, 1957); and George J. Prpić, "The South Slavs," in Joseph P. O'Grady, *The Immigrants' Influence on Wilson's Peace Policies* (Lexington: University of Kentucky Press, 1967). I am not aware of similarly extensive treatments of the strong Yugoslav movement in South America, although Paulová discusses it briefly (pp. 226–35).

3. The first major interpretation of the Yugoslav Committee was Milada Paulová, *Jugoslavenski odbor* [*The Yugoslav Committee*] (Zagreb: Prosvjetna nakladna zadruga, 1925). It remains important, even though it is an *apologia* for Trumbić and the committee. A basic bibliography may be found in the superb study, which is now the standard interpretation of the period, Dragovan Šepić, *Italija, saveznici i Jugoslavensko pitanje, 1914–1918* [*Italy, the Allies, and the Yugoslav Question, 1914–1918*] (Zagreb: Školska knjiga, 1970). The two standard studies in English are Michael B. Petrovich, *A History of Modern Serbia, 1804–1918* (New York: Harcourt Brace Jovanovich, 1976), vol. II, pp. 621–82; and Ivo J. Lederer, *Yugoslavia at the Paris Peace Conference: A Study in Frontiermaking* (New Haven: Yale University Press, 1963), pp. 3–78. Two collections of documents are Ferdo Šišić, *Dokumenti o postanku Krajlevine Srba, Hrvata i Slovenaca 1914–1919* [*Documents on the Creation of the Kingdom of the Serbs, Croats and Slovenes, 1914–1918*] (Zagreb, 1920); and Dragoslav Janković and Bodgan Krizman, eds., *Gradja o stvaranju jugoslovenske države* [*Materials on the Creation of the Yugoslav State*] (Belgrade, 1964). Neither collection was available to me during the preparation of this article. See also Vaso Bogdanov, et al., eds., *Jugoslovenski odbor u Londonu* [*The Yugoslav Committee in London*] (Zagreb: The Yugoslav Academy, 1966).

4. Milorad Ekmečić, *Ratni ciljevi Srbije 1914* [*Serbian War Aims in 1914*] (Belgrade: Srpska kniževna zadruga, 1973), pp. 208–14. See also the solid study by Dragoslav Janković, *Srbija i jugoslovensko pitanje, 1914–1915* [*Serbia and the Yugoslav Question, 1914–1915*] (Belgrade: Institut zu savremenu istoriju, 1973).

5. Šepić, *Italija, saveznici i jugoslavensko pitanje,* pp. 12–13 (map). Pašić's memorandum had been preceded by a note to the allied governments on September 4 in which he had said that the best way to assure the allied war aim, the containment of Germany, was to create a strong national state in the Balkans that would consist of all Serbs, Croats, and Slovenes (Ekmečić, pp. 88–9).

6. Šepić, *Italija, saveznici i jugoslavensko pitanje,* p. 32.

7. As late as October 1918, Pašić said that he had created the Yugoslav Committee and given it money "for propaganda and nothing more" (Šepić, *Italija, saveznici i jugoslavensko pitanje,* p. 358).

8. This is one of Ekmečić's main points. As he puts it, "In the war smoke of 1914, it was seen clearly in Serbia that her five minutes of history had come" (p. 84). For a supportive biography of Pašić, see Alex Dragnich, *Serbia, Nikola Pašić, and Yugoslavia* (New Brunswick, N.J.: Rutgers University Press, 1974).

9. The key statement of the declaration was that Serbia's war aim was "the liberation and unification of all our unliberated brothers: Serbs, Croats, and Slovenes." The Bulgarophile Noel Buxton, who was present, describes the event as follows: "The skupshtina met in a concert hall attached to a cafe. The deputies sat close together on rows of small wicker chairs facing the president. On his right along the wall sat the eight members of the new Cabinet which had just been formed, with a green baize table before them lit by two candles. . . . M. Pasichn . . . then rose. . . . His long grey beard and somewhat threadbare frock coat made him a striking figure as he stood and read by the dim candle light his momentous declaration" (Noel and Charles Roden Buxton, *The War and the Balkans* [London: Allen and Unwin, 1915], pp. 41–2). The basic work on the Declaration is Dragoslav Janković, "Niška deklaracija" ["The Niš Declaration"], *Istorija dvadesetog veka,* X (1969), pp. 7–111.

10. Ekmečić, *Ratni ciljevi,* pp. 214–18.

11. The committe made this fear public at the very end of the war, when Trumbić had lost hope that Serbia would allow the committee to be recognized (Šepić, *Italija, saveznici i jugoslavensko pitanje,* p. 357).

12. Of the two main leaders of the Yugoslav Committee, Frano Supilo and Ante Trumbić, Supilo has occasioned the most interest among historians. Dragovan Šepić published his letters and memoranda from the war period in *Pisma i memorandumi Frana Supila (1914–1917)* (Belgrade: Serbian Academy of Arts and Sciences, 1967) and some further items in *Politički spisi [Political Writings]* (Zagreb: Znanje, 1970). The latter contains an extended biographical introduciton on Supilo's life until 1914. See too Šepić, "Hrvatska u koncepcijama Frana Supila o ujedinjenju" ["Croatia in Fran Supilo's conceptions of Unification"], *Forum,* 7 (1968), pp. 342–81, and Tereza Ganza-Aras, "Frano Supilo u svjetlu najnovijih istraživanja" ["Fran Supilo in the Light of the Latest Research"], *Historijski zbornik,* XXV–XXVI (1972–3), pp. 387–406.

13. Šepić, "Hrvatska u koncepcijama Supila," pp. 355–56; Šepić, *Italija, saveznici i jugoslavensko pitanje,* pp. 43–4; Ekmečić, *Ratni ciljevi Srbije,* pp. 101–3; Paulová, *Jugoslavenski odbor,* pp. 26–34.

14. The provisions of the treaty did not become public until they were published by the Bolsheviks in 1917, but the main provisions were surmised almost immediately by the interested parties.

15. Šepić, *Italija, saveznici i jugoslavensko pitanje,* pp. 89–92.

16. *Ibid.,* pp. 140–46; Šepić, "Hrvatska u koncepcijama Supila," pp. 357–65.

17. For an excellent review of the problems faced by Pašić see Vojislav J. Vučković, "Unutrašnje krize Srbije i prvi svetski rat" ["Serbia's Internal Crises and the First World War"], *Istorijski časopis,* XIV–XV (1963–65), pp. 173–229.

18. Within a short while, however, Supilo realized that if the Habsburg South Slavs were to accomplish their goal of independence, accommodation with Italy was necessary. "I believe," he said, "that the Serbo-Croat-Slovene state, which has

more need of Italian support than any other European power, must compensate for this collaboration with adequate concessions" (Leo Valiani, *The End of Austria-Hungary* [New York: Knopf, 1973], p. 418). Valiani believes that by 1917 Supilo would have conceded Italy dominance of the Adriatic, if not Dalmatia.

19. Supilo read his earlier memorandum of seven points to the committee, but the committee soundly rejected any idea of a separate Croatia as damaging to the ideal of Yugoslavism. For the texts of their statements, see *Nova Europa* [*New Europe*], 13 (1926), pp. 85–6.

20. For Supilo's resignation statement, in which he accuses the Serbian government of supporting the committee with "pretty words" while thwarting it politically, see Paulová, *Jugoslavenski odbor,* pp. 211–14. Supilo's premature death a year later removed him from Yugoslav politics entirely.

21. The basic work is Dragoslav Janković, *Jugoslovensko pitanje i krfska deklaracija 1917. godine* [*The Yugoslav Question and the Corfu Declaration, 1917*] (Belgrade: Savremena administracija, 1967). For the text of the agreement see Petrovich, *History of Serbia,* pp. 644–45.

22. Vučković, "Unutrašnje krize Srbije," pp. 203–23.

23. Šepić, *Italija, saveznici i jugoslavensko pitanje,* pp. 197–205.

24. Petrovich recognizes this: "Trumbić and others may have regarded it as the Magna Charta of Yugoslav unification. For Pašić it was a tactical move in response to given political situation" (*History of Serbia,* p. 649).

25. For a succinct review of Sonnino's career, see Salvatore Saladino, "In Search of Sidney Sonnino," *Reviews in European History,* 2 (1976), pp. 621–33.

26. Christopher Seton-Watson, *Italy from Liberalism to Fascism, 1870–1925* (London: Methuen and Company, 1967), p. 432.

27. English Yugoslavophiles such as R. W. Seton-Watson and Henry Wickham Steed are not discussed in this article, but they had a great impact on the success of the Yugoslav Committee in bringing its ideas before Europe. They founded a Serbian Society of Great Britain, established a journal to forward the cause of East European nationalism (*The New Europe*), and through official propaganda efforts in 1918 popularized the idea of destruction of Austria-Hungary (for the last, see Kenneth J. Calder, *Britain and the Origins of the New Europe, 1914–1918* [Cambridge: Cambridge University Press, 1976]). The fundamental narrative of this activity is Steed, *Through Thirty Years* (New York: Doubleday, Page and Company, 1925). Recently Hugh Seton-Watson has been investigating his father's role in Yugoslav affairs (e.g., "Robert William Seton-Watson i jugoslavensko pitanje" ["Robert William Seton-Watson and the Yugoslav Question"], *Časopis za suvremenu povijest,* II [1970], pp. 75–96. In cooperation with the Seton-Watson family, the British Academy and the Institute of Croatian History of Zagreb University has published *R. W. Seton-Watson i Jugoslaveni: Korespondencija 1906–1941* [*R. W. Seton-Watson and the Yugoslavs: Correspondence, 1906–1941*] (Zagreb-London, 1976), 2 vols.

28. For the following see Valiani, *The End of Austria-Hungary,* pp. 199–256; Christopher Seton-Watson, *Italy from Liberalism to Fascism,* pp. 492–97; Steed, *Through Thirty Years,* II, pp. 183–85; Šepić, *Italija, saveznici i jugoslavensko pitanje,* pp. 289–96; and Paulová, *Jugoslavenski odbor,* pp. 417–43.

29. Valiani, *The End of Austria-Hungary,* p. 240. Paulová's analysis (p. 442) is a good example of how even later supporters of the Yugoslav Committee overestimated its potential positive effect on Italian public opinion and policy.

30. Šepić, *Italija, saveznici i jugoslavensko pitanje,* pp. 337–44.

31. *Ibid.,* p. 358. Seton-Watson became so irritated with Pašić's unwillingness to recognize the Yugoslav Committee that he attacked him in a famous article, "Serbia's Choice," in *The New Europe,* 22 August 1918. "Any Serbian statesman who failed to perceive this truth [that the Austrian Slavs should be treated as an equal factor] would deserve to be regarded . . . as a traitor to the best interest of his race. In Serbia . . . our sympathy and support must be given, not to the old Oriental tendencies, now tottering to their fall, but to those new and democratic elements in whose hands the future of Jugoslavia lies." This was not an entirely fair criticism, since the Radical party had long stood for constitutionalism and civilian government in Serbia, but when Stojan Protić responded that in his opinion "there is more reason to fear that we may encounter semi-Turkish [he is referring to Bosnia and Herzegovina] and semi-Austrian traditions nearer to you in the West," the justice of his reply was drowned out by cries of outrage, and Pašić's reputation was further weakened (*The New Europe,* 26 September 1918). The strong anti-Pašić feeling of the British Yugoslavophiles is obvious in Steed's description of his conversation with Pašić on October 8, 1918 (Steed, *Through Thirty Years,* II, 233–39).

32. For the following see Bogdan Krizman, "Ženevska konferencija o ujedinjenju 1918. godine" ["The Geneva Conference of Unification, 1918"], *Istorijski glasnik,* 1958, no. 1–2, pp. 3–32, and Dragoslav Janković, "Ženevska konferencija o stvaranju jugoslovenske zajednice 1918. godine" ["The Geneva Conference on the Creation of a Yugoslav Union, 1918"], *Istorija XX veka, Zbornik radova,* V (1963), pp. 225–63.

33. Petrovich, *A History of Modern Serbia,* pp. 663–82.

34. Compare the realistic and successful policy that Lenin forced on his unwilling comrades when he cajoled and bullied them into accepting severe losses at Brest-Litovsk but, in the process, saved the Bolshevik Revolution.

35. Some Yugoslav legions were actually formed in Odessa, seeing action in the Dobrudja in 1916, but Sonnino consistently blocked the formation of such units in Italy (Paulová, *Jugoslavenski odbor, passim.*). See Margot Lawrence, "The Serbian Divisions in Russia, 1916–1917," *Journal of Contemporary History,* 6 (1971), pp. 183–92.

7

1. Stojan Cerović in *Vreme,* March 4, 1991, from FBIS EEU-91-051, March 15, 1991, p. 51. John Lampe reported that a friend in Yugoslavia put it this way: "Only the devil's own plan could have designed what we are now doing to ourselves, destroying in a few days what took decades, even centuries to build" ("Yugoslavia from Crisis to Tradgedy," *East European Studies Newsletter,* Woodrow Wilson Center, Washington, D.C., November–December 1991).

2. The Slavic languages include Russian, Belorussian, Ukrainian, Polish, Czech, Slovak, Serbian, Croatian, Slovenian, Macedonian, and Bulgarian. The major non-Slavic languages of Eastern Europe include Greek, Hungarian, Romanian, and Albanian. The major non-Slavic languages among minorities are Yiddish, Turkish, and Romany. The Baltic languages (Estonian, Latvian, and Lithuanian) are not Slavic languages.

3. Milorad Ekmečić, *Ratni ciljevi Srbije 1914* [*Serbian War Aims in 1914*] (Belgrade: Srpska književna zadruga, 1973), pp. 88–89.

4. For an excellent discussion of this period see Ivo Banac, *The National*

Question in Yugoslavia: Origins, History, Politics (Ithaca, N.Y.: Cornell University Press, 1984).

5. In Montenegro, the ousting of King Nikola by the unification party led to a revolt and civil war in 1919 and 1920, and to lasting antagonisms in the interwar years.

6. The decision provoked what amounted to a civil war in Montenegro, the echoes of which reverberated through the 1920s and beyond.

7. The Croatian sabor (legislature) declared Croatia independent and joined forces with the National Council early in November, making Croatia independent for about a month in 1918. This had the effect of legitimizing the council's accession to the new Yugoslav state.

8. At the time of unification Aleksandar was technically prince regent for his father, King Petar, but he had acted as ruler in fact since 1914.

9. Herzegovina is the southwest portion of Bosnia and Herzegovina around the Neretva River. Its name derives from *Herzog*, the German term for "duke," but today simply denotes a geographical region.

10. The Serbian word for the region whose capital city today is Prishtinë (Priština, in Serbian) is *Kosovo*, with the accent on the first syllable. The Albanian word for it is *Kosovë*, with the accent on the second syllable. Since 90 percent of the people who live there today are Albanians, who prefer their own usage, I have used that spelling except when specifically Serbian usage requires otherwise (as in "Kosovo polje").

11. For a brief and balanced discussion of the Ustasha, including good estimates on how many Serbs and other persons died in Yugoslavia during World War II, see Aleksa Djilas, *The Contested Country: Yugoslav Unity and Communist Revolution, 1919–1953* (Cambridge, Mass.: Harvard University Press, 1991), pp. 102–27.

12. Ivo Banac, *With Stalin against Tito: Cominformist Splits in Yugoslav Communism* (Ithaca, N.Y.: Cornell University Press, 1988).

13. Dennison Rusinow, *The Yugoslav Experiment 1948–1974* (Berkeley: University of California Press, 1977), p. 139.

14. See April Carter, *Democratic Reform in Yugoslavia: The Changing Role of the Party* (Princeton, N.J.: Princeton University Press, 1982); and Steven L. Burg, *Conflict and Cohesion in Socialist Yugoslavia: Political Decision Making since 1966* (Princeton, N.J.: Princeton University Press, 1983).

15. Carter, *Democratic Reform in Yugoslavia*, p. 19.

16. Burg, *Conflict and Cohesion*, p. 81.

17. Prof. Dr. Mihailo Djurić, speaking at the law faculty discussion of proposed consitutional amendments in March 1971, quoted by Dušan Bilandžić, *Ideje i praksa društvenog razvoja Jugoslavije* [Ideas and Practice: The Social Development of Yugoslavia] (Belgrade: Komunist, 1973), pp. 287–88. The 1971 discussion at the Belgrade Law Faculty was so volatile that the journal containing the discussion was banned (it was reprinted in 1990) and some faculty members were removed (Robert M. Hayden, "Recounting the Dead: The Rediscovery and Redefinition of Wartime Massacres in Late- and Post-Communist Yugoslavia," in Rubie S. Watson, ed., *Secret Histories: Memory and Opposition under State Socialism* [Santa Fe, N.M.: School of American Research Press, 1993]).

18. Quoted by Burg, *Conflict and Cohesion*, p. 107.

19. "Matica" is difficult to translate. Literally it means "queen bee," but it has overtones of being the basis of something, of being fundamental. Nationalists

might think of "Matica hrvatska" meaning something like "the institutional home of the Croatian national culture and spirit."

20. Dennison Rusinow, "Crisis in Croatia," in four parts, *American University Field Service Fieldstaff Reports, Southeast Europe Series,* 19/1: 15. Rusinow later regretted his use of the inflammatory word *fascist,* which obscured the less prejudicial comparison he had hoped to make.

21. Note that the phrase "the sovereign national state of the Croatian nation" would be offensive to the 600,000 Serbs living in Croatia.

22. Rusinow, *The Yugoslav Experiment,* p. 306. For this paragraph see Rusinow, pp. 296–306.

23. The Yugoslav growth rate in the 1950s was about 7.5 percent per year, about one-third of which can be accounted for by aid from the United States (Bogdan Denitch, *Limits and Possibilities: The Crisis of Yugoslav Socialism and State Socialist Systems* [Minneapolis: University of Minnesota Press, 1990], p. 137).

24. Quoted by Desimir Tochitch, "Titoism without Tito," *Survey* 28/3 (Autumn 1984), p. 16.

25. For a succinct discussion of the Yugoslav economy as "polycentric etatism" with the same problems as other socialist states, see Evan Kraft, "Yugoslavia 1986–88: Transition to Crisis," in *Crisis and Reform in Eastern Europe,* ed. Ferenc Fehér and Andrew Arato (New Brunswick, N.J.: Transaction Publishers, 1991), pp. 455–80.

26. Harold Lydall, *Yugoslavia in Crisis* (Oxford: Clarendon Press, 1989), pp. 83–84. Lydall cites numerous other equally appalling examples.

27. Kraft, "Yugoslavia 1986–88," p. 471.

28. Estimates of the dead ranged from Senator Jesse Helms's propagandistic estimate of sixteen hundred to the probably too low official figure of nine (Elez Biberaj, "The Conflict in Kosovo," *Survey* 28/3 [Autumn 1984], p. 50).

29. For a good discussion of the scanty historical sources for this battle, which contemporaries barely knew happened and did not know who won, and of the creation of the legend, see Thomas A. Emmert, *Serbian Golgotha: Kosovo, 1389* (New York: East European Monographs, 1990).

30. This paragraph is based on Ivo Žanić, "Origins of Political Rhetoric Traced," a series of articles in *Polet,* April 21–May 1989, reprinted in JPRS-EER-89-092, August 17, 1989, pp. 28–44. An example of a genuine epic slogan quoted by Žanić is *Oj, Srbijo / što ti lome krila. / Nisu smeli / dok si jaka bila* (Oh Serbia, / Why have they broken your wings? / They didn't dare / while you were strong). Here is a contemporary poetic description of Milošević arriving at Kosovo polje in April 1987: "But the handsome speaker arrives. / The setting sun sets his bristling hair on fire."

31. Žanić, "Origins of Political Rhetoric," p. 40. Dragiša Pavlović, an opponent of Milošević's ousted in 1987, is also a severe critic of the Kosovo myth. "Defeat cannot be victory, no matter how great it was," he said. Pavlović sees Serbian salvation only in "a rational critique of the Kosovo myth as the traditional Serbian ideology and of every politics that would take it as its framework" (Dragiša Pavlović, *Olako obećana brzina* [Lightly Promised Speed] [Zagreb: Globus, 1988], p. 295).

32. For the 1953 figure, see George W. Hoffman and Fred Warner Neal, *Yugoslavia and the New Communism* (New York: Twentieth Century Fund, 1962), p. 31.

33. Says Serbian writer Milan Komnenić: "Kosovo is Serbia, and that is the

way it has to be. If 20 some have fallen, tomorrow 20 times as many and 400 times as many must fall. We have to defend every foot of our territory, every foot of our spirituality. . . . This is the cherished center of our spirituality and our entire identity." Quoted in JPRS-EER-89-112, October 12, 1989, p. 19.

34. Mark Baskin, "Crisis in Kosovo," *Problems of Communism* 32 (March–April 1983), p. 65.

35. SANU—*Srpska akademija nauka i umetnosti* (The Serbian Academy of Arts and Sciences).

36. Quoted by Ivo Banac, "Yugoslavia: The Fearful Asymmetry of War," *Daedalus* 121/2 (Spring 1992), p. 150. See also the same author's "Political Change and National Diversity," *Daedalus* 119/1 (Winter 1990), pp. 141–59; and "Post-Communism as Post-Yugoslavism: The Yugoslav Non-Revolutions of 1989–1990," in *Eastern Europe in Revolution*, Ivo Banac, ed., (Ithaca, N.Y.: Cornell University Press, 1992), pp. 168–87. These three articles provide a pungent and authoritative analysis of the Yugoslav situation in the late 1980s.

37. Slobodan Stanković, "The Serbian Academy's Memorandum," RFE, Yugoslav SR/11, November 20, 1986, p. 11.

38. For an excellent discussion of Milošević's seizure of power see Branka Magaš, "Yugoslavia: The Spectre of Balkanization," *New Left Review* 174 (1989), pp. 3–31.

39. Pavlović, *Olako obećana brzina*, pp. 308–9.

40. This quotation, as well as some biographical details in this paragraph, is taken from an excellent sketch of Milošević and the Serbian situation just before the outbreak of the civil war: Stephen Engelberg, "Carving out a Greater Serbia," *New York Times Magazine*, September 1, 1991. For a description of the April 24 events and an interesting formal talk by Milošević the next day, see FBIS-EEU-87-080, April 27, 1987.

41. Magaš quotes an article by three Milošević supporters, including the former *Praxis* philosopher Mihailo Marković, which claimed that the majority of Albanians were irredentists who wanted to set up an independent "bourgeois society governed by a pro-fascist right wing regime" ("Yugoslavia: The Spectre of Balkanization," p. 14).

42. Jović to the Serbian Assembly, March 28, 1989, FBIS-EE-89-058, March 28, 1989, p. 54.

43. See Carole Rogel, "Slovenia's Independence: A Reversal of History," *Problems of Communism* 40 (July–August 1991), pp. 31–40.

44. Miha Kovač, "The Slovene Spring," *New Left Review* 171 (1988), pp. 115–28.

45. For the programs of these parties as well as others, including the Croatian Democratic Union (HDZ), see JPRS-EER-89-077, July 7, 1989, pp. 21–48.

46. They used the title "Majniška deklaracija," invoking by that archaic form the May Declaration of 1917, in which Slovenian and Croatian deputies to the Austrian assembly called for the creation of a separate South Slavic unit in the Habsburg Empire (FBIS-EEU-89-096, May 19, 1989, pp. 58–60).

47. Milan Andrejevich, "Slovenia's Alternative Political Groups," RFE, Yugoslav SR/12, December 23, 1988, pp. 15–19.

48. Milan Andrejevich, "Slovenia's Alternative Political Groups," RFE, Yugoslav SR/3, February 24, 1989, p. 23.

49. Milan Andrejevich, "The Spectrum of Political Pluralism in Yugoslavia," RFE, Yugoslav SR/3, February 24, 1989, p. 4.

50. *Keesing's,* 36,900.

51. The most famous case concerned the failure of Agrokomerc, a huge company in Bosnia that left close to one billion dollars of worthless notes behind. On trial for "counterrevolutionary activities," the director of Agrokomerc defended himself by arguing that what he was doing was common Yugoslav business practice.

52. Marković's estimate, FBIS-EEU-91-072, April 15, 1991.

53. For Jović's remark, see FBIS-EEU-91-062, April 1, 1991; for Pučnik's remark, see FBIS-EEU-91-060, March 28, 1991; and for further criticism by Jović, see FBIS-EEU-91-056, March 22, 1991.

54. See Dennison Rusinow, "To be or not to be? Yugoslavia as Hamlet," University Field Staff Report, Europe 1990–1991, no. 18 (June 1991).

55. *Keesing's,* 37,122.

56. The Fourteenth Congress reconvened in May 1990, but without the Slovenian, Croatian, or Macedonian representatives. Its call for a Fifteenth Congress, to meet in September, went unanswered.

57. Quotations from *Elections in Central and Eastern Europe* (Washington, D.C.: Commission on Security and Cooperation in Europe, 1990), p. 76.

58. CSCE report, *Elections in Central and Eastern Europe,* p. 74.

59. According to the *East European Newsletter* of March 24, 1990.

60. Serbian nationalists claim that Izetbegović is a Muslim fundamentalist on the basis of a short book he wrote and went to prison for in 1970 entitled *Islamic Declaration*. In this book he says such things as "establishing of an islamic order is . . . the ultimate act of democracy." On the other hand, he also says "islamic order may be implemented only in countries where Muslims represent the majority," which they do not in Bosnia and Herzegovina. Even though this book was republished in 1990, Izetbegović repudiated it and showed by his actions that he was interested in accommodation. I would like to thank Dr. Jelena Milojković-Djurić for the Izetbegović references. See Misha Glenny, "Yugoslavia: The Revenger's Tragedy," *New York Review of Books,* August 13, 1992, pp. 37–43; and the exchange between Nora Beloff and Misha Glenny, *New York Review of Books,* October 8, 1992, pp. 51–52.

61. Robert M. Hayden, "Constitutional Nationalism in the Formerly Yugoslav Republics," *The Slavic Review* 51 (1992), p. 657. Slovenia and Macedonia introduced similar phrases into their constitutions. Serbia did not, but eliminated any provisions for self-rule in Kosovë and Vojvodina and in fact ran a strictly Serbian government. For an excellent discussion of the structural weaknesses of Croatian political culture that hindered a pluralistic response in 1990, see Vesna Pusić, "A Country by Any Other Name: Transition and Stability in Croatia and Yugoslavia," *East European Politics and Societies* 6/3 (Fall 1992), pp. 242–59.

62. The term "genocide" has come easily to Serbian lips and pens during the Milošević era. Historians in particular have used it regularly, not just when referring to the murders perpetrated by the Independent State of Croatia during World War II, where it is justified, but also as the appropriate general term describing Croatian relations toward Serbs in Croatia over a hundred-year history. In 1989, when an assistant at Belgrade University was found to have published in 1971 a remark critical of the Serbian minority in Croatia in the nineteenth century, for example, he was fired in order to prevent him from spreading "the ideology of genocide" (FBIS-EER-90-023, February 21, 1990, p. 15). Dragoljub Živojinović and Dejan Lučić see the criticisms of Serbs by Catholics in Croatia on the occasion

of the assassination of Franz Ferdinand in 1914 as "preparations for genocide" (*Varvarstvo u ime Hristovo* [Barbarism in Christ's Name] [Belgrade: Nova knjiga, 1988], pp. 52–54).

63. Milošević's speech of June 23, 1990, FBIS-EEU-90-123, June 26, 1990, p. 51.

64. Milan Vego estimated that 103 of the 140 general officers in the Yugoslav National Army and about 9,000 of the 12,100 other officers early in 1991 were Serbs or Montenegrin (talk at the Woodrow Wilson Center, Washington, D.C., April 9, 1991).

65. For some extracts from this document, see Banac, "Post-Communism as Post-Yugoslavism," pp. 183–84.

66. For a balanced discussion of the escalation of violence and the early part of the civil war, see Misha Glenny, "The Massacre of Yugoslavia," *New York Review of Books,* January 30, 1992, pp. 30–35.

67. See Hayden, "Recounting the Dead."

68. Two vigorous accounts of the Yugoslav disaster are Misha Glenny, *The Fall of Yugoslavia: The Third Balkan War* (New York: Penguin, 1992); and Mark Thompson, *A Paper House: The Ending of Yugoslavia* (New York: Pantheon, 1992).

69. For an analysis of U.S. policy, see Paula Franklin Lytle, "U.S. Policy Toward the Demise of Yugoslavia: The 'Virus of Nationalism,'" *East European Politics and Societies* 6/3 (Fall 1992), pp. 303–18.

70. Ivo Andrić, *Bridge on the Drina* (Chicago: University of Chicago Press, 1977, orig. pub. 1959).

8

1. Quoted by Timothy W. Ryback, "Report from Dachau," *The New Yorker,* August 3, 1992, p. 49.

2. Norman M. Naimark, "German-Polish Relations in the New Europe," typescript, has influenced my thinking a great deal. For the treaties and a discussion of them see "Das deutsch-polnische Vertragswerk," *Europa-Archiv,* **13** (July 10, 1991), D309–D334. This phrase appears on p. D315.

3. *Ibid.,* pp. D312 and D328.

4. The figure for German dead is Naimark's, p. 8.

5. Adam Michnik, "Nationalism," *Social Research* **58** (1991), p. 760.

6. *RFE Daily Report,* January 22, 1993.

7. Gordon S. Wood, *The Creation of the American Republic, 1776–1787* (Chapel Hill: University of North Carolina Press, 1969), p. 175; Francois Furet, *La Revolution de Turgot à Jules Ferry 1770–1880* (Paris: Hachette, 1989), pp. 34–5; Wood, *Creation of the American Republic,* p. 109.

8. Alexander Hamilton, John Jay, and James Madison, *The Federalist Papers,* edited by and introduction by Clinton Rossiter (New York: NAL Penguin, 1961), pp. 78–79.

9. *Federalist Papers,* p. 311.

10. Thomas Paine, "Dissertations on Government, the Affairs of the Bank, and Paper Money," in Michael Foot and Isaac Kramnick, eds., *Thomas Paine Reader* (New York: Penguin Books, 1987), p. 168.

11. *Le Moniteur universel,* February 28, 1791, p. 503.

12. Claude Lefort, *The Political Forms of Modern Society: Bureaucracy, Democ-*

racy, Totalitarianism, John B. Thompson, ed. (Cambridge: The MIT Press, 1986), p. 251.

13. Michael Howard, *The Lessons of History* (New Haven: Yale University Press, 1991), pp. 37–38.

14. *Vreme,* March 1, 1993, p. 66.

Part III Introduction

1. The best full-scale presentation of this view is Vladimir Tismaneanu, *Reinventing Politics: Eastern Europe from Stalin to Havel* (New York: Free Press, 1993).

2. Gale Stokes, *The Walls Came Tumbling Down: The Collapse of Communism in Eastern Europe* (New York: Oxford University Press, 1993).

9

1. Teresa Torańska, *"Them:" Stalin's Polish Puppets* (New York: Harper-Collins, 1987), p. 354.

2. Charles Gati, *Hungary and the Soviet Bloc* (Durham: Duke University Press, 1986), p. 69.

3. G. M. Tamás, "Farewell to the Left," *Eastern European Politics and Societies,* 5 (1991), p. 92.

4. Czesław Miłosz, *The Captive Mind* (New York: Knopf, 1981). Miłosz says he found the term "Ketman" in a book by Gobineau dating from the middle of the nineteenth century. Gobineau used it in describing the Shi'ite tradition of *Taqiyya,* or religious dissimulation while maintaining mental reservation.

5. For an extremely interesting argument that heroism in the modern world is the act of surviving, not of storming the barricades, see Terence des Pres, *The Survivor: An Anatomy of Life in the Death Camps* (New York: Oxford University Press, 1976).

6. It is curious that many Hungarian intellectuals do not wish to give the name *revolution* to the events of 1989, despite the fact that they changed almost everything, and insist on using the term for the events of 1956, which consisted in part of the restoration of the parties of 1945 and ended by changing nothing.

7. Milovan Djilas, *The New Class* (New York: Harcourt Brace, 1967; 22nd printing as corrected), p. 69.

8. Mihailo Marković, "Marxist Philosophy in Yugoslavia: The *Praxis* Group," in Gale Stokes, ed., *From Stalinism to Pluralism* (New York: Oxford University Press, 1991), p. 120.

9. Ted Kaminski, "Underground Publishing in Poland," *Orbis,* 31, **3** (Fall 1987), p. 328.

10. Leszek Kołakowski, "Hope and Hopelessness," *Survey,* 17, **3** (Summer 1971), p. 46.

11. Adam Michnik, *Letters from Prison,* translated by Maya Latynski (Berkeley: University of California Press, 1985), p. 86.

12. H. Gordon Skilling, *Charter 77 and Human Rights in Czechoslovakia* (London: Scribner, 1981), p. 211.

13. Václav Havel, *Living in Truth,* edited by Jan Vladislav (London: Faber and Faber, 1968), p. 57.

14. Konstanty Gebert, "An Independent Society: Poland under Martial

Law," *Alternatives,* 15 (1990), p. 359 (quoting his own work originally published in February, 1982).

15. Roman Laba, *The Roots of Solidarity: A Political Sociology of Poland's Working Class Democratization* (Princeton: Princeton University Press, 1991). For another excellent interpretive study of Solidarity see David Ost, *Solidarity and the Politics of Anti-Politics: Opposition and Reform in Poland since 1968* (Philadelphia: Temple University Press, 1990).

16. Laba, *Roots of Solidarity,* p. 65.

17. Stokes, ed., *From Stalinism to Pluralism,* p. 209.

18. Jan Józef Lipski, *KOR: A History of the Workers' Defense Committee in Poland* (Berkeley: University of California Press, 1988), pp. 44–5; and Timothy Garton Ash, *The Polish Revolution: Solidarity* (New York: Allen & Unwin, 1984), p. 280.

19. Havel, *Living in Truth,* p. 31.

10

1. Jeffrey Herf, *Reactionary Modernism: Technology, Culture, and Politics in Weimar and the Third Reich* (Cambridge: Cambridge University Press, 1984), p. 2; Schelling quoted by Isaiah Berlin in "The Counter-Enlightenment," in Henry Hardy, ed., *Against the Current* (New York: Penguin Books, 1982), p. 19.

2. René Descartes, "Discourse on the Method of Rightly Conducting the Reason," in Elizabeth S. Haldane and G. R. T. Ross, trans. and eds., *The Philosophical Works of Descartes,* (n.p.: Dover Publications, 1955), Vol. 1, p. 119; Mihály Vaci, quoted in Ivan Berend, *The Hungarian Economic Reforms, 1953–1988* (Cambridge: Cambridge University Press, 1990), p. 148.

3. Robert G. Kaiser, *Why Gorbachev Happened: His Triumphs and His Failure* (New York: Simon & Schuster, 1991), p. 228.

4. Ralf Dahrendorf, *Reflections on the Revolution in Europe in a Letter Intended to Have Been Sent to a Gentleman in Warsaw* (New York: Times Books, 1990), p. 27.

5. See Walter R. Connor, "Why Were We Surprised?" *The American Scholar* (Washington, DC), Spring 1991, pp. 175–84.

6. Michael Howard, *The Lessons of History* (New Haven, CT: Yale University Press, 1991), quotation taken from Ronald H. Spector's review, *The Washington Post,* Mar. 3, 1991.

7. See Stanley Hoffman, "The Case for Leadership," *Foreign Policy* (Washington, DC), Winter, 1990, pp. 20–38.

8. See James Gleick, *Chaos: Making a New Science* (New York: Penguin, 1987).

9. Václav Havel, "Letter to Dr. Gustav Husák," in *Living in Truth,* Jan Vladislav, ed. (London: Faber and Faber, 1987), pp. 21–22.

11

1. Jiřina Šiklová, "The Solidarity of the Culpable," *Social Research,* 58, **4** (Winter 1991), pp. 765–74.

2. See Adam Michnik, "An Embarassing Anniversary," *New York Review of Books* (June 10, 1993), pp. 19–21.

3. Gordon S. Wood, *The Radicalism of the American Revolution* (New York: Alfred A. Knopf, 1992), pp. 264, 306–7.

4. There is a good deal of pessimism about the European Union today because of recession, the Yugoslav crisis, and the difficulties of securing monetary union. What has been lost in the shuffle is that about 90 percent of approximately 250 laws enhancing European unity that were called for by the Single European Act have been adopted by all parties and are in effect or about to go into effect.

5. Wladek Bartoszewski, in an interview with the author, April 30, 1993.

6. Quoted by Timothy W. Ryback, "Report from Dachau," *The New Yorker* (August 3, 1992), p. 49.

7. For further comments on nationalism and reconciliation, see "Nationalism, Responsibility, and the People-as-One" in this volume.

8. *RFE/RL Daily Report,* April 14, 1993.

9. In that election Csurka's party received less than 2 percent of the vote.

Index